PRIESTS IN WORKING-CLASS BLUE:
The History of the Worker-Priests
(1943–1954)

L. Cunningham
05/ 1987

Oscar L. Arnal

PAULIST PRESS
New York/Mahwah

The author wishes to thank the Social Sciences and Humanities Research Council of Canada and the American Philosophical Society for the research grants used to gather data for this book.

Library of Congress Cataloging-in-Publication Data

Arnal, Oscar L., 1941–
    Priests in working-class blue.

    Bibliography: p.
    Includes index.
    1. Priest workers—History.   2. France—Church
history—1945–   . I. Title.
BX1530.2.A76   1986   253'.0944   86-15062
ISBN 0-8091-2831-4 (pbk.)

Published by Paulist Press
997 Macarthur Blvd.
Mahwah, N.J. 07430

Printed and bound in the
United States of America

CONTENTS

iii

To
Marian Ochkay Arnal,
my beloved wife and partner,
my most precious treasure

ACKNOWLEDGMENTS

"Oscar, do not let them forget us."
—Maurice Combe, worker-priest

To write a history of the original one hundred French worker-priests is a challenging task both academically and personally.

First of all, there is voluminous material on the worker-priests which emerged from their immediate era and its aftermath. Examination of this documentation is very time-consuming, and yet it is like the discovery of gold. Most of these sources—memoirs, newspaper articles, periodical materials, novels, plays, etc.—are partisan and, as such, become source material for the project. Very little has been written about the worker-priests beyond such popular and consciously partisan efforts. The single most important exception is Emile Poulat's *Naissance des prêtres-ouvriers* (1965), a thorough study which describes their origin and pilgrimage until 1948. Beyond a few other brief works, there is no single title which devotes itself exclusively to the worker-priests. This book is an attempt to fill that gap.

However, it is not my intention to write simply a calendar of events, a chronological description of their ministry. My attempt is more ambitious. It is to recreate and portray the very stuff of their life and priesthood, what the French would call their *vie intégrale*. What they were, what they are, what they did and what they experienced deserves to be told in all its richness. This book is my effort in that direction. It will attempt to portray their world, the broader world of their two "fidelties," that of the working class and that of the church in which they were priests. More directly, the book will follow these priests into the working class and will trace the evolution of their life there. It will show how their lives and ideas changed and developed, and it will describe the controversy with the church's leadership which

v

tore them apart. Finally, it will offer some reflections on their historical impact.

Put another way, this book is the history (both personal and social) of a group of radical priests who embodied the "praxis-reflection-praxis" methodology proclaimed so frequently by third world liberation theologians. Indeed, the French worker-priests lived out this incarnational theology in the industrial west two decades before the term liberation theology was coined in Latin America. Consequently, it is appropriate to utilize a holistic methodology in telling their story, a methodology which is both biographical and sociological. In short their daily living and militancy will be examined as the soil out of which their evolving religious concepts emerged. Their pilgrimage had a variety of contexts which defined and redefined them, and these will be described to give flesh and blood to the theological insights which emerged from their ministry and so significantly shaped the post-Vatican II church.

Certainly, there is the danger of distortion and non-objectivity in writing such a history, but I would hasten to add that each research topic and era has its own peculiar dangers. This is no attempt to minimize the problem. I have attempted to surmount it primarily by thoroughness of research. One of my richest sources has been interviews with approximately one-half of the original worker-priests, and one might suggest, with some academic wisdom, that these reminiscences from active participants within the historical drama are suspect. I do not accept that position without elaboration. Rather I prefer to believe what one of these worker-priests said to me about his interview. He called it partial, in the double sense of the word. It means that these personal *témoignages* are a valuable source with a particular perspective, a reality to be found in all source material. Fortunately, I have other sources which can be compared and contrasted with what former worker-priests told me. These include other interviews with non-worker-priests (bishops, theologians, journalists, trade unionists, communists), books, periodical publications, private papers and the like. After all the comparisons had been made, I found that the worker-priests' recollections had stood the test of time.

The final danger of writing such a contemporary history is that of the author's own partisanship. There is no doubt that I have been touched deeply by these men, by their daily heroism, by their cause, by their humanity and by the testimony of their entire lives. I make no apologies for that. They welcomed me into their humble dwellings; I sat at their tables; they treated me like a brother and a comrade; and they entrusted me with their private papers and their personal pilgrimages. I felt honored and deeply grateful, and these feelings have not left me. Yet I hasten to add that these very experiences strengthen my resolve to avoid partisanship, to avoid romanticizing or eulogizing their lives. I owe that to them, to myself and to my readers. Their story speaks for itself. For that reason, I have tried, within the framework of my ability, to allow this book to be a channel through which that story may flow—no more, no less.

In researching and writing this book, I have accumulated a mountain of indebtedness to many fine people. The advice of French scholars and journalists, who have been involved both intellectually and personally in these events, has been invaluable. Pierre Nautin, René Rémond, Georges Hourdin, Maurice Montuclard, Jean-Marie Domenach and especially Emile Poulat must be included in this context. I owe a special debt to Father Joseph Debés, both a scholar and a committed Catholic liberationist, for his tireless kindnesses and for the documentary materials he permitted me to use. In addition, I am indebted to the many participants in the great events surrounding the worker-priest experience who permitted me to interview them: Louis Augros, Daniel Perrot and Jean Vinatier of the Mission de France; the auxiliary bishops Mgrs. Robert Frossard, Daniel Pezeril and, above all, the worker-bishop, Prado's Alfred Ancel; the theologians Yves Congar and M.-D. Chenu; former lay militants in Catholic Action Joseph Jacquet, Louisette Blanquart, André Villette, René Boudot and Roger Cartayrade; the communist militants and C.G.T. activists Jean Bratteau, Lucien Trilles and André Moine; and priests involved in other missionary apostolates during the period under investigation, Fathers Jacques Hollande, Yvan Daniel, Georges Mollard, Maxime Hua and Jean Villain. Further personal thanks to the library staff of the Jeunesse Ouvrière Chrétienne and to Father Francis Corinwinder of the Mission de France for permitting me to utilize and photocopy important and irreplaceable documents.

In the English-speaking world I am grateful to a number of scholars who have encouraged or helped me with this task over the last five years. These include Father Joseph N. Moody, Father Francis Murphy, John Cammet, Sandi Cooper, David Schalk, Robert Soucy, Allen Douglas, John Hellman, Robert Young, Donald N. Baker and Eduard Gargen. Gregory Baum's vital assistance to me at critical junctures of this project is remembered with deep gratitude. Still other historians have added their friendship and personal support as well as their expertise. So I thank Dean O'Donnell, Patricia Howe, Stewart Campbell,

William Irvine, Jane Bond-Howard, Jean Knoll, Mark Gabbert, Henry Heller, Jim Osen, my dissertation advisor and mentor Seymour Drescher and my alter-ego and colleague since student days Joel Blatt.

Without material support from various granting bodies, this effort would have been impossible. Consequently I express my deep gratitude to the Humanities and Social Science Research Council of Canada, to the American Philosophical Society and to Wilfrid Laurier University for the four grants which allowed me to conduct vital research in France.

I am indebted to my colleagues and students at Waterloo Lutheran Seminary and Wilfrid Laurier University who have encouraged my work and have borne patiently any excessive time and zeal I have spent on the project. Many thanks to my typist Maureen Nordin for her diligence, patience and fine work. The assistance of Jean Hiesberger, John Farina and Gloria Capik of Paulist Press merits grateful mention also. To Dr. Andrew Coppolino and to my friend of twenty-five years, Edward Madura, I owe a special thanks for the important emotional support they rendered for the duration of this project. The solidarity of my house church brothers and sisters was invaluable for my work as well. Above all, I am grateful for the consistent patience, support and encouragement of my wife Marian and my two boys William and Bradley who had to endure unjustly prolonged periods of an absentee husband and father.

There is one final tribute to be rendered; that is to the worker-priests themselves. To their dead and to their living I say thank you from the bottom of my heart. I will remember always their kindness, their welcome to a stranger, their hospitality and their trust to the point of opening up their personal lives and vocations. This is not the place to mention their names. The reader will meet and come to know them personally in the pages of this book. They have left their indelible mark upon me, and for that I am profoundly grateful. This book is my gift and tribute to them. Where I have misunderstood or misconstrued them inadvertently, I beg their forgiveness, and where I have portrayed them accurately and sensitively, I rejoice over the honor and privilege of having been able to tell their story.

I

THE PARADIGM OF THE WORKER-PRIESTS: LIBERATION IN THE INDUSTRIAL WEST

"The church without the working class is not the church of Jesus Christ."
—A. Deman, *Témoignage Chrétien*

Shortly after the Second World War about one hundred French and Belgian Catholic priests entered factories to take up manual work as an essential facet of their ministry to the industrial work force. This resulted from an awareness by the French church that the proletariat had become alienated from the traditional religiosity of the nation. The crisis of war and German occupation produced corresponding opportunities for more creative ventures to cross this gap between the church and the laboring classes. The worker-priest experiment would become the most well-known of these efforts; within ten years their clerical witness had stamped itself on the sacred memory of western Christianity.

Worker-priest, as a term, has been adopted throughout the mainline denominations and denotes any member of the clergy involved in a specialized form of ministry which draws a salary from agencies that are not part of the institutionalized church. However, in the purest and most historical sense of the idea, it is a misnomer to call such people worker-priests. Instead, the original bearers of that name were those clergy who fulfilled their mandate by engaging in full-time manual labor as a priestly manifestation of the church's commitment to embrace the working class of their respective nations.[1] This particular mission was able to survive two papal condemnations, one in 1954, the other in 1959, until the very idea of priests working (*prêtres au travail*) was vindicated by the delegates of Vatican II.

1

Since then both Catholic and Protestant churches have experienced a resurgence of what in North America has been called the social gospel. Throughout the latter 1950s and the 1960s the dormant conscience of the western churches has been stirred by the civil rights surge, the peace movement, native rights, feminism and assorted efforts to assert the cause of ethnic identity. The names of Martin Luther King Jr., William Sloane Coffin, Jr., Daniel Berrigan and James Groppi were some of the more notable clergy involved in the justice struggle "for the least of these." Prosperous North America's underside was pushing itself to the forefront as a living example of a new language coming from Latin America which spoke of a "priority option for the poor."

The protest-euphoria in the United States and Canada reached its peak in the late 1960s and early 1970s, and it is no surprise that this movement was able to form links with the Central and South American theology of liberation which was emerging at this time. The works of Gustavo Gutiérrez, Rubem Alves, Helder Camara, Camilo Torres and Paulo Freire were not only going through English translations, but their ideas were being linked with the radical theologians of hope from Europe such as Johannes Metz and Jürgen Moltmann. A serious dialogue of radical Christian thinkers and practitioners from Canada, the United States, Latin America and Europe had begun in earnest just as the American troop involvement in Vietnam was drawing to a close.[2]

This dialogue reached a critical watershed with the Theology in the Americas Conference held at Detroit in August, 1975. The Chilean liberation theologian Sergio Torres managed to bring together radical Christian leaders representing the wide spectrum of the Christian left in North and South America. Very quickly it was discovered that liberation theology was pluralistic; the various contexts of oppression out of which people spoke demanded equally particular brands of theology to address these situations. From the United States and Canada came voices crying for the liberation of blacks, women, Chicanos and indigenous people. Though stunned by this diversity, the Latin Americans gave to the conference a theological perspective that was sorely needed. They defined a consciousness which insisted that theology must speak out of a concrete reality, more specifically, the reality of oppression. For them, the gospel was a message of justice, hope and liberation for the poor, oppressed and marginalized of society. History and revelation were viewed from society's underside rather than from the top down. In this context of doing theology from the soil of real oppression emerged a methodology that was intensely incarnational, an approach that spoke of "praxis-reflection-praxis." In line with this method, Gutiérrez called theology the "second act" (*actus secundus*), that is, a "reflection on the struggle for emancipation" of oppressed peoples. It is a consciously incarnational and participatory approach which challenges directly the more academic and supposedly neutral theology of North America.[3]

In both the United States and Canada Christian theologians and activities have responded positively to this theological challenge. Reacting to the Detroit congress Gregory Baum of Toronto has called for theologians to form links with the marginalized of their own world and "to come to a more Christian understanding of their society by rereading its history from the viewpoint of the oppressed peoples." From the United States the Protestant Robert McAfee Brown has issued a similar mandate to Christian academics. Reacting to his own experience at the Detroit Conference, he resists the impulse of many U.S. thinkers to treat liberation theology as simply one other fad or commodity for the American intelligentsia to consume. Instead, he insists that no other "issues on the theological or human scene" are "more important than the ones liberation theologians are raising."[4] Brown proceeds to move from this challenge to a description of the salient principles of the emerging Latin American thinkers. They speak of the poor as the priority point of theology; they use radical social analysis, much of it Marxist; they accept conflict and class struggle as legitimate and often necessary; and they insist that Christians must militate actively for and with the poor. Brown not only accepts these suppositions but also expects Christian academicians to adopt them by living them out vocationally. He calls for a recovery of sacred memory among first world Christians which portrays the church's history from the perspective of these liberation themes. Understandably he cites the radical Anabaptists and the North American social gospel as examples,[5] but with equal justification he could have heralded the French worker-priests.

These laboring clergy represent a unique and potent response to a set of forces long ignored by the church—the Industrial Revolution. Throughout the centuries Christianity developed structures which responded to a western society that was largely decentralized socioeconomically and built upon the base of rural and small-town life. To a very great extent the parish is an institution which grew out of and thrived in that type of social setting. The Industrial Revolution, however, wreaked havoc with this pattern, and the church resisted the world of industry and the massive work force that it created. The evils of the city were excoriated, and Christian orators raised eulogies to an idyllic pastoral world which was becoming obsolete.

This is not to suggest that the worker-priests were the sole effort on the church's part to proclaim a liberating gospel to a proletariat created and ravaged by the rapidly industrializing west. There are note-worthy attempts to do just that before and after the worker-priests. The Methodists of England turned to the brutalized workforce of the textile mills with their gospel of hope, and Methodist Sunday Schools eventually became the laboratory out of which a self-educated militant working class movement would spring. Wesleyan theology would be radicalized by Methodist working class activists in the Chartist movement and by coal-miner preachers (worker-priests in their own right) who organized the British coal pits as union agitators.[6] The U.S. and Canadian social gospels were also a response to the ravages of industrial capitalism. Theologians such as Washington Gladden and Walter Rauschenbusch insisted that the Christian message demanded social reform at the workplace. Rauschenbusch himself developed a systematic critique of capitalism and offered a humane socialist alternative in its place. The Presbyterian minister Norman Thomas began his career in the inner city slums, a ministry which led him eventually to run several times for the United States presidency under the banner of the Socialist Party. In Canada the social gospel followed similar lines. Clergy activists James S. Woodsworth, William Irvine, William Ivens and others moved from urban reform to labor activism and finally to socialist politics.[7]

North American Catholicism as well as Protestantism was sensitive to labor's plight during the initial stages of the Industrial Revolution. Much of the work force in the United States and Canada had immigrated to the New World from Catholic countries, and parish priests were acutely aware of the suffering of their people in the urban ghettos. Soon a number of progressive bishops, such as James Cardinal Gibbons of Baltimore, lifted their voices in support of the rising labor movement. Until the Second World War the North American Catholic Church was mostly cautious and timid on labor questions, but the pioneering work of Father John A. Ryan, a Minnesota seminary professor, sowed the seeds which would bear fruit during the Depression, World War II and beyond. Increasingly, these global events began to radicalize Catholics. In the United States Peter Maurin and Dorothy Day formed the Catholic Worker movement, while in the Canadian Maritimes, Father Moses M. Coady provided the impetus for substantive social reform through his Antigonish Movement. Behind these efforts stood the authority of papal social doctrine. The two encyclicals *Rerum Novarum* (1891) by Leo XIII and *Quadragesimo Anno* (1931) by Pius XI were product of and inspiration for pro-labor Catholics throughout the industrial west. Though an ambiguous blend of social conservatism and radicalism, these papal letters served as a last line of defense for Catholics who dared to challenge capitalism and show solidarity with worker resistance toward it.[8]

Since World War II the Christian churches Protestant and Catholic have intensified their efforts for the victims of industrialization throughout the first world. Catholic labor unions and Catholic Action among young proletarians have built upon their prewar efforts in Europe, and in North America the work of Dorothy Day and Moses Coady reached its full fruition after VE Day. Pro-labor priests, such as Msgr. Charles Owen Rice of Pittsburgh, have been on the increase, and church social doctrine on behalf of the working class has become more public and more partisan. The 1975 statement of the Appalachian bishops on behalf of their poor, and the string of increasingly radical statements from Canadian bishops reflect both a groundswell of avant-garde Catholicism and the increasingly progressive character of the social encyclicals since John XXIII. Mainline Protestantism has adopted official positions which have graduated from timid reformism to substantive social democracy and structural reform. The United Church of Canada has condemned the economic excesses of multi-national corporations, and the Lutheran Church in America's statement on "Economic Justice" (1980) is a far cry from traditional Lutheran quietism. More recently, a number of Lutheran pastors linked to a labor-church alliance, called the Denominational Ministry Strategy and the Network to Save the Mon-Ohio Valley, have been jailed because of their refusal to abandon a ministry for the unemployed and against the corporate power in Pittsburgh, Pennsylvania.[9]

This is the over-all historical and social context out of which the worker-priests emerged. They are one of the most unique responses of organized Christianity to the ravages of the Industrial Revolution. Standing between the earlier efforts of the social gospel and the latter struggles of such people as Cesar Chavez, Msgr. Rice and Dorothy Day, the French worker-priests serve as a unique and bold paradigm of a lived theology in struggle for "the least of these." Two decades before liberation theology spoke of a faith based upon concrete reality, of a consciousness emerging from *praxis*, of a partisan commitment to the poor and of a gospel dedicated to the militant struggle for justice, French and Belgian laboring clergy were articulating and practicing such a faith. The worker-priests were a living example of liberation theology well before the term was coined. Their experience and testimony became a model along the lines suggested by the Christian theologians at Detroit, namely an example of a lived theology which is relevant to the oppressed peoples who reside in the white west. Robert McAfee Brown put it this way: "Our task is not to imitate theologies from Third World situations but to develop an indigenous theology for our situation."[10] Unknowingly, the worker-priests operationalized this mandate forty years ago when the ravages of World War II and its aftermath had darkened the face of Europe. They were a creative and bold venture of the first world Catholic church in response to the needs of the industrial working class. In this sense, they reacted to a third world situation in the midst of the prosperous capitalist west. As such, they are one paradigm, one significant model, of the gospel of liberation lived and articulated among the first world laboring classes. For these reasons their story deserves to be told—in its historical context, in its fullness and in its impact.

II

THE FRANCE OF THE WORKER-PRIESTS
(1943–1954)

"The Union Sacrée of the Resistance was over . . . The Liberation was over . . . We were in the midst of the Cold War!"
—Joseph Robert, worker-priest

The worker-priest pilgrimage grew out of the soil of troubled France. German occupation, Liberation and the French Fourth Republic were the immediate political contexts for this clergy and the church which mandated them. Depression, the rise of fascism and World War II were volcanic not only for France but also for the entire globe. France herself, the nation which spawned the worker-priests, was torn apart during these years by war, defeat, military occupation, collaboration, resistance, revival, disillusionment and Cold War. It was in this troubled context, from the mid-1940s to 1954, that about one hundred Catholic priests undertook full-time manual labor in order to render the gospel present in the midst of the industrial toilers. Their bold experiment was born in France, and in that national soil were found the roots and events out of which they grew and thrived. That France was a nation in the midst of crisis from the economic collapse of the 1930s until Charles de Gaulle came to power in the late 1950s.[1]

A decade before the birth of the Parisian worker-priest communities France was in the midst of the world-wide Depression which had struck Wall Street in 1929. Government scandals and the ultra-rightist press had brought legions of right-wing protesters onto the streets on the night of February 6, 1934. By midnight, fifteen people lay dead and another fifteen hundred were wounded. Not since the famed Paris Commune of 1871 had there been so much carnage in the city's streets. Fearing a fascist plot, the French left united for the first time since the ill-fated split of Socialists and Communists at Tours and mounted a counterdemonstration on February 12. The always fragile French Third Republic was on its way to becoming a hopelessly divided nation.[2] Under Soviet pressure and in response to its own rank-and-file, the French Communist Party adopted a broad policy of anti-Fascist defense and New Deal social reforms by joining with Leon Blum's Socialists and Edouard Daladier's Radicals to form an electoral coalition called the Popular Front. It was swept to power in the spring of 1936 in the midst of a euphoric leftist élan, and faced with massive factory occupations, it enacted some trail-blazing social legislation which benefitted the nation's working class. However, within a year, a continuing financial crisis, the Spanish Civil War and divisions within the leftist coalition ground the Blum government to a halt. Once again the Communists became pariahs within the nation, and the Popular Front limped along in name only, ruled by events rather than controlling them. Czechoslovakia fell; Spain fell. An aggressive Nazi Germany was on the march toward European hegemony, and a divided, defensive France, symbolized poignantly by its Maginot Line, was not prepared for the Wehrmacht onslaught of the 1940s.[3]

In spite of the growing national collapse, the 1930s were marked by intense intellectual ferment.[4] Young academics from the middle classes were stirred to commit their skills and craft to the great political causes of that day, and in that sense, these men and women added explosive fuel to the fires which were blazing in a divided nation. It was the era of *engagement,* the decade that saw the rise of such giants as Jean-Paul Sartre, Albert Camus, Simone Weil, Simone de Beauvoir, Paul Nizan, Robert Brassillach and Emmanuel Mounier.[5] Catholicism could not avoid being caught up in this ferment and polarization. Indeed, Emmanuel Mounier himself, a profound influence upon the liberationist Paulo Freire, was a devout Catholic, and it was this faith which was the very foundation of his *engagement.* Since 1927 French Catholicism had embarked on what has been called the Second Ralliement. With the papal condemnation of the right-wing royalist Action Française, the French church became liberated from its sterile reactionary politics, and its progressives, democrats and pluralists took heart. Consequently, throughout the late 1920s and 1930s, these elements expanded and became a recognized, albeit minority, voice for change within a church which was abandoning its pre-French Revolutionary mentality with a great deal of reluctance. The formerly condemned Christian Democrats, symbolized by the tribune Marc Sangnier, witnessed a resurrection, and a more progressive and pluralist Catholic press emerged, embodied by the weeklies *Vie Catholique* and the Dominican *Sept.* Catholic trade unionism entered the mainstream of national life, and Catholic Action, through the creative Jeunesse Ouvrière Chrétienne, made a concerted effort to bring the Christian gospel into working-class life. In spite of the fact that these ventures were timidly reformist, for the most part, formidable opposition to them arose among Catholics in massive proportions. The two-million strong Fédération Nationale Catholique replaced the now suspect Action Française as a more official voice of Catholicism, and most of the church's hierarchy and its quasi-official newspaper *La Croix* were, at best, hesitant and timid toward the newly emerging face of French Catholicism. The forces of the Second Ralliement were thrown on the defensive by the events which grew out of and followed the Popular Front. Crusading anti-Marxism dominated most of the French church's articulate sectors, and those progressives inclined to be open toward the Popular Front and the Communist offer of friendship to Christians found themselves isolated, persecuted and sometimes condemned by major forces within the church. By the end of the 1930s the cautiously liberal Second Ralliement was in shambles and would not emerge again with strength until the Resistance.

Most of the worker-priests were adolescents or in early manhood during this period of national division and turbulence, and although many were not obviously shaped by these events, the Catholicism which would support and nourish them in the 1940s and 1950s was experiencing its birth pains during these troubled years.[6] Although this movement within the church was a far cry from liberation theology, nonetheless, it set the stage for more radical developments to follow. A massive tank blitzkrieg through the Ardennes in 1940 altered the nation drastically, and humiliated France experienced four years of German occupation, collaboration and resistance. Traumatized by a massive and rapid military defeat, the Third Republic voted its own burial and gave full powers to Maréchal Philippe Pétain to negotiate an armistice with the victorious Germans and to set up a new regime that would give the definitive coup de grace to the now-hated republic which was blamed for the defeat. The price of peace was exhausting to France. The nation lost two-thirds of its territory to military occupation and was forced to pay the costs of this foreign presence. A nominally autonomous authoritarian regime was set up under Pétain at Vichy, and it governed the rump one-third of the land under the watchful and guiding eyes of the Germans. Until its demise when the Wehrmacht absorbed it in November, 1942, it pursued a policy of collaboration with the occupiers in the name of self-justifactory patriotic pragmatism. Any residual autonomy of Pétain and his underlings, such as Pierre Laval, was erased with the nation's full occupation. Collaboration abounded until the bitter end, and the more fascist sectors of Pétain's National Revolution became increasingly powerful as the fortunes of war turned against the Third Reich. The Liberation of the land brought shame, degradation, trial and often execution for those public figures who had followed the path of collaboration.[7]

But there was another France, a France which kept honor through its dark hours of shame, the France of the Resistance. Symbolized personally by Charles de Gaulle and his refusal to accept a regime of defeat, the nation's active resistance was embodied largely by the Third Republic's two most prominent pariahs—the Communists and the Catholics. The slumbering wounded Popular Front spirit reemerged under fire, and slowly but surely sectors of French society turned actively against the occupiers and their Vichysoisse shadows. Initially, individuals for a variety of reasons rose up to resist, but within a year, it was apparent that the forces of opposition were dominated by the Communists and by lay Catholics who earned their progressive credentials during the ill-fated Second Ralliement of the 1930s. It was not the French hierarchy, nor *La Croix* nor the Fédération Nationale Catholique who joined the Resistance. In fact, they had welcomed Pétain's National Revolution, its peace, its hierarchical conservative values and its repudiation of the anticlerical Third Republic. Even with the passage of time these conservative Catholic forces stood by the collaborating regime until its demise. Noted exceptions, like Msgr. Saliège of Toulouse, who had backed the Resistance quietly, could not change the fact that the very ecclesiastical forces which had harassed the fledgling Ralliement of the 1930s were also the staunchest supporters of collaboration in the 1940s. Nevertheless, all Catholics did not acquiesce. Christian Democrats, such as Georges Bidault, leader of the National Resistance Council; sectors of the Jeunesse Etudiante Chrétienne; former Catholic trade unionists; Catholic progressive journalists, like Francisque Gay and the founders of the *Témoignage Chrétien* movement, and masses from Jeunesse Ouvrière Chrétienne locals, who were subject to the forced labor requisition program called the Service du Travail Obligatoire, all these formed the backbone of the Catholic resistance. In the face of a common enemy they forged links with the once-hated Communists and laid the ground-work for an esprit de corps which would inspire the construction of a new and more humane France. Louis Aragon, the resistance poet, praised this wartime solidarity by honoring the Communist martyr Gabriel Péri and his Catholic counterpart Gilbert Dru.[8]

The courage of these Catholics and their relentless pressure against the occupiers and collaborators inspired some timid gestures on the part of certain prelates to endorse and adopt avant-garde missionary apostolates to the dechristianized working class, apostolates which would include the Mission de Paris and the worker-priests. It was during the dark night of occupation that Emmanuel Cardinal Suhard of Paris and other bishops struggled to bring to life the Mission de France seminary, to authorize the clandestine chaplaincy to Germany via the Service du Travail Obligatoire and to adopt the controversial study by J.O.C. chaplains Godin and Daniel, *France, pays de mission?*, which would give rise to a Parisian mission to the proletariat. It was within this context of national and ecclesiastical crisis that the worker-priests would be born and experience their baptisms of fire.[9]

When Charles de Gaulle led his Free French troops into Paris in the summer of 1944, the forces of the resistance began in earnest to pool their resources in an effort to rebuild their shattered nation. France would be reborn out of the ashes of defeat and war in the image of the National Resistance Council. Those who had fought together would link arms now to create a nation of *liberté, égalité, fraternité,* a nation which would wipe away forever the shame and humiliation of the the previous four years. Former enemies Catholics and Communists would continue the unity they had forged under fire and would join with the Socialists to rebuild and govern the nation. This three-fold coalition of resisters bore fruit in France's first free elections since the war. With an astounding 26.6 per cent of the vote, the Communists emerged as the number one party of France, while the hastily assembled Christian Democratic Mouvement Républicain Populaire garnered a hefty 25 per cent. Even the Socialists' disappointing third-place 24 per cent was healthy enough to allow a relatively equal partnership among the three parties of the left.

Between the autumn of 1945 and 1947 these parties attempted to govern together according to their earlier resistance visions. This effort called *tripartisme* proved far more difficult to implement. The roots of suspicion and earlier hostility could not be uprooted so easily. Both Communists and Christian Democrats jockeyed for position with the Socialists caught in the middle. Initially, in the process of constitution-making, the Socialists joined with the Communists to endorse a constitution which was unacceptable to the M.R.P. It was rejected by a bare majority at the polls, and the *tripartiste* coalition was sent back to the drawing boards. However, by that time the resistance élan was mortally wounded, and when a compromise constitution, drafted by a Socialist-M.R.P. alliance, was adopted by a weak plurality of the voters, the war-time unity was hopelessly dead. The Fourth Republic emerged at the end of 1946, a discouraging carbon copy of the Third.

Charles de Gaulle, his goal for a strongly executive republic rejected, went into voluntary exile. The Communists became increasingly isolated within the government, and the M.R.P., under the pressure of its voters and events, moved rapidly toward the political center and right center.[10]

When the Communists were ejected from the governing coalition in 1947, the Cold War phase of the Fourth Republic had begun and would last beyond the Fourth Republic into the Fifth which was largely the creation of Charles de Gaulle in 1958. The rise of national economic blueprints, the entry of the Marshall Plan into European life, the first steps toward European integration, the rise of NATO and the wars in Korea, Indochina and later Algeria were the major events which characterized the Fourth Republic after the outbreak of the Cold War. Much of this period was marked by "third force" alliances, shaky coalitions of moderate or centrist politicians led by the M.R.P. and the Socialists. These governments were determined to isolate the growing Gaullists on their right and especially the Communists on their left. They were committed heavily to the United States and European alliance structure, and their increasing conservatism was reflected in the electoral reform legislation of 1951 which repudiated proportional representation for a mixed system favoring the centrist and governing parties. The deterioration of French fortunes in the Indochinese War, the collapse at Dien Bien Phu in the spring of 1954 and rightist army rumblings led to a political crisis which was resolved successfully by a new government led by the Radical Pierre Mendès-France. When the crisis repeated itself with greater intensity in 1958 over the colonial war in Algeria, the Fourth Republic could not resolve the conflict. Right-wing sections of the army were in revolt in North Africa, and Charles de Gaulle's demand for full power to resolve the crisis was voted by the National Assembly on June 1, 1958. In effect, on that day the Fifth Republic was born. The voting of its constitution almost four months later was recognition of a fait accompli.[11]

However, in all of this, the isolation of the Communists was less than successful, since they retained their popularity with the voters. Throughout the Fourth Republic the Communist Party remained the largest political grouping in the land and was the obvious party of most of the nation's industrial proletariat. Furthermore, its effective control of the country's largest and most militant trade-union federation, the Confédération Générale du Travail, insured its working-class reputation and its capacity to use strike action for wider purposes than simple bread-and-butter issues. The massive work stoppages of 1947, 1948 and 1953 are ample demonstration of this. In addition, the Party scored a great political success through its leadership and dominant role in the Peace Movement from 1948 to well into the 1950s. Not only did this movement become world-wide; also it attracted large numbers of noncommunists to its ranks, including prominent progressive Catholics.[12]

And the nation's Catholics, where were they in the midst of this turbulent transition from resistance unity to Cold War? Like the 1930s they were divided, but this time the forces of the Catholic left were notably stronger. More conservative elements within ecclesiastical circles had been tarnished frequently with the collaborationist stain. The hierarchy was not well received in the nation as a whole, and its moral suasion over militant believers was at a low ebb. *La Croix,* Catholicism's most prominent newspaper, adopted a more moderate position in the postwar period, but its circulation plummeted by over one hundred per cent to a figure between 100,000 and 150,000. The weekly *France Catholique* retained a respectable circulation of about 50,000, but this was a massive decline from its earlier Fédération Nationale Catholique days.

By way of contrast, left-leaning Catholics emerged from the Resistance much stronger and more militant. Unlike the 1930s they had moved over to the offensive and were no longer a beleaguered minority. The Mouvement Républicain Populaire had surprised everyone by its stellar showing at the polls, and for one brief moment in 1946, it was the largest party in the nation. Its daily newspaper *l'Aube,* a tiny and financially harassed paper in the 1930s, attained a circulation of 200,000 in the first years of the Fourth Republic. To the left of the more moderate M.R.P. were some influential Catholic voices embodying varying socialist positions. *Témoignage Chrétien* survived the war and became the respectable leftist weekly of the French Church. Although its circulation did not exceed that of *French Catholique,* it had surpassed any other Catholic social democratic newspaper of the earlier period, and a number of progressive prelates welcomed it favorably. Emmanuel Mounier's *Esprit* was thriving, and a few new and creative periodicals were being published by Catholic groups who were advocating a continuation of the war-time alliance between Catholics and Communists. Most noteworthy of these were the Union des chrétiens progressistes, Maurice Montuclard's Jeunesse de l'Eglise movement and the newspaper *La Quinzaine.* Finally, it was during this immediate postwar period that the French Church expanded its creative home missionary activity begun in the 1930s and 1940s. Working-class Catholic Action, youth and adult, continued its previous work, and the theological renaissance, begun in the 1930s, was reaching its maturity after the war. The Mission de France was expanding, and the worker-priest movement was entering its most creative phase. French Catholicism was consciously expanding its interest in the nation's working class.

However, with the advent of the Cold War and with the expulsion of the Communists from the government came also a shift of much of the church toward more conservative and traditional positions. The M.R.P. became a party of the center right and was characterized by a growing anti-Marxist mentality; French bishops paralleled this rightward drift. Once more, progressive Catholics were being isolated. A turning point was marked on July 1, 1949 when the Vatican's Holy Office condemned Communism and collaboration with it. Although the French cardinals softened this position to some extent, they adopted a harder line toward those Catholics dedicated to Marxist-Christian cooperation. From that moment until the end of the Fourth Republic, church progressives found themselves on the defensive. *Témoignage Chrétien* was under fire on a number of occasions not only by conservative Catholics but by members of the hierarchy as well. In their turn, the Union des chrétiens progressistes, the Jeunesse de l'Eglise and *La Quinzaine* were condemned by church officials. The radical Mission de France seminary was closed for a year from 1953 to 1954, and progressive Dominicans were disciplined in 1954. Efforts were made throughout the early 1950s to circumscribe more carefully working-class Catholic Action, and in late 1953 and early 1954 both the Vatican and the French hierarchy acted to dismantle the worker-priest movement. The church's commitment to working class liberation had been softened considerably.[13]

This was the nation into which the worker-priests were born, thrived, struggled and anathematized. It was a France of decline and division, creativity and destruction, war and defeat, collaboration and resistance, liberation and disillusionment, rebirth and Cold War. The worker-priests found themselves within this context, and it could and would not leave them unaffected. Political crisis created the national, ethnic and ecclesiastical environments out of which they would emerge, but there were two other worlds which shaped them more directly. The first was the one from which they came, the world of progressive Catholicism.

III

THE WORLD FROM WHICH THEY CAME: MISSIONARY APOSTOLATES TO THE PROLETARIAT

*"We do not have to put God into this world. He is there . . .
We are in solidarity with this world."*
—Daniel Perrot, Mission de France

National crisis alone could not produce the worker-priests. What it did was provide the means to upset the balance between progressives and conservatives within the French church. In this way an atmosphere was created which allowed the Catholic avant-garde to press for changes. The worker-priests benefitted from this new situation directly, but their origins were rooted in a more distant past. For over seventy years forces within the church had recognized the need for a special ministry to the victims of the Industrial Revolution. Sometimes members of these movements were called social Catholics or Christian Democrats; others were described as belonging to specialized Catholic Action or missionary apostolates. However, no matter what terminology was used, it was this gradual sensitivity of the church's avant-garde toward the working class which prepared Catholicism for the worker-priest experience of the 1940s and 1950s. Certainly, these efforts reflected various value perspectives. Some were reactionary and socially paternalistic; others were reformist; and still others were radical, clear forerunners of liberationist approaches. However, they were all part of the gradual evolution of French Catholicism's growing commitment to the liberation of the oppressed working class. In this sense, they were the most important ecclesiastical nursery which brought the worker-priests to birth and maturity.

Some seventy years earlier two conscience-ridden aristocratic army officers inaugurated a program to liberate the proletariat. These pioneers realized with great sorrow the deep chasm which existed between traditional Christianity and the growing industrial work force. While they were war prisoners of the Prussians, Count Albert de Mun and Marquis René de la Tour du Pin discovered the need for Catholics to dedicate themselves to social reform. Toward that end they vowed to create structures designed to win the working class back to a pre-French Revolutionary Christianity through the medium of social charity. With that in mind they created in 1873 small groups of workers and employers called Oeuvre des Cercles Catholiques d'Ouvriers. These bodies, set in motion after the destruction of the Paris Commune, served as meeting places for study, spiritual development and conflict resolution between bosses and workers. There owners (*patrons*) and their employees would develop a cooperative spirit prompted by Christian justice and inspired by Christian charity. In short, the foundation of the Cercles was inspired by social paternalism, the genuine good will of the "haves" to nurture the "have nots" placed under the care of their social superiors. They called this noblesse oblige the "love of the smallest" and the "devotion of the elevated classes."[1] The organization's own publication described its task as the "propagation and defense . . . of a work organization whose Christian principle of owner duties toward the worker would be its foundation." No wonder the more radical Marc Sangnier, one of De Mun's leading social Catholic competitors, could say of De Mun, "He goes to the people, but he is not one of them."[2]

In spite of this reactionary aloofness, both of these aristocrats laid the necessary groundwork for French social Catholicism and its subsequent evolution in more radical directions. La Tour du Pin, largely through the review *Association Catholique,* became the movement's chief theorist, and de Mun, for the next forty years, would be its leading activist through his writings, through the organizations he founded and in parliament. The limitations of their vision were obvious, but half a century before Cardinal Suhard's patronage of the worker-priests, it was Albert de Mun who uttered this prophetic claim, "There is a chasm between the priest and the people, and because of that the Christian life no longer spreads in France.[3]

Soon a number of committed social Catholics moved beyond the paternalism of la Tour du Pin and de Mun. Rejecting both the noblesse oblige and anti-French Revolutionary principles of their aristocratic forebears, these Christian Democrats, as they were called, sought to amalgamate their dedication to republican democracy with social reform. Although it would be dishonest to call them radicals, these Catholics were moving gradually from platforms "for" the workers to programs "with" and "by" the workers. From the 1890s a number of priests and prominent laity attempted to organize groups to implement these principles. Factory owners, such as Léon Harmel, the naval officer Emmanuel Desgrées du Loû and the priests Hippolyte Gayraud, Jules Lemire, Pierre Dabry, Paul Naudet and Félix Trochu struggled to form political networks and newspapers which would spread progressive Catholic ideas and practices among the dechristianized sectors of the French populace. To be sure these early Christian Democrats espoused a mélange of discordant views, anti-Semitism, social paternalism, radical reforms and some social democracy, but from this unworkable mix emerged notions which contained seeds of the radical liberationist ideas lived by the worker-priests.[4] For example, Father Charles Calippe published a serial novel in *La Démocratie Chrétienne* (1902–1903) in which the priestly hero was an effective witness to Socialists by virtue of his factory work. Paul Naudet, priestly editor of a Breton Christian Democratic newspaper, advocated a worker-priest ministry, and his clerical colleague in parliament Jules Lemire stated, "Let us do what St. Paul did . . . earning a living from the hard labor of the fields."[5] Thus, by the dawn of the twentieth century, some Catholic reformers were flirting with the idea of a priesthood which would identify fully with the working class via manual labor.

Most influential and most visionary of all the Christian Democrats was the well-to-do Marc Sangnier, founder of Sillon, a militant organization dedicated to his mystical Catholic and social democratic principles. In a variety of ways Sangnier made concrete his commitment to "the reconciliation of Christ and the people, of Catholicism and the suffering of the revolutionary masses." He formed study groups of workers and radical bourgeois Catholic youth; he created consumer cooperatives, hostels and popular educational institutes; and he disseminated Sillonist ideas through a monthly review *Le Sillon* and a weekly newspaper *L'Eveil Démocratique*. Especially visionary were Sangnier's notions of working class justice. He rejected the separatist Catholic trade unions, calling instead for Sillonist workers to join the more revolutionary Confédération Générale du Travail (C.G.T.) because it was "an instrument of social transformation." He supported the right to strike, accepted the reality of class struggle and upheld the necessity for "the free and conscious worker [to] possess in common the instruments of their [sic] work." Although the Vatican and French hierarchy repudiated his efforts in 1910, Sangnier's work was prophetic. His insistence on the non-Christian character of modern industrial society and his call for "a new social order in conformity with the exigencies of Christianity" foreshadowed the trenchant observations of the more radical Catholic progressives who created and welcomed the worker-priests in the early 1940s. Sangnier was a man well ahead of his time. His analysis of working class oppression, and the means he advocated to overcome it were adopted years later by both the worker-priests and numerous liberation theologians.[6]

During the same era emerged two study groups of progressive Catholics, both dedicated to the christianization of the proletariat and the amelioration of its lot. Beginning in the 1890s a number of Catholic laymen in the Lyon area proceeded to publish a social Catholic review called *Chronique des Comités du Sud-Est*. Led by a mystic celibate silk worker named Marius Gonin this group adopted Christian Democratic principles of social reform and soon drew fire from more reactionary foes. Although the review changed its title a number of times, it settled upon the name *Chronique Sociale de France* in 1909. From that moment it appeared monthly throughout the Third and Fourth Republics. Beginning in 1904 its leaders organized annual study weeks which brought together the nation's leading social Catholic thinkers and activists. Throughout the next half century these Semaines Sociales provided the most important locus in France for the exchange of socially progressive ideas within the church. Although neither the *Chronique* nor the Semaines Sociales were dedicated exclusively to proletarian concerns, they studied carefully such diverse issues as socialism, class struggle, a managed economy, strikes, factory injustices and the total liberation of the working-class.[7] However, the theoretical nature of this organization prevented it from having any serious impact in the arena of industrial reform. Its influence would be felt in exclusively Catholic circles where it would act as a gadfly challenging the dominant social conservatism within the church.

The Jesuit-based Action Populaire would play a similar role among the faithful. Founded by a Lille Jesuit Henri-Joseph Leroy in 1903 and assisted by his confrere Father Gustave Desbuquois, it became "a team of religious, aided by some laity," involved in developing "a center of study and social information." Over the next fifty years its headquarters moved first to Reims, then to Paris and from there to the Parisian suburb of Vanves. There it remained until the present, save for a brief Lyon sojourn during the German occupation. Although this educational and missionary apostolate evolved over the years, its consistently most valuable contributions were its publications in the fields of social Catholic thought and practice. This blend of the theoretical and technical made Action Populaire perhaps the most broadly based source of Catholic social thought in France. Its pamphlets, monographs, and reviews provided thoughtful analysis on such varied topics as working class dechristianization, Marxism, trade unionism, factory life, the missionary structures of the church in popular milieus and other related topics. Like its counterpart the Semaines Sociales it remained theoretical and somewhat socially conservative, but it is important to note that a number of Jesuit worker-priests were temporarily under its tutelage.[8]

Similar to much of the work debated and published by both Action Populaire and the Semaines Sociales were the efforts of individual authors concerned with the need for priests more adapted to an emerging secular society.[9] However, it was the rise of the sociologists of religion that added a new dimension to these inquiries. Although there were some parallels with respect to the issues under investigation, these researchers gave a priority to scientific pursuits rather than missionary concerns. The pioneer in this emerging field of religious sociology was Gabriel Le Bras. To be sure, he was a man of faith aware of the church's apostolic needs in a rapidly secularizing society, but his sociological work was a natural outgrowth of his university vocation in the history of Christian institutions. His methodology was clearly that of scientific sociology. In his seminal two-volume *Introduction à l'histoire de la pratique religieuse* (1942–1945) and his later *Etudes de Sociologie Religieuse* one can see the work of a precise social scientist examining how French Catholics practiced their faith from the Middle Ages to the present. This methodology and its concern with objective research reached a culmination in the postwar period with the appearance of the review *Archives de Sociologie des Religions.* Published by the Centre National de la Recherche Scientifique, this scholarly journal studies religious sociology from the perspective of the social sciences. In this sense, it represents a strand of that discipline which was not part of the ecclesiastical milieu out of which the worker-priests emerged.[10] However, both the content of Le Bras' investigation and the results he unearthed were of immediate concern to the "pastoral sociologists" who were inspired by the missionary needs of the church in France. Father Fernand Boulard set the tone for this mode of sociological work. Although his initiatives were directed toward rural dechristianization, he paved the way for subsequent efforts in urban research. Boulard edited a review for rural clergy called *Cahiers du clergé rural,* but his seminal work *Problèmes missionnaires de la France rurale,* published in 1945, served as a model in the years to come for the systematic study of religious practice in the nation from an ecclesiastical perspective. Unlike Le Bras and the later articles of the *Archives,* Boulard broke with the social scientific intentions of these other sociologists.

His concerns were openly evangelistic; his purpose was to use this data as a shock (*choc*) to inspire the church to mount effective apostolates to meet the problem of dechristianization. In this sense his work reflected the "pastoral sociology" of urban missionaries as well. The investigations of Fathers Henri Godin and Yvan Daniel which produced *La France, pays de mission?* are one example of this. It was these "pastoral sociologists" who formed a direct link with those who were prepared to combine sociological research with militant programs designed to ameliorate the lot of the workers.[11]

These latter figures could be called participatory or incarnational sociologists. A number of them were not researchers by profession, but the ability and passion which enabled them to write about their life within the French proletariat had a direct impact upon the more sophisticated work of the other participatory sociologists. Simone Weil was Jewish in background, but in the latter years of her brief life she was attracted passionately to the Christ figure and the Catholic faith. Her revolutionary devotion to the causes of the poor and the proletariat led her to abandon a professional teaching career for factory work and the militant working class movement. Her reflections on these experiences, published under the title *La Condition ouvrière,* as well as her personal and theological ties with Gustave Thibon, had direct impact on the church's missionary apostolates of the 1940s and 1950s. Especially important was her influence upon the Economie et Humanisme team and its docker-priest Jacques Loew. Madeleine Delbrêl was an unmarried social worker who ministered to her neighborhood in the Communist industrial ghetto of Ivry just southwest of Paris. She arrived in 1933 and served there for over three decades until her death in 1964. Although her two major works reflecting on this experience were not published until after the worker-priest controversy, her witness at Ivry and her ideas were promulgated by Jacques Loew at Economie et Humanisme in Marseille and utilized by the Mission de France seminary, which trained so many of the worker-priests.[12]

In fact, it was this Marseille-based team (*équipe*) which represented most clearly the practice of incarnational sociology. The inspiration behind Economie et Humanisme was Louis-Joseph Lebret, a Dominican who had been in apostolic mission work since 1929. In that year he helped to organize the Jeunesse Maritime Chrétienne, and throughout the 1930s he studied the economic, social and moral life of fishermen while he lived in their midst. From 1938 he dreamed of organizing a team of Catholic sociologists inspired by the twin goals of missionary and social transformation. Led by these visions, he and his colleagues would do their scholarly research in the midst of human problems. In 1941 this hope bore fruit with the founding of Economie et Humanisme. The new team published a manifesto in 1942 which described in detail its commitment to "observe human facts methodically with the view of assuring a more happy life for humanity." Both liberal capitalism and socialism were decried as false solutions to human deprivation and dislocation; instead the équipe called for "an economy of a humane order" based on natural groupings and communities (*communautés de destin*) which would be nurtured and supported by some governmental regulation. Toward that end Lebret, Loew and the others dedicated themselves to highly sophisticated techniques of sociological analysis and research which demanded, above all, investigation in the very day-to-day experience of the subjects to be studied. A masterpiece of this methodology is Jacques Loew's own *Les Dockers de Marseille,* a powerful blend of history, data and personal testimony. In two significant ways Economie et Humanisme had moved beyond the other Catholic sociologists toward a liberation model which would be adopted by the worker-priests. First, it identified with the oppressed by living among them, and second, it called for a substantive social transformation which would obliterate that oppression. That its team members did not adopt the militancy necessary to accomplish that task does not negate the significant steps they had taken in the direction of a liberation *praxis* for and with the proletariat.[13]

The Jeunesse de l'Eglise *équipe,* the child of another Dominican Maurice Montuclard, shared the concern of Economie et Humanisme for the marginalized and disinherited, but its analysis and program were significantly more radical. This team of both clergy and laity evolved in roughly two phases. From 1936 to 1942 it sought to unite the various fragments of specialized Catholic Action and to develop a relevant and active spirituality for "the use of the laity." After some disciplinary reorganization by Cardinal Gerlier of Lyon, Montuclard broke up the community but maintained a team dedicated to publishing research on "the problems of the church and the world" and the relationship between the two. By the end of the war Montuclard set up residence with his collaborators at Petit-Clamart, a Parisian suburb. There until the church's condemnation of its efforts in 1953 and 1954, Jeunesse de l'Eglise produced a number of specialized studies as well as a newsletter. These publications called "Collection Jeunesse de l'Eglise" contained a series of articles centered around such particular themes as the problem of the established church, poverty and human liberation. One of the books, *Les Événements et la foi,* authored by Montuclard himself, was instrumental in convincing members of the church's hierarchy that Jeunesse de l'Eglise should be condemned. Its advocacy of the revolutionary working class movement in the name of the gospel and its support of Christian-Marxist collaboration may have been received with joy by radical Catholics and some worker-priests, but the church's clerical leadership was wary at best.[14]

Indeed, Father Montuclard was part of a wider theological renaissance in the French Church which had begun with such Thomistic figures as Jacques Maritain and Etienne Gilson in the 1920s. The weekly newspaper *Vie Catholique,* founded by the Christian Democratic publisher Francisque Gay, heralded the advent of an era of Catholic intellectual pluralism. This explosion of creative theological energy blossomed in the 1930s and reached its fruition in the late 1940s and early 1950s. It was a theology of openness to the world and of challenge to the church. One found it in the *équipe* of Emmanuel Mounier which gave birth to the avant-garde journal *Esprit* in 1932. It emerged in the Dominican Order in the 1930s in the forms of liturgical innovation (*Vie Spirituelle*) and intellectual reflection (*Vie Intellectuelle*). Also a number of theological forerunners of Vatican II began their illustrious careers in this era. These thinkers were determined to move beyond the fortresses of academia into active involvement (*engagement*) in both the church and the world. Although their earlier efforts were cautious and timid, they created an atmosphere for the philosophical radicalism which emerged from the war and resistance to the Germans.[15]

Most important of these theological innovators were the layman Emmanuel Mounier, the Jesuits Henri de Lubac and Jean Daniélou and the Dominicans Maurice Montuclard, Yves Congar and Marie-Dominique Chenu. Not all of these thinkers linked their avant-garde notions to proletarian issues. Indeed, Father de Lubac was relatively unconcerned with either the worker-priests or the working class apostolate, and both Daniélou and Congar, although sympathetic, were only involved marginally. Such was not the case with Mounier, Montuclard and Chenu who were dedicated passionately to these concerns. Inspired by the unity forged in the Resistance, Emmanuel Mounier spoke of "a fraternal presence in the working class world that we have the moral duty to uphold," and toward that end, he insisted that Christians cooperate with the Communist Party because it was the "most dynamic party of the working class." In his *Pour une théologie du travail* M.-D. Chenu developed an intellectual rationale for integrating the church's message of creation and redemption with industrialization and the struggles of militant toilers. "The proletarian masses are destined to produce in their own being this will and this hope [for human community]," affirmed Chenu. "They will redeem the world."[16] This burst of intellectual vitality impacted upon both the worker-priests and later liberation theology in two ways. More generally, it was part of an increasing atmosphere of inquiry which presaged the open ecumenicity of the Second Vatican Council, and in the specific instances of Mounier, Montuclard and Chenu, there were direct ties of empathy and commitment to the worker-priests and proletarian justice issues.

Even the more cautious hierarchy was caught up in this new spirit which had peaked in the Resistance euphoria. Prior to the war a number of high-level prelates had established a reputation for sympathy toward the working class. Jean Verdier, the cardinal archbishop of Paris, and Achille Liénart, the cardinal bishop of Lille, were the most prominent of these. As early as 1929 Bishop Liénart had endorsed and supported an effort by Catholic trade unionists near Belgium to raise money for the material needs of suffering families involved in a local strike of textile workers. Verdier committed himself publicly to working class missions by the construction of chapels in Paris' industrial suburbs and by espousing openly the need for justice in social matters. However, these earlier acts were rare and were limited to charitable gestures.[17]

Nevertheless, these initiatives laid the groundwork for the postwar hierarchy's more concentrated efforts on behalf of social reform. After the national soil had been liberated France's leading cardinals, Liénart of Lille, Pierre-Marie Cardinal Gerlier of Lyon, the aging Jules-Gérard Cardinal Saliège of Toulouse, Emmanuel Cardinal Suhard of Paris and later his successor Maurice Cardinal Feltin led the church's leadership into open advocacy of proletarian missions and justice for the workers. Under their direction the 1945 Assembly of French Cardinals and Archbishops condemned "the scandal of the proletarian condition," its "state of insecurity" and "its misery" as well as the capitalist system with its "primacy of money" and "profit" over and above "the human person of the workers." Using the papal social teachings of Leo XIII, Pius XI and Pius XII, the church's princes demanded property for the workers, proletarian participation at all levels of factory life and strong working class organizations. On other occasions these same prelates, both singly and collectively, defended the legitimate demands of the workers in the midst of their strike actions. In this respect the French cardinals had moved beyond their halting gestures of the 1930s. This and the support they gave to the church's missionary efforts to the proletariat created an ecclesiastical atmosphere which allowed the worker-priests and other Catholic progressives to maneuver with some flexibility.[18]

However, the situation was much more complex than that. A profound conservative and defensive spirit continued to define and shape the hierarchy's dedication to the proletariat. The same churchmen who defended the workers had also welcomed the authoritarian collaborationist regime of Philippe Pétain which had closed down the trade unions. Indeed, a deep anticommunism colored the cardinals' perceptions of working class needs to the extent that they advocated policies which would create and promote *de facto* divisions within the proletarian movements. Their notion that the Catholic trade unions should be a competitor of the communist-led unions, and their and the pope's condemnation of collaboration with communists (1949), are two examples of that. Such a stance created many difficulties for militant Catholics involved in direct working class protests. Among those most seriously affected were the worker-priests.[19]

In spite of this ambivalence toward the working class with its values, demands and organizations, the nation's prelates were avid promoters of significant efforts to penetrate the working class in the name of Christian mission. To be sure men like Suhard, Liénart, Gerlier and Feltin carried this mix of progressive and defensive ideas into their dealings with the missionary apostolates, but their affection for these experiments cannot be denied. These movements form the immediate context out of which the worker-priests grew. Indeed, as far as the church was concerned, the worker-priests were part of one coordinated effort to win the proletariat to Christ.[20]

Suhard himself realized that specialized missions to dechristianized workers both rural and urban required specially trained priests. Consequently he promoted a mission-centered seminary which the French cardinals and archbishops created at Lisieux in 1941. From the fall of 1942 until Rome granted it an apostolic constitution in August, 1954, the Mission de France seminary prepared priests for the difficult and creative work required by the non-Christian arenas into which the church would send its special clergy. Under the direction of the Sulpician father Louis Augros, the seminary and the clerical communities which grew out of it became centers of research and radical innovation for clergy and theologians involved in direct work with the rural poor and the industrial proletariat.[21]

The structures, values, and personalities linked with the Mission de France overlapped the worker-priest movement itself. Many of these laboring priests received all or part of their formal training at

Lisieux. The atmosphere at the seminary and its evolving program were exceedingly imaginative. Pedagogically Augros and his fellow professors were dedicated to a mode of open inquiry which they called *recherche*. In this format, traditional lectures in classical theology were augmented by group work and discussion in Bible and church history. The historical sense of God's revelation was stressed as well as the interrelated character of human and divine activity. Students were encouraged to read Karl Marx and other communist materials, and daily breakfast included reflective exercises on current events as reported in popular newspapers. All spiritual and academic activities were exercised in small groups called *équipes,* and these demonstrated the Mission's emphasis on community living. A similar pattern was practiced by the mission teams in the field whether urban or rural, and these groups of priests gave to the French church some of its most creative and avant-garde forms of ministry. Perhaps the most innovative of all the seminary's programs was the controversial *stage.* Ever since a number of its students had returned from German prison camps, pressure to send seminarians into the fields and factories became the norm at Lisieux. Fathers Chenu and Depierre, one of the first worker-priests, promoted this idea with Father Augros as well. The *stage,* or brief period of manual labor for seminarians, was viewed as an integral part of priestly missionary formation, "a more profound way" than simply study for discovering "the human life of the people just as it is." These innovative practices in combination with each other were forerunners of the praxis-reflection-praxis methodology employed by the liberation communities of Latin America, but in France they were used in the context of an industrialized society. Thus it is not surprising that there was a direct link between so many of the worker-priests and the Mission de France.[22]

Mission de France values reflected similar ties to both the worker-priests and later liberation theology. The notion of "the law of incarnation" and the conviction that God was accomplishing his redemptive purpose within the world and history are two examples of this. One of the seminary's professors Father Lévèsque called these views expressions of the church's "nuptials with the world." Father Daniel Perrot of the Mission summarized these ideas in a language echoed by later liberation theologians and practiced by the worker-priests:

We must enter the working class movement to evangelise the worker or become a sailor with the sailors. In every case we must enter into the hopes, efforts, quests (*recherche*), creations, enthusiasms of the modern world to there discover the

action of God and reveal it to men. We do not have to put God
into this world. He is there. But we must perceive His presence and aid our brothers to recognize Him. Further we must
enter into the struggles and temptations of this world. We
must, like Christ, carry its sins. We are in solidarity with this
world.[23]

As far as the hierarchy was concerned, top priority in missionary
efforts to the proletariat was linked to the parish. The vast majority of
the nation's 41,000 priests were involved in that form of ministry. Consequently the hierarchy chose to concentrate on this institution in the
hope that it could be rendered truly missionary in both structure and
commitment. Sharp criticism of the parish was rampant among the
church's avant-garde leaders, but all of them were convinced that the
neighborhood church could have a significant impact upon the industrial ghettos of France.[24] Indeed, throughout the 1940s and 1950s
a number of churches in urban proletarian neighborhoods were renovated to meet the special needs of the dechristianized workers who
lived within the territory of these parishes.

Most famous of these was Sacre Coeur found in the heart of the
Parisian industrial suburb Colombes. During the critical growth years
it was pastored by two priests from the Fils de la Charité order,
Georges Michonneau and Louis Rétif. Michonneau was the senior pastor and Rétif was his vicar until 1947 when the latter became the leader
of the priestly *équipe* in his own right. He continued to serve the Sacre
Coeur parish throughout the worker-priest years and was himself
caught up in the controversy of that era. Both men were committed to
ministering fully to their slum neighborhood of almost 30,000 inhab-
itants. During the German occupation they created soup kitchens and
consumer cooperatives, gathered packages for war prisoners and
helped the destitute families of the deported.[25]

By 1945 both priests were prepared to adapt the parish to meet
the spiritual needs of a proletarian environment alienated from the
church. Door-to-door visits were organized within the parish boundaries, and the active members of the church were involved in reflection
sessions geared to instituting renovations which would render church
life more communal and relevant to the working class world. Toward
that end much of the liturgy was put in the vernacular and structured
to increase participation on the part of the worshipping community.
Specifically ecclesiastical activities were reduced so that greater emphasis could be placed upon specialized Catholic Action and direct
neighborhood visitations. Distinctions between marriages and funer-

als based on the ability to pay were abolished, and financial appeals were reduced to a minimum. During the Rétif years Sacre Coeur was a center of coordination for working class apostolates in the Colombes-Nanterre area. In addition to missionary parish activities Sacre Coeur had militant Catholic Action groups and links with many of the Paris-based worker-priests.[26]

Throughout the 1940s and 1950s other missionary parishes were organized in industrial ghettos throughout France. A number of these were created by the Mission de France. Daniel Perrot himself gave up his seminary professorship to lead the parish team of St. Hippolyte in a working class neighborhood in southern Paris. The church became deeply involved in all the social and political reforms of the entire sector and remained committed to the coordination of all the missionary apostolates of the area. Other missionary parishes were dedicated to mining communities, and still others ministered to the dislocated workers constructing large hydroelectric dams in isolated rural areas.[27] For the most part, the clergy of these parishes avoided any direct advocacy of working class radicalism. Their overriding concern was to adopt a mode of being that reflected the culture and life of their working class neighbors. In this way they hoped to attract the proletariat to the church. However, the very compassion which permeated their parish reforms also intensified their growing openness to proletarian struggles. Because of this many of them were strong supporters of the worker-priests throughout their controversial career.

Specialized Catholic Action, dating from the 1920s, was more controversial and potentially more radical than the renovated parishes. Its oldest and most prominent missionary apostolate was created in 1925 by a Belgian priest named Joseph Cardijn. He took his idea of a working class Catholic youth organization to Pope Pius XI, and the pontiff himself became the patron of the new Jeunesse Ouvrière Chrétienne. Two years later Father Georges Guérin found a unit in France. By the late 1930s the J.O.C. had a membership in excess of 65,000, and its major newspaper *Jeunesse Ouvrière* had a circulation of roughly 270,000. Throughout the 1930s it spread rapidly in the industrial centers of France so much so that by the outbreak of the war it was the single most important proletarian youth group in the nation. After the military defeat of 1940 the Jociste leadership welcomed the authoritarian Pétain regime, and the J.O.C. was accepted under the umbrella of Vichy youth organizations. However, when Nazi Germany forced France into a labor requisition program which compelled Pétain to send masses of French workers to German factories, many rank-and-file Jocistes joined the Resistance while those already in Germany formed factory cells which included militant Communists. After the war the J.O.C. continued its collaboration with Marxists until an atmosphere of cold war prompted it to return to its prewar anticommunism. By the mid-1950s it was declining and beset by internal difficulties, but it continued to promote social reforms designed to help proletarian youth.[28] This checkered history is one indicator of the self-definitional problem faced by the J.O.C. in its first thirty years of life. Though potentially radical by virtue of its proletarian character, in reality it vacillated between defensive anti-Marxism and social democratic reformism. In this respect, it reflected the ecclesiastical forces which sponsored it.

This tension was revealed in the consciously adopted two-fold task of the J.O.C., namely the establishment of justice for the working class as well as its conversion to Jesus Christ. Roger Cartayrade, a war-time Jociste leader, insisted that "the goal of the J.O.C." was that of "remaking our brothers into Christians" in "their life context . . . a Christianity which participates in this life and which does not separate the youth from the social context of the working class nor from the workers' movement." However, this two-fold goal was most difficult to achieve. The social doctrine of the church was class collaborationist and anti-Marxist, whereas the industrial proletariat was conscious of class struggle, with its most militant sectors being resolutely Marxist. Jocistes strove mightily to integrate their Christian and proletarian commitments, but it was not easy. At one moment they could appeal to "an atmosphere of unity between factory owners and workers," and in another instant, claim that the bosses have forced "the workers into a class struggle."[29] Twenty-five years did not resolve the tension, yet by 1952 a more mature J.O.C. was prepared to recognize this painful ambiguity:

> As persons, we are in a unique *engagement,* involved (*engagés*) in the world, in the working class movement in so far as we are militant workers, and involved (*engagés*) in the Kingdom of God in so far as we are militant Christian workers: active members of the church and active members of the temporal realm. Sometimes we suffer an internal dislocation; this is the fatal tension of those who are crucified. But we are sure that, in struggling for justice, for liberty, for love, our unique effort is valuable and efficacious . . . for the Kingdom of God and the human order as well.[30]

On the practical level this tension hampered the effectiveness of the J.O.C. in both its social and missionary endeavors. Structurally it was linked to the church's hierarchy with the bishops retaining their influence through the chaplains whom they appointed to advise the Jocistes at every level. Although many of these chaplain advisors were sensitive to proletarian needs and supportive of a growing autonomy for the youth they counseled, many others were overbearing and oppressive. In addition, the Jeunesse Ouvrière Chrétienne was hampered by internal debates about the proper milieu for most of its activities. Initially its members seemed most comfortable in ecclesiastical structures, such as the urban parish, but soon feeling alienated there, they moved into massive neighborhood activities such as mutual aid, education and leisure programs. In the professional arena, they organized political lobbying campaigns for social benefits, and they were effective advocates for relevant apprenticeship courses for young proletarians. However, even in these areas, they hesitated to move beyond the patterns of reformist behavior.[31]

In addition, their presence was weak and often divisive on the factory floor. By the late 1940s and early 1950s they had organized cells in the postal, railroad and mining industries, but results were only substantive among the postal workers at this time. In heavy industry the Jocistes were isolated, and their influence was minimal. Even here they stood out quite often by their unwillingness to unite with the more militant sectors of the French proletariat. The organization's persistent anticommunism was perhaps the chief reason for its reluctance to espouse the more radical forms and strategies of its laboring comrades. Although increasingly rank-and-file Jocistes joined the ranks of the communist dominated C.G.T., the national leadership continued to promote openly the Catholic trade union federation. This same hesitancy was found concerning strike activity. Certainly Jocistes had been militants in every major work stoppage since the factory occupations of 1936, but once again the organization itself was very cautious. It advocated limited and professional strikes designed, as a last resort, to pressure for purely economic and social gains. The notion of a broad-based or political strike in the name of social transformation was anathema to Jociste officials. This cast the Jeunesse Ouvrière Chrétienne in a reformist light which made it suspect in the eyes of the industrial proletariat to which it belonged and for which it claimed to advocate. In spite of these difficulties the J.O.C. remained one of the most innovative and influential organs within progressive Catholicism which championed the cause of the proletariat. Over the years its rank-and-file had become increasingly radical in spite of the resistance of both its leadership and the hierarchy of the church.[32]

Inspired by its success with the Jocistes, the church expanded its efforts by creating adult forms of specialized Catholic Action among the nation's toilers. As early as the 1930s the Ligue Ouvrière Chré-tienne was formed by those who had been Jocistes before their adult-hood. Although the new organization achieved some prewar success, it was not satisfied with being simply an adjunct of the J.O.C. Turning more and more to political efforts, the L.O.C. lost the favor of the church and was forced to leave Catholic Action. In 1941 the organi-zation changed its name to the Mouvement populaire des familles so that it could advocate for the workers in the name of the family and thus avoid direct persecution by Pétain's authoritarian state. The new movement was successful during the war years both in terms of growth and social aid programs to proletarian families. Much like the J.O.C., the M.P.F. had the dual goal of evangelization and social justice for the proletariat, hence its formula "by the worker families, with the worker families, for the worker families." With the liberation of France the M.P.F. had become both decentralized and relatively autonomous with respect to the hierarchy and priests of the church. In addition, its members were increasingly active collaborators with their former com-rades in the Resistance, including communists in both the party and the C.G.T. As the Cold War intensified in France so did hierarchical pressure make itself felt upon an increasingly independent M.P.F. Consequently, in 1950 the church reorganized its adult working class apostolate into a new Action Catholique Ouvrière which would be more effectively shaped by the ecclesiastical leadership and less sus-ceptible to Marxist elements.[33]

The new A.C.O. viewed itself as "a collection of priestly teams and lay (*équipes*) . . . in the service of the church and the working class world." A certain autonomy was granted to the militants within the or-ganization, but it was very clear that with the church's "mandate for the evangelization of the workers' world" came the mechanisms of episcopal control through the A.C.O. chaplains and the diocesan com-mittees. Nevertheless, the pluralism of the A.C.O. was never repu-diated. Its members were required to be active participants in a proletarian organization outside of the A.C.O., and that was left to the individual's discretion as long as his choice was not a group con-demned by the church. The A.C.O. was to gather together all adult militant Christian workers into one organ of spiritual and missionary formation. There they would be religiously strengthened and trained so that they could be an effective Christian presence in their union or worker organization. Like the J.O.C. these adults received their eccle-siastical character from Catholic Action; unlike the J.O.C. they expe-rienced their working class militancy outside of the institutional apparatus of the church. This relative autonomy allowed A.C.O. activists the opportunity for more radical participation in the liberation of the proletariat. Consequently, many of them would be found among the ranks of the worker-priests' supporters.[34]

Last of all, there were a number of small religious orders dedicated specifically to apostolic endeavors in the midst of the toiling poor. Although there was some overlap between these groups and the worker-priests, the organizations were essentially evangelical in outlook. For that reason, they were committed to adopting the grim lifestyle of the proletariat. Militant action to change that oppression was, at best, a secondary matter as far as they were concerned. The first of these orders, the Fils de la Charité, was dedicated to parish reform in working class neighborhoods and included the well-known priests Georges Michonneau and Louis Rétif. Henri Godin, considered the impetus to the worker-priest ministry, served in the order briefly, and Bernard Lacroix was the first of this group to enter a factory.[35]

The Prado order, which had direct links to the worker-priest movement, was founded in Lyon (1856) by a Father Antoine Chevrier. He felt called to a mission in which he would "link up with the poor, wherever they were, in order to bring Christ to them." Prado was created to fulfill this need; consequently, it located in the worst slums of that city. Alfred Ancel, the first worker-bishop, was the superior of the order during the 1940s and 1950s. As auxiliary bishop of Lyon, he had the ear of Cardinal Gerlier and helped him develop working class apostolates in the archdiocese. Ancel set up Prado *équipes* of priests and laymen in urban slums so that they could be a visual presence of Christ in the neighborhood and factory. A number of his priests, including Paul Guilbert, Jean Tarby and René Desgrand, toiled in Lyon-based industries. After the worker-priests were condemned in 1954, Father Ancel was able to receive permission from his archbishop to set up a Prado team in the urban slum of Gerland. Ancel himself lived on the premises and ran a small workshop part-time. His priests were allowed to labor a few hours each day, but the lay brothers were able to be employed full-time at a factory. For Ancel manual labor was a testimony of the presence of Christ among the poor and not an occasion for militant social change. At the heart of the matter were Chevrier's words, "I will be in the midst of them [the workers], and I will live their life."[36]

Like Prado the Petits Frères de Jésus are an order of clergy and laity devoted to incarnating Christ fully in the midst of the proletariat. Founded in 1936 the Petits Frères were inspired by the thought and life of Father Charles de Foucauld who, at the end of the nineteenth century, committed himself to the lifestyle Jesus had experienced in the carpentry workshop of Nazareth. De Foucauld became a desert hermit in French North Africa determined to adopt "the life of Nazareth in its simplicity" by being a presence of God among the poor and disinherited Moslems of the Sahara. The order which adopted his vision organized small clergy-laity *équipes* prepared "to lead a life of poverty, prayer and work, going into the milieu of the most abandoned sectors of the population, in order that the love of Christ might shine there." Thus, by the time of the worker-priests, manual labor had become of the very essence of the Petits Frères apostolate. For them, work was necessary to bring the gospel to the proletariat. Father René Voillaume, the order's superior, defended the manual labor of a Petit Frère priest in this way: "Work is the act of naturalization which allows him to enter the proletariat. Without this work, the priest will remain a stranger. A priest who does not earn his bread will remain suspect." Voillaume and his order remained on the fringes of the more militant apostolates, but they developed a theology of priestly manual labor which would be adopted by many of the worker-priests themselves.[37]

Behind all these efforts to render the church present in the midst of a dechristianized proletariat was the official social doctrine of the popes. Since 1891, with the publication of *Rerum Novarum* by Leo XIII, Catholicism had committed itself openly to the amelioration of the workers' lot both materially and spiritually. The emergence of Pius XI's *Quadragesimo Anno* forty years later established the continuity of Leo's earlier dedication, and both Pius XI and Pius XII became involved actively in a number of working class apostolates. Although the papacy reflected the same ambivalence as the French hierarchy toward the church's more radical grass-roots expressions, it cannot be doubted that the papal encyclicals in these matters were inspired by and supportive of those pioneers who, since Albert de Mun, had dedicated their lives to crossing the chasm which existed between the church and the working class.[38]

Certainly the worker-priests were not the immediate product of all these efforts to integrate Catholicism into the French proletariat, nor did this seventy years of activity produce a full-blown liberation theology applicable to the industrial west. Nevertheless, the groundwork had been laid. The worker-priests and the liberation theology they came to embody emerged from a particular ecclesiastical context, a context characterized by a massive explosion of missionary apostolates to and with the proletariat. What had begun with Albert de Mun and Marc Sangnier continued and expanded in the 1930s until its full flowering of the 1940s and 1950s. Research teams, renovated parishes, a mission seminary, militant Catholic Action and specialized religious orders were rich soil conducive to the growth of a worker-priest ministry. The mood was ripe for such an experiment. Catholic missions to the working class were the matrix in which the worker-priests were born; proletarian life itself would become the caldron in which they would be defined and shaped along more radical liberationist lines. Progressive Catholicism allowed them to be priests for the laboring masses. The factories and urban ghettos would transform them into worker-priests.

IV

THE WORLD TO WHICH THEY CAME: THE FRENCH WORKING CLASS

*"The proletariat goes through life
like a motorist without a spare tire."*
—Jacques Loew, docker priest

Inspiration to enter the working class was rooted in the worker-priests' consciousness of their faith, a faith nurtured in sectors of the church dedicated to proletarian mission. However, it was the oppressive milieu to which they came that most profoundly radicalized the worker-priests and provided them with liberationist conceptions of their collective vocation. The workplace and the industrial neighborhoods were decisive in forging their identities, and all the preconceived ideas they brought with them would be either abandoned or recast in light of the environment into which they were plunged. Their uniform testimony, much like that of later liberation theologians, was that the shocking experience of manual labor and the daily life molded by it demanded a totally new assessment of their mission.[1]

A description of this environment is absolutely essential for understanding the life and values which grew out of the worker-priest ministry. In spite of the productivity and the apparent prosperity of western industrial society, there were always pockets of poverty and uneven development not unlike the barrios of Latin America. In France, the laboring classes represented this darker, more grim, side of the expanding capitalism which followed the devastation of World War II. The French proletariat was a microcosm of the third world in the macrocosm of the first.

The kind of work they were forced to undertake was one significant example of this oppression. Testimony after testimony revealed that factory toil was perceived to be dehumanizing and brutal by those

34

who performed it. Simone Weil observed that "work is too mechanical to offer any material for thinking." Indeed, it is "a perpetual and humiliating degradation." The reduction of the human being to one cog in the machinery of production was the direct result of Taylorism or automated assembly line labor. Each worker was assigned one mechanical job in a vast production line and was expected to maintain a rapid and mindless cadence in keeping with the speed capacity of the machinery. This monotonous rhythm, argued Weil, gave to the toilers a single clear message: "You are nothing here. You don't count." You are "a simple intermediary between the machines and the factory parts made." Consequently, she asserted: "The worker, though indispensable to production, counts for almost nothing, and this is why each suffering, each imposed mutilation, each disregard, each brutality, each humiliation, however small, is a reminder that he doesn't count and that he doesn't belong."[2]

Others, who labored side by side with the worker-priests, described the same unrelenting toil. The assembly line worker was a slave to the machine and the clock. It was the equipment which produced the piece. And the worker, "he must regulate it, watch over it and make a certain number of elementary and identical gestures for each piece." This alone tied him to time and its rhythm. A work pace was set according to the machine's capacity to produce the item it was designed to manufacture. Sleep, meals, travel time and, above all, labor on the line were subject to the minute ticking of the clock. "We must arrive five minutes before the doors close in the morning, . . . and begin work on the assembly line at the exact hour," stated a woman employed at a military equipment plant in Paris. She recalled the loud whistle which blew every three minutes to mark production time for the brass helmets she helped to assemble. She lamented the brief span of fifteen minutes allowed "to go to the washroom and have a snack" and remembered the "frequent nervous breakdowns and many accidents" which resulted from the fatigue created by this kind of labor.[3]

The menial and rote character of such toil tended to demean the work relationship between the laborers and their bosses. Reports of disparaging comments about workers were not uncommon. "You've been gone for ten minutes," said one foreman to a woman at his plant. "If you're sick, get lost." About a laborer with tuberculosis, another foreman stated abruptly: "You know, we don't need a dead dog around here." Two other comments by managers seem to summarize the notion that workers are simply replaceable parts. "The worker is like a lemon that you squeeze. When it is no longer of service, you throw it out the window." Similar to this statement was the remark, "take care of the machinery, for I can't replace it. People I can."[4] This harsh reality lent credence to the summary of proletarian life reported by the worker-priest *équipe* at Limoges:

> He [the worker] is totally dependent.
>
> On the bosses (*patrons*) who employ him; on the foreman who regulates his work; . . . on a time schedule which he has not determined; on the tram which he takes two to four times a day; on a landlord to whom he pays a rent which he has not fixed; on neighbors who make noise when he wants to relax.[5]

Although most of the worker-priests were engaged in menial toil, they were employed in a variety of trades. Heavy industry dominated their experience, and much of it involved metallurgical labor. Most innovative in iron and steel production in France were the Renault automobile plants nationalized immediately after the war. The center of this the nation's largest enterprise was the factory found at Boulogne-Billancourt, a Parisian suburb. This particular plant was the first in France to utilize assembly line production. Further it developed increasingly sophisticated adaptations of this work mode to the point where an entire automobile could be fabricated in one mass automated process. At the time, all seventeen Renault factories employed 37,000 people, and the Billancourt factory alone increased production from 11,994 cars in 1945 to 274,057 in 1956. Most Renault workers were classified as specialized (*ouvrier spécialisé*, O.S.), but, in fact, an O.S. was largely responsible for servicing and repairing machinery. The older sense of craftsmanship had been systematically obliterated by technological development.[6] Other important metallurgical industries, which came to include priests among their work forces, were the aviation trades, electrical construction and the large iron foundries and smelters mostly located at Lorraine in the Moselle Valley. This region alone in the 1940s accounted for 64.5% of the nation's steel production and contained two-thirds of France's furnaces which produced over 250 tons of steel daily.[7]

Manual labor at the ports and in textile mills were two other areas in which priests might be found earning a living. At the nation's largest seaport Marseille the docker's life was especially difficult. The entire city's economy was centered on the ports, but its working class had been reduced from a well-organized labor aristocracy to a largely unorganized mass of day laborers, many of whom were immigrants. Although wages were occasionally high for dockers, the work was insecure, and unemployment was an ever present threat. Housing and health conditions were deplorable, making the entire Marseille port area a hotbed of infant mortality. The Lille-Tourcoing-Roubaix triangle in northern France was the center of the nation's textile industry. Lille was the most working class city in all of France, containing five mills which employed over one thousand people each. Eighty thousand workers were employed in the textile trades alone. Unlike the toilers of Paris and many other industrial areas in France, most textile laborers lived in the neighborhoods in which they worked. These crowded ghettos were rampant with unhealthy housing, alcoholism and infant mortality. The working and living conditions of other industrial centers where worker-priests toiled presented similar conditions. These grim realities paralleled the industrial boom towns so characteristic of postwar Latin America. In fact, the French urban ghettos and the factory life they reflected were vivid examples of third world life in the midst of the first world.[8]

Although job insecurity was especially endemic to dockers, layoffs and unemployment were ever present specters for the entire industrial work force in France. This was even more the case for immigrant labor. Unemployment was a perpetual threat to the stability of the proletariat, even though France did not experience massive layoffs in the decade immediately following the war.[9] Moreover, the assurance of work alone could not guarantee the stable life which the industrial workers dreamed of obtaining. Inadequate wages and rapidly rising living costs rendered this hope illusory. The workers' basic wages were relatively low, and the unpredictability of their income added to the dilemma. Bonus money was based on increased production, and it was usually the younger workers who were most able to profit from this extra source of revenue. However, older married workers with families, who needed the resources more, were often unable to maintain the physical endurance of their younger single comrades. Most unskilled workers earned about 35,000 francs monthly with skilled workers averaging close to 40,000 francs. Nonetheless, large numbers of laborers earned significantly less than that. The tragedy of these figures is that they reveal a working class in relative economic decline, unable to earn enough to live comfortably and humanely. Government figures at the time demonstrated that most proletarian earnings fell below the necessary monthly minimum required for a decent life, and inflation was so rampant that worker purchasing power was 20–50% less than it had been in 1938. After food, lodging, clothing and utilities had been paid, few laborers had more than 4% of their budget left to pay for leisure or emergency needs. When contrasted with all other urban classes of French society, the lot of the worker was especially appalling. A monthly wage of 20,000–30,000 francs compared to that of a large factory manager's c.800,000 francs was one more shocking example of class disparity between proletarians and *patrons*.[10]

In this context of privation and ruinous monotony the working class sought to ameliorate its condition by collective endeavor. Mutual help and leisure societies sprang up in the crowded neighborhoods, but no proletarian organizations could claim the importance that the trade unions came to play in the twentieth century. Chief among these was the Confédération Générale du Travail, created in 1895 at the Congress of Limoges. The new C.G.T. was a less than perfect amalgamation of the anarchistic Bourses du Travail and the more socialistic union federations. Only the two-fold promise to remain "outside of every political school" and to endorse revolutionary class struggle allowed this shaky unity between anarchosyndicalist and Marxist workers to survive. However, the reality of the pre-World War I C.G.T. was largely defined by its practice of pragmatic reformism, a *de facto* repudiation of the twin ideological forces which heralded its birth.[11]

War and the rise of Bolshevism in its wake forced the C.G.T. to deal with Communists within its ranks for the first time. During the massive strikes of 1919 and 1920 the minority, which controlled the union's newspaper *Vie Ouvrière*, advocated mass class struggle tactics and endorsement of the Russian Revolution. In the C.G.T. congresses, these *minoritaires* pressed for their program. The ensuing split left the more reformist C.G.T. dominated by functionaries, postal workers and teachers. The more militant unionists, led by the *Vie Ouvrière* group, formed the Confédération Générale du Travail Unitaire. This new C.G.T.U. was Communist in leadership and thought, and until it rejoined the C.G.T. in the euphoria of the Popular Front (1935), it had achieved a high degree of success in organizing workers in the newer mass production industries. Massive sit-down strikes in May and June, 1936 involved about 2,000,000 of the work force, and the success of these actions led to a rapid increase in union membership. The C.G.T. alone peaked at over 5,000,000. However, the Popular Front gains were illusory. By the outbreak of World War II, membership had fallen to 800,000 and the Communists had been pressured out of the union. The more conservative leadership of Léon Jouhaux and the Daladier government had forced Communist unionists into clandestine activity even before the Vichy government of defeat had outlawed trade unionism altogether.[12]

With France occupied by German troops or ruled by the authoritarian government of Philippe Pétain, the moment was ripe for trade unionists to forget their differences and unite against the common foes. Pétain's Charte du Travail (October, 1941), which obliterated the union movement in France, created the soil out of which resistance unity could spring. By the end of the war Communists had been welcomed back into the C.G.T., and soon they came to dominate it. In September, 1945 the C.G.T. had in excess of 5,000,000 members and 15,040 locals. It had been active in the Resistance and, as a result, had become one of the forces invited to participate in the reconstruction of the nation. Most characteristic of the postwar C.G.T. was the dominance of militant Communists at every level of the organization. For the first time, the union had a Communist for Secretary-General, Benoît Frachon, a position he shared with the older Léon Jouhaux. However, this sharing of leadership was an act of Communist diplomacy and not a reflection of the union's reality. The Communists controlled the first postwar convention by a ratio of four to one, and they were more disciplined and organized than their disparate opposition. Although parity was maintained between Communists and non-Communists in the executive organs of the union, both the industrial and regional federations were overwhelmingly Communist at their power bases.[13]

This close connection between the C.G.T. and the French Communist Party was a source of grave anxiety to other unionists who felt that such a fraternal relationship was a violation of their organization's apolitical status so clearly defined by the Charter of Amiens in 1905. Of all the opposition to the weight of this Communist presence in the C.G.T. none was as important as the Force Ouvrière movement led by Léon Jouhaux and Robert Bothereau. The newspaper *Force Ouvrière* was a continuation of an earlier resistance publication, but after the C.G.T.'s congress of 1946 it became a rallying point for opposition against Communist control of the union. "*Force Ouvrière* is at the service of independent trade unionism," reported one editorial, and another announced its dedication to the "real interests" of the workers "independent of political interferences." For a year the conflict deepened until acrimony caused by the mass strikes of 1947 led to a public rupture. In December of 1947 Léon Jouhaux and his supporters organized a new union, the Confédération Générale du Travail-Force Ouvrière. Jouhaux claimed that the Communist-led union was "no longer the C.G.T. save in name only" because it had "abandoned the true principles of traditional unionism." The constituting convention for the new union was held in April of the following year, where F.O. claimed a membership of about 1,000,000. Although the new union was pluralistic in its values and although it contained Trotskyists and revolutionary syndicalists within its ranks, it behaved conservatively and cautiously. It was dominated by civil service and white collar employees, and its anticommunism made it a *de facto* tool in the political interests of the Cold War. Benoît Frachon's dream of "one working class, one C.G.T., one union, one union section in each plant" lay in shambles. In this sense the creation of Force Ouvrière was a setback for the French proletariat.[14]

Unity with Catholic trade unionism was a more intractable problem for the C.G.T. Socially conservative Christian unionism had always presented difficulties for more revolutionary proletarian organizations. From small beginnings at the end of the nineteenth century until the formation of the Confédération Française Démocratique du Travail (1964), Catholic unions faced a continual definitional crisis much like the Jeunesse Ouvrière Chrétienne. Were they chiefly Catholic organizations with an underlying religious purpose, or were they autonomous organizations of French labor dedicated chiefly to erasing the injustices of working class life? The tension between those two possibilities was manifest from the very beginning with the formation of the Syndicat des Employés du Commerce et de l'Industrie (S.E.C.I.) in 1887. Although it won its autonomy from the church in purely professional matters, membership was open only to Catholics in good standing, and moral formation of the organization was under the supervision of religious brothers. Nonetheless, the pressure toward independence by the lay leadership was relentless; non-confessional autonomy was achieved by 1891. Workers who joined had merely to acknowledge the precepts of Christian social morality. Although growth and accomplishments were checkered for the next thirty years, the S.E.C.I. had laid the groundwork for the more mature Christian trade unionism of the interwar years. It had developed a clear ideology, organized pressure for reforms, created mutual aid and educational groups and had trained such well-known Catholic unionists as Gaston Tessier and Jules Zirnheld.[15]

Immediately after the Great War the S.E.C.I. and numerous independent Catholic unions formed a national federation. The Confédération Française des Travailleurs Chrétiens, born in 1919, brought together 350 different organizations and about 140,000 members. Throughout the next decades the new union would experience steady growth. By the Popular Front period its numbers would reach nearly half a million in 2,384 separate unions. Clerical workers constituted the largest single bloc of members, but sectors of industrial laborers, mostly from the textile mills and mines of the Catholic Nord, became increasingly important. With the influx of new members in the mid-1930s the C.F.T.C. became a more genuinely proletarian union federation. Nonetheless, it remained an ideological preserve for a social Catholicism characterized by cautious reformism and class collaboration, positions which were anathema to the more militant sectors of the French working class. Catholic union leaders spoke of the need for "social pacification" and "the struggle against socialism," and its organizational values endorsed action "based on social Christian principles" and not "through class struggle." Such a philosophy made cooperation with other trade unions extremely difficult. By the fall of France in 1940, the C.F.T.C. had not resolved the tension between its Christian and proletarian concerns.[16]

The postwar period provided the C.F.T.C. with a golden opportunity to accomplish that task. Negotiations between the C.F.T.C. and C.G.T. began at the war's end to search for ways in which trade union unity might be achieved. However, even Resistance solidarity could not remove the historic suspicion which had risen between Marxist and Catholic unionists. Gaston Tessier described this chasm in great detail even during the height of cooperation between the two federations. He spoke of bringing to "the organized proletariat . . . the enrichment of Christian thought," and although he lauded the unity of clandestine activities with the C.G.T., he repudiated "complete unity by the immediate fusion of the two federations." His reasoning involved what he called "a profound difference" in both theory and practice between the two bodies.[17] Maurice Bouladoux, one of the C.F.T.C.'s leading moderates, summarized Tessier's judgment in the following manner:

> The problem which is posed today . . . is to know whether it is possible to reconcile spiritual principles, which are at the foundation of our movement, with the doctrine of materialism, on which the C.G.T. is built, whether it be Marxist, Proudhonian or simply opportunistic. To pretend to neglect this fundamental aspect of the question . . . would be not only an unforgivable sin but also a kind of treason against those who, by coming to us, have taken a posture which proceeds from one of the basic liberties of our democratic system.[18]

With the advent of the Cold War after 1947, these differences were accentuated sharply to the point where even unity of action was exceedingly difficult. Hostile attacks were published frequently by the union leadership at the two central offices, but cooperation among local cadres in specific working class struggles survived in spite of the acrimony between the national executives.[19]

Internally the C.F.T.C. wrestled mightily with these tensions in order to reconcile its Christian ideology and history with the needs of mass industrial unionism. Rapidly the federation split into two camps. Gaston Tessier and Marcel Poimboeuf, leader of the Fédération des employés, techniciens et agents de maîtrise (E.T.A.M.), engineered the fight for the traditional status quo position. They defended the confessional character of their federation and sought to retard the growing strength of their industrial mass unions vis-à-vis the white collar and clerical unions which had dominated the C.F.T.C. for so long. Leading the struggle for nonconfessional mass industrial unionism were Paul Vignaux of the Syndicat Général de l'Education Nationale (S.G.E.N.), Fernand Hennebicq of the gas and electricity federation, Albert Detraz of the construction industry and Charles Savouillan from the metallurgical trades. These younger union militants, shaped largely by the Jeunesse Ouvrière Chrétienne, organized what they called Groupes Reconstruction. Throughout the postwar worker-priest period and beyond it, the Reconstruction *équipe* fashioned local and regional groups throughout the C.F.T.C. Further, they published bulletins and study papers designed to convince the rank-and-file membership that radical change was necessary. First of all, the Reconstructionists sought to eradicate all confessionalism from their union by eliminating Christian language from official documents, by removing all ties with the church's hierarchy, by obliterating links with the Christian Democratic M.R.P. and by joining a secular international instead of the Christian one to which the C.F.T.C. belonged already.[20] Secondly, the radicals attempted to reorganize their union structurally. They wanted a more democratic organization that would be grounded upon the realities of modern industry, with a double federalism both territorial and professional. The fight was a long and difficult one, but victory passed finally to the Reconstructionists who captured the union in the mid-1960s. What had been the C.F.T.C. came to be called the C.F.D.T. The name Christian was dropped, and only a small conservative minority bolted and retained the original C.F.T.C. title along with its social Catholic heritage. However, even by the strike wave of 1953 a sense of victory was in the air. Gaston Tessier relinquished his leadership to the more moderate Maurice Bouladoux; Christian rhetoric was being abandoned rapidly to give way to social democratic ideas and language; and structural reform was advancing slowly but surely through the greater number of Reconstructionist personnel to be found in the higher echelons of the union. The C.F.T.C. was becoming increasingly proletarian and class conscious at some cost to its traditional Christian heritage.[21] Conflicts between the worker-priests and Catholic unionism's hierarchy reflected this basic struggle. The priest toilers were dedicated to revolutionary rank-and-file unionism, and as such, they were either in the communist C.G.T. or the reconstructionist wing of the C.F.T.C.

In spite of these divisions within the French trade union movement, the working class had risen to defend itself in the midst of deep social and political strife. Largely through its unions the proletariat fought a number of significant battles which were part of its collective pride during the important worker-priest years. The first of these were the massive sit-down strikes and factory occupations which followed in the wake of the leftist Popular Front victory in the 1936 national elections. The strike wave of May and June, which began with provincial metallurgical workers, spread rapidly into 17,000 separate conflicts involving almost 2,500,000 laborers. In the face of such militancy the government of Léon Blum pressured the owners and the C.G.T. to sign the Matignon Accords in June which brought unprecedented social benefits to the working class. Among these were the forty-hour week and paid vacations. Equally important was the sense of collective strength experienced by the labor force. One worker put it this way: "In 1936 I fought. Not with fists but in action. That was a formidable élan." Simone Weil heralded the strikes, in which she participated as well. In a June, 1936 letter she penned these words: "I think that it is good for the oppressed to have been able for just a few days to affirm their existence, to lift up their heads, impose their will and obtain some deserved advantages by means of more than just generous condescension."[22]

Resistance against the occupying German forces and the Vichy government of Philippe Pétain was another great moment for the nation's proletariat, a moment experienced personally by a number of the men who would become worker-priests after the war. Even prior to the German invasion the Daladier government had taken punitive action against the Communists both in the parliament and the C.G.T. Consequently large numbers of Communist workers were already involved in clandestine activities before the notorious armistice signed by Pétain in the spring of 1940. Meanwhile the reformists of the C.G.T. and the C.F.T.C. sought initially to cooperate with the collaborationist regime, although a number of rank-and-file militants were in active opposition from the beginning. However, the destruction of all unions by Vichy's Charte du Travail (October, 1941) led to a joint protest by the C.G.T. and the C.F.T.C. called the Manifesto of the Twelve. As time passed and as Vichy and German rule became increasingly onerous, trade union resistance grew more effective and more united. By the final years of the war the Communists had reentered the C.G.T. via a clandestine trade union alliance, and all the unions were represented in General de Gaulle's National Resistance Council. Further, they had been active in war-time propaganda, massive strike action and even armed combat. The working class had emerged from the war basking in its well-earned patriotic credentials.[23]

Finally, during the worker-priest era, the nation's industrial work force participated in a series of massive strikes which resembled the earlier grass-roots actions of 1936. A number of work stoppages occurred in 1947 and 1948 which paralyzed the nation for a number of months. They were largely a response to a precipitous plummet in the workers' buying power. In late April and early May, 1947 up to 30,000 Renault workers had responded to wildcat strikes inaugurated by two shops in the Boulogne-Billancourt plant. By the end of the year even more massive work stoppages were in process. Beginning at Marseille in November they spread rapidly to the rest of the nation until two million had laid down their tools by the end of the month. Although Cold War anticommunism was used as a rationale for calling in the militia and passing anti-strike legislation, this did not prevent new outbursts of militancy in the following year. In October and November, 1948 the miners refused to work for five weeks, and their dissatisfaction spread to the ports. Once again police and military power was utilized to force an end to the protests. The great strikes of August, 1953 were the direct result of government decrees designed to weaken unions in the public sector. Protests began with the Force Ouvrière postal workers at Bordeaux, but rapidly the strike became general involving most major industries and all three union federations. By August 21, both the C.F.T.C. and F.O. had signed separate accords with the government leaving the C.G.T. virtually holding the reins of a defeated strike. August, 1953 proved to be a dark moment for French trade unionism. It left the unions hopelessly divided and weak, and the ensuing acrimony intensified existing hostility between the unions which would take over a decade to repair.[24]

Working class militancy found further expression in the peace movement of the latter 1940s and early 1950s. After the advent of the Cold War the Communist Party sought to break out of its isolation by utilizing its militants, discipline and organizational skills in service of this Mouvement de la Paix. Although some leftist elements in the C.F.T.C. called for an end to the Korean and Indochinese conflicts, the abolition of atomic weapons and a halt to the remilitarization of Europe, it was largely the C.G.T. which devoted itself to these particular causes. Through its various locals and federations it created the vital mass base needed to make the peace movement effective.[25] These great issues of the day and the heroism called for in moments of emergency were vital components of working class hope and inspiration, and as such, they became part of the worker-priests' collective *engagement*.

However, these memorable events should not be allowed to conceal the day-to-day efforts by the labor movement to insure that the needs of its constituency were met. Economic and professional concerns, such as wages, layoffs and accidents, were always at issue, and unions were forced to have structures able to address these problems in a militant and effective way. Most typical, the C.G.T. was organized along two lines—professionally according to particular trades and regionally in various Unions Départmentales. The basic unit of the whole movement was the union local which selected its own administrative council. Locals could be either factory or neighborhood units. Regional federations grew out of these locals through an elective representative process, and at the national level, federations were both industrial and geographical. National convention delegates, chosen by representation, elected permanent bureaus to handle the executive and daily affairs of the union; indeed in any of these bodies, some officials received full-time wages for performing their designated chores. Hence they were called *permanents* as contrasted with all elected leaders (*responsables*), many of whom were not paid.[26]

Finances were always an issue with the unions; there was never enough money. Consequently, recruitment and the collection of dues were continual concerns. Subscriptions through the selling of union stamps were the chief source of revenue. Both the C.G.T. and the C.F.T.C. provided monthly stamps. In addition, annual membership cards were sold, but in every instance, dues were kept purposely low and tied to the workers' wage scales. Recruitment into the union was usually handled informally, the direct result of factory camaraderie or daily struggle. Of course, the union was greatly concerned with the effectiveness of its propaganda. Courses were held and leaflets distributed; programs were frequent in the union halls; and training sessions were designed for proletarian militants.[27]

Much of daily union activity was involved with conflict resolution between labor and management. Postwar *tripartisme*, the moderate leftist governing coalition fresh out of the Resistance, was able to legislate machinery to resolve such differences in a regular fashion. Disputes concerning dismissals, job classifications and wage payments could be brought before the *conseils de prud'homme*, organizations which dated from Napoleonic times. Composed of an equal number of employers and labor representatives, it had the authority to mediate or adjudicate conflicts, but it had little power to reverse injustices already committed. The governmental Ministry of Labor made some provision for conciliation of disputes as well.

However, the most important sources of grievance settlement came from legislation which grew out of the Popular Front and postwar era. These were the shop stewards (*délégués du personnel*) and the plant committees (*comités d'entreprise*). Shop stewards, elected by the workers themselves, were the first persons contacted on the factory floor by laborers when grievances in professional matters needed to be settled. These militants brought before management, at least on a monthly basis, concerns about wages, health, safety and social benefits. In addition, the worker could call upon the support of his/her plant committee delegate. These *comités d'entreprise*, composed of both managers and workers, were set up in February, 1946 in factories employing over fifty people. Unions hoped that the committees would become a forum of economic democracy, but the fact that they remained advisory bodies only in such vital matters as production and investment undermined this hope. In reality, they came to run factory cafeterias, cooperatives, sports clubs, day nurseries and the like, and they conducted mutual aid activities, as well as surveillance over apprenticeship programs. Thus, over a brief period of time, the forces of management had successfully reduced the potential of these committees to be a source of substantive industrial reform.[28]

Even though the law designed the *comité d'entreprise* to conciliate labor-management differences, it became instead one more arena of conflict between the two groups. The bosses undermined union input in the committees, withheld vital information from worker representatives and persecuted delegates sent by labor to serve on the committee. In spite of all the machinery designed by the government to bring labor peace to the workplace, conflict between labor and management was endemic to the factory system. The strike remained the ultimate weapon for the proletariat in this continual struggle. Conventional work stoppages, prepared in advance, were the most common form of strike employed by the unions. In addition, a number of more spontaneous modes were employed by angry grass-roots militants who had reached their collective boiling point. These included walkouts, work slowdowns, short demonstrations, wildcat strikes and occasional sabotage. The daily life of the active union militant, involving both organizational chores and conflicts with management, became part of the normal experience lived by Catholic priests who entered the work force. As union activists in their own right, they too were caught up in the day-to-day battle for justice at the workplace.[29]

Although the daily work routine and the struggles which arose from it defined the proletarian's life, the neighborhood also had a vital role to play. The worker had a residence where he or she ate, slept, shopped, raised a family and engaged in leisure activities. Invariably these homes were found in the vast urban sprawls that embraced the industrial basins of the nation. Crowded and dirty, these proletarian ghettos were a hotbed of illness, infant mortality and deplorable living conditions. This was especially true in the Parisian area where the largest group of worker-priests made their residence. By the interwar years the entire suburban ring of Paris, save for the west, had been transformed into an urban nightmare by a rapid influx of people seeking work in the large industrial plants of the area. Makeshift shantytowns (*bidonvilles*) sprung up almost overnight to meet the housing needs of these impoverished workers coming from rural France, northern Africa and other Mediterranean countries. Streets were often unpaved, lighting was poor or nonexistent, and health and police protection were notably absent. Things began to improve after the war, but the nation's need to repair its basic rolling stock forced production of vitally needed working class housing to a virtual standstill.[30]

By 1954 proletarian lodging was still in a crisis stage. Single workers were often housed in one of the tiny rooms so characteristic of the high-rise rentals called *hôtels meublés,* and lodging for families was not much better. Well over half of working class families lived in substandard housing, and 50% of their dwellings had only one or two rooms. Often this meant adults and children sleeping in the same room, with the necessity of converting the bedroom into a sitting room at the beginning of each day. As late as 1954 over 10% of the resident buildings had been constructed prior to 1871, and less than two-thirds had been built after 1914. Only about 20% of the workers owned their own homes, and barely two-thirds of proletarian dwellings had running water. A mere 12% had hot water, and only 6% could boast of possessing a bathroom. Around 5% had refrigerators, the rest being forced to market daily since food could not be stored safely. Private toilet facilities were especially rare. Some families paid subsidies to nearby cafés to use their facilities; others would sneak into public buildings to relieve themselves; and most others would share a common toilet with a large number of neighborhood families. This crowding itself constituted a serious health hazard. Housing needs were so critical that working families were forced to pay inflated rentals for the worst hovels. Situations like this were rife with slum landlordism, and harassment against tenants by their proprietors was not uncommon. In these ways injustice experienced at the workplace was carried over into proletarian residential life, one more example of third world oppression in the midst of first world France.[31]

Food was the single most important item in the workers' family budget with one-half to two-thirds of wages going for nourishment alone. Immediately after the war shortage of food was so great that laboring families were forced to pay the ruinous prices found on the black market. Even when this issue was resolved price inflation of food remained over 10% higher than the corresponding rise of skilled wages, let alone those of the common laborer. The requirements of daily marketing and the lack of transportation forced working families to buy goods from neighborhood shops where costs were habitually higher than elsewhere in the center city. Garden produce, grown on tiny plots of ground by over 50% of the workers, was a vital source of nutrition for families without the financial resources to purchase fresh greens. More than half of the workers polled in the mid-1950s felt that they did not have sufficient red meat, and soup, bread, cheese and other cheaper foods were more normal fare for those toiling in the nation's factories. The very nature of their work and the lack of financial resources forced many of them to eat packed lunches. Consumption of alcoholic beverages was characteristic of proletarian life. Both the positive role played by wine in socializing and its destructive impact upon family breakdown were common in urban ghetto life.[32]

During the worker-priest era French laborers had two weeks of paid vacation, with the unions advocating for one or two more. However, insufficient wages limited the leisure possibilities for workers and their families. The unions and some neighborhood organizations were able to provide a few opportunities for camping and day excursions. Organized sports furnished some outlet for the young men, and neighborhood festivals were pleasurable occasions for the whole family. Nevertheless, most leisure was of an individualistic nature with married women suffering the most deprivation in this area. Bistro sitting, sentimental movies and local dance halls were the chief sources of habitual recreation, and church and union alike were convinced that the influence of these was largely negative. Family life suffered severely under the strains of a labor system which required so much toil and paid so little in benefits. Add to this the crowded living conditions and the atomized leisure, and it is easy to see why drunkenness, physical abuse, divorce and abandonment were so prevalent in proletarian families. Even schooling was not viewed as a realistic means of escape from this grim reality. Over 80% of the workers had no more than a primary school education, and apprenticeship programs were too few and too poorly organized to be of much help. Local libraries, courses and popular universities did much to raise the class consciousness and pride of those laborers who felt educational needs, but these did little to open the door for better economic opportunities. All in all proletarian life was incredibly grim, marked by monotonous toil and daily systemic oppression.[33] This was not unlike the existence characteristic of the shanty towns found in Latin America.

It is difficult, perhaps, to believe that dreams and noble visions took root in such squalor. In fact, they did, and those who have studied the French proletariat bear testimony to that reality. To be sure, the selfishness, aggrandizement and violence which spring from misery were present as well, but these did not conceal the powerful human values that were characteristic of the laboring masses. Workers developed a sense of loyalty and generosity to their work comrades and neighbors quite unlike the more rampant individualism found in the professional classes. Realizing daily that their existence was precarious, the workers were inclined to provide immediate help to others as it was needed. This sense of solidarity with those of his class led the worker to a feeling of revolt against a labor system which was degrading him. Although this passion brought with it an intuitive anger toward the "bosses," its chief characteristic was "a very acute sense of justice" and the need for "a new world, just, fraternal and without privileges."[34] In time, the proletarian milieu would impact upon the worker-priests in similar ways.

With such notions, it is not at all surprising that the class conscious workers were attracted deeply to Marxism in general and Communism in particular. The sense of revolt and the "magnificent faith in human struggle against all alienation," provided by Marxism, gave to the proletariat a philosophical base for both its misery and its hope. French Communism provided the organizational apparatus in which these values could be exercised. One C.G.T. plant secretary put it this way:

> The militant French worker is a very intelligent person. He is generous, intelligent, understanding, a good leader. The Communists have captured almost all I know, because they give these workers a chance to be educated, to be trained and to be creative.[35]

Le Parti, as it was called, had both active factory and neighborhood cells in which recruitment, propaganda, educational and social activities were provided on a regular basis. Although party strength declined from the 1940s to the mid-1950s, it still had half a million members in 1954 and could count on the electoral support of almost one-half of the nation's industrial work force. Communism was especially strong in the major cities, and it controlled the political life of the "red" suburbs surrounding Paris. This influence inspired the more militant workers to take a pro-Soviet, anti-American stance during the Cold War years. Marxist communism was so prevalent in the French proletariat that it took on the character of a religious faith. A local labor leader described this sense of faith when he made the following testimony: "Marxism gives us power. It must not be underestimated in the importance it has for people who want to know more about themselves and about the world they live in. For it gives us new means of sight."[36]

Industrial life, the values which grew out of it and commitment to philosophical and practical Marxism were all signs of the French proletariat's alienation from the Catholic Church. For almost half a century church activitists and researchers had been pointing to that unpleasant reality. Concretely this was noted in the sharp decline of traditional religious practice among proletarians. In working class neighborhoods attendance at Mass was limited largely to women, children, the elderly and members of other classes. Very few working men participated in worship services with any regularity. There was even a measurable decline of worker involvement in the sacramental rites of passage provided by the church. Baptisms, first communions, marriages and burials, though practiced rather habitually in industrial neighborhoods, were still diminishing in frequency among working families. Even where practiced, they were treated by workers casually or with some superstition. By way of example, in the Longwy iron basin less than 5% of the adults practiced their Catholicism in any manifest way although 95% of them had attended their first communion as children. In the Parisian red suburbs attendance at Mass was even lower. National statistics of the mid-1950s demonstrated that almost half of the proletariat had abandoned Catholic religious practices totally and that another 36% were mostly indifferent to the church. Over 50% of the workers had no contact with any member of the clergy, and only 13% had regular dealings with any priest. Even at the rudimentary level of external religiosity, the French proletariat could not be called Catholic with any degree of seriousness.[37]

In the realm of attitudes the chasm between the church and workers was even wider. Pragmatic atheism, demonstrated by non-participation in church life, was buttressed frequently by its philosophical counterpart. In place of faith in God most of the militant working class had a profound faith in humanity and its capacity to build a better, more just world. This atheism was expressed habitually as indifference to God; social concrete justice and the proletarian struggle were all that mattered as far as these militants were concerned. One worker told a sympathetic priest from his neighborhood, "If God exists, as you say to me, then I am not afraid to appear before Him, for I, who do not believe in Him, am less unfaithful than they [church goers] are, because I have supported the working class." To be sure, a number of workers were impressed by the Christ figure, but for them, he was a socialist and advocate for the poor rather than the divine Son of God.[38]

Meanwhile the overwhelming attitude of the proletariat toward organized religion was a negative one. Overall, workers felt that the church was alienated from their struggles and daily existence. A 1950 report by the Limoges worker-priests summarized this reality for their bishop:

> Religion appears to them as a constraint, not as a liberation . . . It is not the cross, nor the sacrifice, nor renunciation that prevents their adhering to the Christian message . . . In the church they have found formulae, rituals, gestures . . . The working masses do not believe in the sincerity of the church's wish to change working conditions because the Christians are those industrialists who want only to conserve their privileges.[39]

This conviction was re-enforced by incidents and contacts between the worker families and the church. Priestly condemnation of proletarian social life, insistence that certain fees be paid for church activities, the church's obvious wealth, its intellectualized theology, its individualistic spirituality, its preference for middle class clothes and manners and its anti-union practices on the local level all contributed to the proletariat's rejection of the Catholic religion.[40]

Especially apparent was the workers' contempt for the priest. Anti-clericalism had a long history in France which predated the French Revolution, but it took certain forms among industrial laborers which were characteristic of the setting in which they lived. Testimony after testimony by workers demonstrated graphically the antipathy felt toward the clergy. Priests are "hypocrites" and engaged in sex just like anybody else were common opinions held in the urban ghettos. A priest had "a soft job" and didn't know a stitch about real toil. His "hands are too white," proclaimed one militant, "and if I would speak to him about my misery, he wouldn't know what to say to me." He led a bourgeois life with bourgeois tastes, and because of this he was "the ally of money power and of the capitalist." One Christian worker illustrated the depth of this alienation most poignantly. He told of the wedding of Victor and Denise, a young couple who had suffered as deportees in Germany. "They were married by a vicar in a somber corner of the church. Not a word on the Christian sense of their marriage. The prayers are murmured in Latin. Since they don't have a cent, it is a marriage which lasts only five minutes."[41]

Certainly there were priests, such as Fathers Michonneau and Rétif, who cared and related with sensitivity to their proletarian neighbors. However, they were far too rare, and their impact was slight. The overwhelming reality was a vast gulf between the church and the working class, and this was felt most acutely at the clerical level. A growing awareness of this tragedy was the most immediate context from which the worker-priests arose. Initially the salvation of souls took precedence over the liberation of the oppressed. Missionary apostolates were the womb out of which these clergy were born, but it was the overwhelming grimness of proletarian life which baptized them, brought them to maturity and reshaped their goals along more radical lines. Nonetheless, the very irreligiosity of the working class provided the specific impetus which set in motion the events surrounding the origins of the worker-priests.

V

THE WORLD OF WORKER-PRIEST ORIGINS

"I discovered the misery of the workers, not in books, but by living it myself."
—Albert Gauche, worker priest

Until they faced the squalor and monotony of proletarian life daily, the worker-priests found themselves defined by the wider contexts of war-torn France, the explosion of working-class apostolates and the rampant dechristianization which characterized the French working class. It was this last reason which most immediately explained their creation. The church which sent them into the foreign land of the proletariat had an agenda of evangelism not liberation. Consequently, those priests who would be toiling in French and Belgian factories by the late 1940s were a most manifest response by French Catholicism to the discovery that there was "a wall between the church and the working class."[1] Although pioneers such as Albert de Mun, Marc Sangnier and the Jeunesse Ouvrière Chrétienne had brought this to the attention of their Catholic comrades over a period of seventy years, these cries had fallen largely on deaf ears.

Such was not the case with the controversial booklet *France, pays de mission?* which appeared in 1943. This sociological study of the alienation of the proletariat from the church was the work of two Paris-based Jociste chaplains Yvan Daniel and Henri Godin. Daniel was largely responsible for the book's data, while Godin was the recognized interpretive spirit of the study.[2] He was born in 1906, the son of a poor Catholic family from the Jura foothills, and these humble origins marked his entire vocational life. "I was born from the people," was his frequent cry. In spite of his poor health or perhaps because of it, Godin was drawn to the priesthood by his intense Marian piety. His seminary life was a painful experience. He was a shy "loner" who suffered from migraine headaches. It was during this difficult solitude that he began to sense the call "to go to the disinherited." "I want the apostolate of the poor whom Jesus preferred," he noted in a journal. During one summer vacation he was converted to such a mission. He had come to feel a closer tie with the workers than with his own classmates. "I didn't think of them [proletarians] any longer as 'they' but rather as 'we'," he told a friend. "I felt a sense of revolt. I wanted to remain one of the people." Of his classmates and his seminary education he made the following harsh judgment: "They're bourgeois now. They don't care about the working classes. They're deserters. There ought to be a seminary for workmen where they'd stay workmen when they become priests. All priests are bourgeois." The groundwork had been laid. Henri Godin, with his growing liberationist convictions, was fast becoming that priest who would be the source of inspiration for the birth of the worker-priests.[3]

Godin's subsequent career served to intensify this earlier commitment. He entered the Fils de la Charité order which was well-known for its parish work in proletarian ghettos, and his first assignment was such a church in Clichy. There, in addition to the usual parish activities, he oversaw the budding Jeunesse Ouvrière Chrétienne in his neighborhood. Soon he became disenchanted with his order and its penchant for parish work. Convinced that mission activity in the midst of the proletariat demanded detachment from the classical structures of the church, he left his order and worked full-time for the J.O.C. By 1940 he was living alone in the rue Ganneron apartment which would become the informal headquarters of the worker-priest collectivity called the Mission de Paris. There he welcomed his neighbors, provided temporary housing for recently married workers and engaged in clandestine activities against the occupying Germans.[4]

However, in all of this Godin could not quiet his restless critical spirit. His deepest conviction was that the church had not yet discovered the means to penetrate the heart of the working class. He had become beloved among those toilers with whom he lived, yet he was driven to do even more to close the gap between the church and the working class. He was harassed constantly by the question, "Can I be a real Christian while leading this bourgeois life when our Lord has made me understand so clearly that it displeases Him?" Driven by his passion for the proletariat and by his own harsh self-critique, Father Godin became convinced that even the J.O.C. had failed to become a genuine part of the working class milieu. These burning convictions led him to join with his fellow chaplain Father Daniel in producing the controversial study which would rock the church and revolutionize Catholic missions to the proletariat.[5]

Beyond the statistical demonstration that the French urban working class existed in a world apart from the church, *France, pays de mission?* was a passionate plea for new and radical mission forms to reach this alienated sector of French society. Starting with the shocking assumption that "France is a mission country" Godin and Daniel suggested that the task of conversion must be milieu directed rather than individualistically oriented. "The entire working-class apostolate is hampered . . . by this problem of a parish milieu," they charged. "The parish and the proletarian worlds are not merely separated; they are also utterly different." Indeed, these two priest activists were convinced that the entire parish structure was so permeated with bourgeois values and practices that it could no longer serve a missionary function among workers.[6]

Something drastic was demanded, or the proletariat would never be converted to Christ. In essence that more novel approach could be described as incarnational or what Godin and Daniel called a "leaven in the lump." "What is needed," they insisted, "is a small Christian community living in the milieu and radiating Christianity from its very midst." To accomplish this Godin and Daniel were convinced that men with a strong sense of missionary vocation required specialized training so that they could be sent into the proletarian world which was "not their own." Half-way houses for new converts were to be established; genuine leaders from the working classes had to be brought to Christ and then become missionaries themselves; and proletarian Christian communities needed to spring up in the urban ghettos without the more bourgeois control of the parishes.[7] Nowhere did Godin and Daniel suggest that priests should be involved in manual labor. Worker-priests were not on their agenda, but in their incarnational notions they laid the groundwork for this more radical missionary form:

> Christ became man like ourselves in all things except sin, and our missionaries must adapt themselves to the ways and manners of the pagan peoples they are evangelizing.
>
> The Good News must find its incarnation in their [workers'] human actuality.
>
> Missionaries who become 'of the people' (and how else can they penetrate among the people?) must be prepared to be a little suspect even in the eyes of their fellow priests. They have changed worlds.[8]

These innovative notions of proletarian evangelization would have remained stillborn without intervention from high places. Specifically, *France, pays de mission?* would have been solely the critical musings of two Jociste chaplains within Catholic Action circles had not the archbishop of Paris decided to act in response to their observations. Emmanuel Cardinal Suhard, in many respects, seemed an unlikely candidate to be the patron for such novel ideas. He had been reared in the piety of rural Catholic France, and his seminary training was of the traditional classic type. Like his episcopal colleagues he welcomed Pétain's authoritarian regime of defeat and played the role of pragmatic collaborator with the Germans. In spite of this strain of ultra-conservatism, Suhard was a visionary dedicated to missionary endeavors. From his first years as bishop of Bayeux and Lisieux he sought to promote a more missionary oriented training for priests as well as sensitize his clergy to Catholic Action and social issues. Indeed, during the war years he was aware of and encouraged priests in moderate clandestine activities against the Germans.[9]

This unique blend of conservative and visionary made Cardinal Suhard the ideal patron for the church's missionary explosion of the 1940s, and as his nation's leading prelate, he was at the heart of all these endeavors. Not least of these was his active support of *France, pays de mission?* Not only had he commissioned the study initially; also he had sent eighty copies to select ecclesiastical personalities to get their responses prior to the book's publication. Eventually it reached the public where it achieved sales in excess of eighty thousand. Its success was assured. Even in the midst of the controversy which followed this popularity, the aging cardinal was resolute in his support of Godin's and Daniel's assessments.[10] *France, pays de mission?* had served as both manifesto and inspiration for those clergy who would become worker-priests or would emerge as their most vocal supporters. Many of these laboring clerics recalled how significantly the book had impacted upon their vocation. Their reading of it either intensified an already existing commitment to a proletarian mission or led them in that direction.[11]

Meanwhile Suhard did not end his patronage with an endorsement of the controversial book. Immediately, he set in motion structures designed to implement the radical suggestions of the two Catholic Action chaplains. His previous support of Georges Michonneau's missionary parish and his efforts to create a mission seminary at Lisieux a year earlier had already established his reputation as a trailblazer. In order to continue this momentum and to give practical direction to the avant-garde ideas of *France, pays de mission?*, he announced an organizational retreat to be held at Lisieux during the Christmas holidays of 1943. From December 19, 1943 to January 16 of the following year, the leading progressives of the French church met, first at Combes-la-Ville near Paris and then at Lisieux, there to create a concrete mission to the working class of the Parisian basin. Included among these high-powered thinkers and activists were the theologians Jean Daniélou and M.-D. Chenu, Georges Michonneau, Father Maxime Hua of Catholic Action, Louis Augros and Father Lévèsque of the Mission de France, Father Jean Villain of Action Populaire and four leaders of the new Mission de Paris, Fathers Godin, Daniel, Jacques Hollande and André Depierre, one of the first worker-priests.[12]

For twenty-one days and in fifty-seven meetings, these clergy brought their expertise to bear in the creation of the Mission de Paris. Discussions centered around such diverse topics as the failures and successes of the J.O.C., new methods for missionizing the masses, the importance of incarnational methods adapted to the proletarian social milieu, the role of clergy in this atmosphere and the need to create special missionary communities for the conversion of the working class. Some speakers went so far as to suggest that the priest in such a setting might even abandon his clerical garb and do some temporary factory labor. However, this notion was clearly ancillary to the main thrust of the retreat. Its real contribution to the birth of the worker-priests was a spirit of innovation and experimentation which later became characteristic of the Mission de Paris.[13] Cardinal Suhard's concluding address baptized this avant-garde *esprit*. "The direct goal of the Mission de Paris is to convert the unbelievers," he affirmed. "Its indirect goal is to show to the Christian community that it must take a new attitude. A shock (*choc*) must be produced. Much has been done for fifteen years, above all with Catholic Action. We must go further, and this Mission should show the orientation."[14]

Suhard expected his Mission de Paris to be a model for all the church's efforts to win the working class to Christ. Toward that end he mandated Henri Godin to lead this movement from his modest apartment at rue Ganneron in Paris. It would not be so. In an almost prophetic statement Godin confided to Father Depierre concerning the Lisieux retreat, "It's a miracle the way everything has been arranged. Now I can vanish. The Mission can now take place without me." The next morning Father Godin was found dead in his apartment, the victim of fumes from a faulty coal stove. Long before, he had prayed to the Holy Mother, "My Queen, deliver me from becoming a bourgeois priest," and he had vowed two days before his death, "I make an oath to consecrate my entire life to the christianization of the Parisian working class." His prayer had been answered; he had kept his vow. Henri Godin was laid to rest in a poor man's grave among the dead workers of greater Paris. He had given his life to the dream of effective proletarian missions, a dream which would become the worker-priests.[15]

Meanwhile other events were laying the foundation for the worker-priest movement as well. The German occupation and the ensuing privation that it caused could not leave the Catholic Church and its clergy unaffected. Many priests, as prisoners-of-war, were languishing in German concentration camps or factories. There they encountered a whole new world, the world of factory labor. Over four thousand French priests spent some time as war prisoners in Germany, and this experience marked their vocational life deeply. The situation was compounded when the Nazi government in collaboration with the Vichy prime minister Pierre Laval instituted the Service du Travail Obligatoire, a forced requisition program which transported French workers to German factories. For the first time since Maréchal Pétain had taken power, the church reacted with massive resistance to the civil authorities. The Jeunesse Ouvrière Chrétienne suffered most immediately from the S.T.O. Large numbers of Jocistes were sent to Germany, and the J.O.C. leadership protested vehemently. Even the more conservative hierarchy did not remain silent. Achille Liénart of Lille declared his opposition publicly, and Cardinal Suhard and others quietly approved of those Jocistes who went into hiding or joined the Resistance to avoid the S.T.O. The situation became so serious that Cardinal Suhard sought ways in which his church might fulfill its priestly functions in this abnormal situation. He was aware that over seven hundred thousand workers were in Germany and that, among them, there were some four thousand priests and over three thousand seminarians.[16]

To meet the spiritual needs of these French Catholics in Germany the archbishop of Paris suggested to his fellow cardinals and archbishops that a clandestine chaplaincy be established. This controversial act of civil disobedience was approved by these prelates in April, 1943 and placed under the direction of Father Rodhain who had already served in the capacity of chaplain organizer for prisoners-of-war. Very quickly he had twenty-six volunteers willing to go to Germany; by the end of the war there were two hundred and seventy-five. The suffering and privation of these clandestine chaplains and the other priests and seminarians in Germany had a deep effect upon the growing sense that the church must reach out to the working class. Priests and clerical candidates in German camps and factories came to know the harsh life of the working class first hand. When they returned they brought with them a burning zeal for a priesthood cast in the lifestyle of the proletariat, a priesthood which would be dedicated to working class liberation as well as evangelization. They carried their message back to the Mission de France and the other seminaries; they took it to their bishops; and they influenced the future worker-priests both directly and indirectly.[17]

The impact of these deported clergy was far wider than their immediate contacts. A number of them put their experience into writing, and these public memoirs had a wide circulation in progressive Catholic periodicals, both as books and as articles.[18] A brief examination of two such examples serves to demonstrate how their content both reflected and added to the proletarian mission fervor which was laying the foundation for worker-priest endeavors. Father Hadrien Bousquet's *Hors des Barbelés* (1945) is a description of his life as a clandestine chaplain in a German airplane factory from 1943 to 1945. From his ordination in 1926 he dedicated himself "to the evangelization of the popular masses." He was struck by the plight of the miners and by the gulf which separated his life from theirs. As a Franciscan he became involved in social issues, and his order gave him permission to work in an Ivry iron forge in June, 1939. His mobilization into the army a few months later ended his brief stint as a worker-priest, but the idea had taken root. Cardinal Jean Verdier of Paris and the famed St. Sulpice Seminary were discussing the matter favorably, and some seminarians were earning money in factories during their summer vacations. For his part, Father Bousquet remained committed to the proletarian mission. He was assigned to the chaplaincy corps under Father Rodhain, and by the beginning of 1943 he was toiling in a German factory.[19]

The content of his memoirs, which appeared in 1945, coincided with the concerns of both Cardinal Suhard and *France, pays de mission?* Bousquet spoke of the suffering and brutal life of the laboring classes, a life of soup lines and malnutrition, of low wages and miserable lodging. But he was impressed also by working class solidarity and courage, characteristics which manifested themselves in acts of resistance to tyranny and in the sharing of goods in common. In the following words he advanced the cause of their liberation from oppression: "We do not have a right to ignore their [proletarians'] just aspirations and demands. Tomorrow in a reorganized world, we must work, above all, to suppress this immense proletariat, the object of paternalism from some and charity from others." To reach this oppressed class Bousquet argued for a renovated church, more communalistic and more innovative than the individualistic and traditional church of which he was a part. One form which appealed to the Franciscan chaplain was that of the worker-priest. He justified this particular mode of ministry in Germany because it helped "to create . . . a clandestine church which would live like the catacombs, to reconstitute forbidden movements, to unite believers and unbelievers, to make a treaty of union between workers, prisoners and deported." These convictions would be lived out and developed further by the worker-priests in the years to come.[20]

The memoirs of the Jesuit Victor Dillard paralleled those of Father Bousquet in many ways. Like Bousquet, Dillard was deeply involved in social issues during the 1930s. He worked with the Jesuit-based Action Populaire and was well-known in the field of economics in both France and abroad. However, his deep concern over the fate of the proletariat led him to volunteer for the clandestine chaplaincy. His priestly identity was discovered by the Gestapo at his factory in Wüpperthal, and he was sent to Dachau where he became ill and died in January, 1945. His memoirs, called *Suprêmes Témoignages*, were published posthumously. Much like Bousquet, he described his discovery of proletarian existence from the inside, and he felt it was an "immense advantage to live as completely as possible the working class life." He came to understand the meaning of work as both an art and a life struggle, and he became convinced that there was an international class consciousness among these proletarians. These discoveries led him to believe that Christ's incarnation as a worker centuries before was a necessary part of God's plan. Indeed the need to bring the gospel to the working class demanded the recognition that France was a mission land and that the church must adopt radical means to enter this alien world of the proletariat. "Our manner of living, our ceremonies . . . our literary, artistic and philosophic cultures are attached to capitalism, which is attached to a bourgeois civilization. . . . If France is a mission land, it should have methods adapted properly to our present situation." In this way he was advocating a missionary stance adopted a few years later by the worker-priests. His martyrdom prevented him from fulfilling that dream personally.[21]

All of these factors played pivotal roles in the formation of the Mission de Paris and the worker-priests. Henri Godin's *France, pays de Mission?*, the Lisieux retreat, the person of Emmanuel Cardinal Suhard and the proletarian existence lived by priests and seminarians in Germany were the immediate momentous events and the grand personalities which were fundamental to the creation of the worker-priests. However, only those who had tasted the bitter wormwood of working class oppression had any real sense of the radicalism which was inherent in this new missionary impulse. Godin, Daniel, Suhard and the Lisieux theologians were only advocates of a missionary presence (*présence*) of priests in the midst of a working class which needed Christian conversion. The thought of *engagement* for the proletariat's liberation was far from their minds.[22]

This was not altogether the case with a fair number of the men who became worker-priests in the years to follow. Beyond the larger events which brought this novel ministry to birth were the personal and private pilgrimages which led one hundred men to adopt manual labor as the defining mark of their priesthood. Biography is also a vital context of this story, and although these men did not create the worker-priest ministry on their own, they did bring to it a passion and richness which would move it beyond the narrow walls of ecclesiastical mission. Many of the reasons which attracted them to a non-traditional priesthood would lead them also along more radical roads. Their earlier lives were, to a great extent, schools of training for their later dedication to the liberation of the proletariat. In light of this, it is necessary to ask just who these men were as individuals. What was their personal biography, the experience, the "formation" which led them ultimately to take up factory life? Why did they embark on a road uniquely different from the more traditional priestly role adopted by more than thirty-nine thousand of their clerical brothers? To be sure they were shaped by wider events in church and nation, but they were also products of their narrower more personal life pilgrimages. It is to these that we now turn.

Most of the worker-priests were young when they embarked on their special mission. They had been born in the period between 1920 and 1924 and were thus in their mid-20s by the time they entered the factories. Of course, there were some notable exceptions. Jacques Hollande (born 1901) was already forty-three years old when he replaced Henri Godin as the superior of the Mission de Paris. Father Roger Deliat, a Renault metallurgical worker, was born in 1907, and the oldest Mission de Paris priest Auguste Rosi (born 1892) was already in his fifties when he joined this apostolate. Nevertheless, youth remained the dominant age characteristic of most of these avant-garde priests.[23] Perhaps this was one reason why so many of them were prepared to embark on ventures beyond the landscape of the more traditional priesthood.

Social origins were another, perhaps more important, factor in shaping the vocational choice of these clergy. Not surprisingly the remembrance of humble beginnings accounted for the desire of some of them to serve the proletariat in new and risky ways. André Depierre recalled that his poverty-stricken peasant parents had no voice in their local parish, and this memory intensified in him the task "to give responsibility to the poor within the church." Albert Bouche was born into a family whose working class credentials went back five generations. His choice of an intellectual and priestly life was made in the midst of privation, and the sacrifices demanded of himself and his family stirred within him a conscious desire to be a working priest. Joseph Gouttebarge of St. Etienne (born 1924) came from a poor peasant family. His father died when Jo was only 3¹/₂ years old and when his mother was pregnant with her third child. All his life Jo felt like an orphan, deeply missing "the father he didn't know." He recalled the grinding poverty caused by the death of his father. He spoke of his mother, "a widow with three children after five years of marriage, and I, a companion of this misery until eleven years of age. . . . I remember when I watched cows for three months . . . [with almost no pay] . . . or the time when, for all my family, I went begging, but with head high, because my dignity was intact, to get six cents worth of milk, or the time when, as a timid and fearful boy, I crossed the threshold of the school, not knowing a word of French. . . . It is from this lump that God has made a priest." Gouttebarge was not the only worker-priest impoverished by the loss of a father. Both Maurice Combe and Henri Perrin were orphaned by virtue of the Great War; neither man ever knew his father.[24]

Other worker-priests were born into strictly proletarian families. Jean Volot's father was a common laborer who could neither read nor write, and Bernard Cagne's father worked on the railroads because he could not make ends meet on the farm. Both of Henri Barreau's parents toiled in a shoe factory, and his father organized a C.G.T. local there in 1920. In almost every instance worker-priests of proletarian heritage remembered their forebears with pride. "I am of working class origin," declared Charles Pautet. He spoke of his father's lifetime at the factory and affirmed proudly that even after his father died, "my mother still worked to earn her livelihood." The Dominican Joseph Robert made a similar testimony. "I am from a working class family," he affirmed. "My father, my two brothers and my two brothers-in-law are workers, metallurgists. . . . I lived my entire childhood in a working class city. . . . When I grew up I experienced all the working class suffering of the period after the Great War." For these reasons, he affirmed, "I grew up with a working class conscience."[25] Even before these men became worker-priests they had lived the grim reality of the proletariat. As a result, they were prepared in advance for their new field of labor and the liberation from social oppression that it demanded.

Although so many of the worker-priests were from the proletarian, peasant or petit-bourgeois classes, a few came from the more privileged sectors of French society. Jacques Loew was born into a middle-class Protestant family of some prominence, and Bernard Tiberghien was the son of an established bourgeois Catholic family made wealthy by the textile industry of the French Nord. The Dominican worker-priest Jacques Screppel reflected a social heritage similar to that of Father Tiberghien. Screppel's family belonged to "the great industrial bourgeoisie" but this only served to intensify his later devotion to the proletariat's liberation. He was convinced that this wealth and privilege was instrumental in driving him to identify with the working class. He recalled the days when his mother walked him through industrial ghettos to a private school. "I was struck by the contrast . . . between the very beautiful house of my parents . . . and the very miserable houses [of the workers]. . . . I decided, at that moment, that the fortune of my parents came from their [the proletarians'] work, and that I had a debt to these workers who provided my parents' fortune." Although this experience did not lead Screppel directly into the priesthood, he was convinced that his discovery of the harsh contrast of rich and poor oriented him "toward concern for the working class world," toward his "*engagement* as a worker-priest."[26]

In other instances worker-priests felt that earlier gainful employment had led them to their specialized form of ministry. Often this reality was simply a necessary outgrowth of a previously impoverished life. This was certainly the case with Jean Volot, Bernard Cagne, Jean-Marie Lepetit, Charles Pautet, Henri Barreau, Roger Deliat and Joseph Gouttebarge. Father Barreau labored in the same shoe factory as his parents, and Roger Deliat toiled as a hotel bellboy, salesman, cook and fitter's apprentice before he entered the seminary at age twenty-five. "Sadly I lived the constant humiliation of the poor," he noted in his memoirs. Charles Pautet reported that factory labor shaped his very notion of the priesthood. "I didn't enter seminary until I was twenty years old after I had worked for four years," he recalled, "and I could never imagine my life as a priest other than in a factory." Jo Gouttebarge was so impatient to begin his working class apostolate that he sought proletarian employment even during his seminary training. Before his graduation he was both a packer and an electrician's helper. On the day of his ordination he arrived by bicycle from the Fives-Lille plant in Givors just in time for the service. This memory of earlier oppression at the workplace prepared these men for the radical *engagement* they would undertake as clergy among the toilers.[27]

Many of the worker-priests chose their apostolate consciously as the result of an intellectual search or spiritual experience. Among their classmates they were often more restless and critical in spirit; they were ready for the new wave of progressive thinking which was finding its place in the church. Henri Perrin was one such example. His interest in theology and the social question drove him into the pages of the progressive journals *Sept, Vie Intellectuelle* and *Esprit*. He fell under the spell of the J.O.C., the Semaines Sociales and Action Populaire, and he praised the theological work of his Jesuit comrade Henri de Lubac. André Depierre was captivated equally by the intellectual currents of his day. "From the beginning, I was ... a man of inquiry (*recherche*)," he remembered, and this mood of theological search served only to intensify his commitment to the poor. Part of Jacques Jaudon's discovery of his vocation to "the poorest, to the workers" was precipitated by his study of the review *Jeunesse de l'Eglise* and the newspaper *La Quinzaine*. Jean Gray was converted to the gospel as a teenager, and his reading of Paul Claudel's poetry caused him to consecrate himself to the evangelization of the dechristianized proletariat. Father Francis Laval, the only priest-miner, experienced his call to the priesthood after a rather intemperate life. He felt led to a ministry among the poor by reading the works of Claudel, Charles Péguy and Georges Bernanos. Not surprisingly many of these clerics had been inspired directly by *France, pays de Mission?* Bernard Tiberghien testified that it had "made an enormous impression" upon him, and Father Laval recalled that it had led him to enroll at the Mission de France seminary. In fact, Laval was so overwhelmed by the book that he went to Paris to meet Fathers Godin and Daniel. Godin had died already, but Father Daniel introduced the young Laval to Louis Augros, the Lisieux seminary's superior. This encounter led Laval to enroll in that missionary institution.[28]

In fact, a full twenty-five percent of all the worker-priests had, at least, some specialized training at the Mission de France. In many cases, their total vocational preparation was at Lisieux. Among these were Philbert Talé, Jean Laudet, Maurice Droesch, Joseph Gouttebarge, Francis Laval, Maurice Combe, Bernard Striffling, Jacques Vivez, Gabriel Gential, Jacques Jaudon, Jacques Riousse, Yves Garnier, André Chauveneau, Albert Guichard, Jean Gray and the Belgians Louis Flagothier and Albert Courtoy. All testified to the positive impact of this seminary training upon their worker-priest apostolate.[29]

In particular, Albert Guichard was attracted to the Mission de France because "it represented . . . a wind of revolution in the church . . . a renovation in every domain." Jean Gray spent four years at the seminary as a professor of theology, yet while there, his strongest desire was to enter a factory as a priest. In one instance, the hope for work at Lisieux was thwarted by a more radical commission. The young intellectual Father Emile Poulat sought employment as a professor at the Mission de France seminary, but Louis Augros convinced him that his talents would be utilized more effectively at the Mission de Paris. Augros felt that Poulat was too avant-garde even for the Lisieux seminary; the young priest agreed and arrived at the Mission de Paris in October, 1949.[30]

Strangely enough, in some cases a negative seminary experience served to intensify vocational interests in proletarian mission work. A number of the worker-priests from humble backgrounds felt alienated by classical priestly training. Roger Deliat had to spend long hours to catch up to his more prosperous and better educated comrades at the seminary. He got sick and almost abandoned his vocation twice, but by sheer persistence he managed to survive. Almost forty years later, he remembered those years in these poignant words: "I felt so small, miserable and clumsy. . . . No one seemed interested in the social aspect of the gospel, except one old professor who was isolated by his ideas. In many instances, I asked myself if I had not taken a wrong road. How could I speak to workers the liberating message of Jesus Christ by a training limited to dogmas and intellectualized apologetics?" The Dominican Joseph Robert survived his traditional training by constantly reminding himself of his more radical vocational dreams. "When I entered the seminary," he recalled, "I had the conviction not only that my life would be given to the working class milieu but that also one day . . . I would become, at the same time, a worker-priest."[31]

Much like Fathers Bousquet and Dillard, large numbers of worker-priests had been influenced deeply by their discovery of the working class in German war camps and in resistance activities. Because of this, such men as Jean Gray, Jacques Riousse, Paul Guilbert, Bernard Chauveau, Bernard Striffling and the Jesuit Georges-Pierre Puységur carried into their worker-priesthood an already existing conviction that the church should assist the liberation of the laboring classes.[32] Albert Gauche, a Marseille-based worker-priest, discovered the proletariat in a German P.O.W. camp. This convinced him to adopt a ministry to that disinherited class. "Yes, I found the misery of the workers, not in books, but by living it myself," he said. "This life in the camp, in the midst of the working class . . . made me decide to concentrate all my existence to bring faith and solace to this class held in misery." Henri Barreau felt that his P.O.W. years in a Hanover camp marked his life so definitively that then-and-there he "decided to become a worker-priest." Joseph Robert found that his years of captivity gave him the definition of the priesthood which would guide his life. A priest was to be "one of them [the workers], sharing all their sufferings and all their human hopes. . . . In a word, it is by a communion of life and destiny . . . that the church has rendered itself present (*présente*) behind the barbed wire."[33] Much as later liberation theologians would claim, the reality of oppression cried out for values and lifestyles which would address this concrete situation. The experience of these particular men was a living testimony of that assertion. However, it was Henri Perrin who provided the most detailed description of how prison and proletarian life led him into the worker-priesthood. In a testimony following the pattern of both Bousquet and Dillard, he described the misery and Christian life of his camp comrades, but it was his discovery of work and the laboring classes which led him to more radical conclusions. He came to see "the worker commanded, devoured by his machine," but he also saw him in heroic form as the voice for "the suppression of outrageous social inequalities." He was convinced that militant communists served the cause of justice and that the church should "make the social revolution in the name of the gospel." Toward this end he advocated a ministry of clergy in factories: "For several years a current of priests has stood out who, in full accord with their bishops, wish to live as workers . . . in order to continue the incarnation of Christ. . . . These worker-priests . . . are ready to give this testimony of their hands before the world." Perrin's experience as a German P.O.W. had radicalized him along liberationist lines even before he became a worker-priest in Paris.[34]

Similar discoveries would be made by those worker-priests who found their baptism of fire in the resistance. Both Robert Pacalet and Jean Volot were in the *maquis,* and André Depierre served with the armed resistance in the Jura Mountains. The Dominican Father Robert engaged in acts of opposition to the Nazis from within a German concentration camp, and the entire family of Francis Vico was in the Normandy resistance. Although his parents were arrested and deported for such activities, Vico continued their courageous work at age twenty by hiding Jews and Allied aviators who had been shot down by the Germans. These and similar activities brought these young men into contact with militant proletarians in the Resistance, and such encounters predisposed them to the worker-priest ministry which they later embraced.[35]

Finally, a number of worker-priests were influenced in their vocational choice by direct contact with specialized Catholic Action or by ministry in working class parishes. As a vicar at Notre Dame de Lourdes in Nancy Michel Bordet learned his missionary orientation from the J.O.C., while others, such as Michel Lemonon, Jean Cottin, Jo Gouttebarge and Pierre Riche, merely enhanced their earlier radical commitments during their stints as Catholic Action chaplains. Joseph Robert was convinced that his Jociste activities helped shape his future vocation. "At eighteen years of age," he recalled, "I had my first contact with the newly-born J.O.C. which conditioned my priestly orientation. . . . It was my task as a Jociste chaplain which made me decide for the factory."[36]

Similarly parish duty in working class ghettos led some of these young priests to adopt the more radical form of worker-priesthood in order to establish more meaningful contact with their proletarian neighbors. Bernard Striffling wrote that his "presence as a vicar . . . in a working-class suburb" imposed upon him "this fact of people living outside the church," and Albert Gauche testified that his vicarage in a proletarian parish led him "to discover what was really the life of the working class." For Jo Guttebarge, a parish ministry among the poor of St. Etienne brought back all the painful memories of his childhood and reinforced within him a total commitment to "the most disinherited." In some instances, frustration with parish life, even in its most innovative forms, drove some of these men to a worker-priesthood. Roger Deliat, commenting on his ministry at Nanterre, stated: "I tried by every possible means to go to the non-Christian masses," but he felt "beaten by the parish cadres, the principles, the methods, the 'good people' and the parish clergy." For him, the Mission de Paris was his "last chance." At Nancy, Father Robert Pfaff felt oppressed by a similar reality, and Father François Vidal, ministering in a North Marseille parish, felt deeply the contradiction between his parish duties and his life as a worker-priest. In spite of these negative feelings, the working class parish had given these men a taste of their growing vocation to reach the proletariat. Yet they felt compelled to move beyond the church's institutional confines. This they did by going to work.[37]

No single reason prompted these men to become worker-priests. Usually a complex of events and experiences had driven them willy-nilly to their destiny. For some it was almost a single conscious event and choice, but for others the soil had been prepared since birth. Each had his own individual story, his own pilgrimage to the factory. The intertwining of humble origins, work experience, war-time privations, a searching restlessness, Jociste activity and working class parishes brought these men together upon a common road which led to the workplace. In practically every instance their individual pilgrimages had begun an evolution which would drive them toward increasing militancy in the cause of working class liberation. Subsequent history would immortalize the bold choices they made to construct a new world of justice with the oppressed proletariat. Collectively they would be remembered as the worker-priests.

Nevertheless, the road to manual labor by these men was neither a single corporate act, nor was it immediate. Instead, it was the gradual product of their experience in the proletarian environment. Becoming a worker-priest grew out of collective "brainstorming" among the men, much like the "praxis-reflection-praxis" sessions described by later Latin American theologians of liberation. Gradually these missionaries among French workers were able, on a case-by-case basis, to convince their religious superiors to mandate them to earn a living by common toil. Jacques Loew was laboring on the docks as early as 1941, and small groups of worker-priests began their existence in 1944. In that year the Mission de Paris had one priest at the workplace and only five by 1947. But this year was the turning point as increasing numbers of priests began to work full-time. By the end of that year there were twenty-five worker-priests, sixteen in the Mission de Paris, some in various missionary orders and still others located in industrial centers outside of Paris. By their highpoint between 1952 and 1954, they numbered approximately one hundred, about eighty in the secular priesthood with the remainder in the Franciscan, Capuchin, Jesuit, Dominican, Pradosian and other religious orders. About half of the worker-priests were centered in the Parisian area, while the remainder were scattered in provincial industrial centers such as Lyon, Marseille, Lille, Limoges, Toulouse, Bordeaux, Nancy, Le Havre, Dunkerque, Liège (Belgium) and others. Some were even located in rural areas at the construction sites of hydro-electric dams.[38]

Thus it is clear that the worker-priest form of ministry began gradually, and until the end of 1947 it was rare indeed. In a very real sense most of these men and the groups to which they belonged were groping for the most appropriate means to make the gospel relevant to the proletariat. Manual labor and all that went with it was their final choice, a choice they adopted almost unanimously by 1948. Until that time they experimented with different approaches. This trial by error method can be seen most readily in the early efforts of the priestly members in the Mission de Paris. Internally there was early strife at rue Ganneron over questions of leadership and personalities. Some were suggesting that charismatic figures such as André Depierre or Georges Michonneau should replace the more lack-luster Jacques Hollande. Others were afraid that a cult of personality would emerge if Hollande were dropped. There were discussions advocating an openness of their weekly meetings to a selected Catholic public, a move which brought such prominent theologians as M.-D. Chenu into the life of the worker-priests. Methods of penetrating the neighborhoods were discussed regularly. A rough consensus developed in which it was felt that Christian communities should be organized in the various industrial quarters of Paris which would become an integral part of the people's lives. In February, 1946 one of the Mission's reports defined that task in the following way: "We desire to plant the church where it has not been, that is, *to insert* Christianity into the natural communities of work, neighborhood and leisure. We are trying to penetrate these communities, their human currents, carrying with us only the witness of an authentically Christian life."[39]

How to accomplish this goal in a pragmatic way was much more difficult. Initially, the Mission de Paris priests engaged in some flashy activities. Open air masses were held at city halls; Christmas sermons were preached at local markets; street corner addresses were given; and leaflets were delivered at factory gates and subway entrances. However, the Mission de Paris soon recognized that patience, long-term efforts, "the capacity to work in a team (*équipe*) and live in poverty" were more vital to missionary success than a hasty series of ostentatious programs. Consequently these priests turned to home visitations and neighborhood activities to make their presence felt. Each priest set out to accomplish these tasks in his own particular sector.[40]

Most well-known of all these Mission de Paris groups was the one at Montreuil under the direction of Father André Depierre. This tiny Christian ensemble would become the model and most publicized example of the Mission de Paris communities. Depierre's leadership qualities, his writing skills and his wide contacts with the French Catholic avant-garde made him the natural spokesperson for the fledgling worker-priest movement. However, most of his time was spent in Montreuil where he sought "to create . . . veritable communities outside of the general institutional structure of the church" in the areas of "neighborhood, work and city." Toward that end he joined with both Christians and communists in mutual aid organizations like the Mouvement Populaire des Familles. These activities brought him to the attention of the communist officials who governed Montreuil. They welcomed him heartily, and he was soon involved in municipal programs concerning health, family and youth issues. He participated in neighborhood street carnivals and festivals, such as the open-air dances characteristic of Bastille Day. Also Depierre was convinced of the value of personal contacts. This commitment prompted him to visit homes regularly and to spend hours in local cafés with the men from his factory. As of 1979 Father Depierre still lived in Montreuil as a worker-priest. In spite of bad health he continued to toil at a full-time job. After all, though a priest, he was still a worker, and a worker was required to earn a living.[41] The Christian community which he had built over thirty years before was a forerunner of the well-known grass-roots parallels which emerged among the poor in Latin America and elsewhere.

During these early years the Mission de Paris provided the first worker-priest martyr Father Camille Folliet. Ordained in 1932 he served in a working-class parish where he became active in the budding Jociste movement. During the war he sold the resistance newspaper *Témoignage Chrétien,* hid Jews and formed links with the armed *maquis.* After his arrest by the Gestapo and a brief stint in an Italian prison, he used forged papers to join the Mission de Paris sector at Argenteuil. He took up arms to help liberate Paris in August, 1944 and died in the spring of 1945 from wounds received fighting the retreating Germans in the French Alps. Camille Folliet may have been the worker-priests' first martyr, but he would not be their last. But the others would not fall in the recognized heroism of war. Instead they would be the victims of firings, lay-offs, bad health, strikes and work accidents, namely the everyday martyrdoms of that proletarian oppression so characteristic of the industrial west.[42]

In addition to the Mission de Paris other worker-priest ministries sprung to life during the mid-1940s. One of these was the Fraternité des Ouvriers de la Vièrge des Pauvres in Liège, Belgium. The inspiration behind its birth was Father Charles Boland, a priest dedicated to proletarian missions since his ordination in 1921. Very quickly he recognized that to be effective the church must "return to the workplace no longer to make a study but rather to render Christ to these workers." He felt that one way to accomplish this task was for the priest to engage in factory toil in "homage" to 'Jesus' life as a carpenter. For years he sought permission from the church's hierarchy to undertake the task himself. Over a period of time he won sympathy from key Vatican officials, but his bishop Msgr. Kerkofs of Liège refused him permission to work full-time until 1943. Now forty-eight years of age, Charles Boland had waited twenty-two years to fulfill his vocational dream. Finally, he had become a worker-priest. His vocation was fulfilled. At last, he cried enthusiastically, "I was admitted to share (*partager*) the working class condition, to enter the movement of the working masses."[43]

Joining with Father Damien Reumont and a militant Jociste Hector Cools, Boland organized his religious fraternity that same year. He dedicated this O.V.P., as it was called, to the "Virgin of the Poor," because its task was to be a Christian leaven in the lump of the dechristianized proletariat. By 1946 two other priests had joined the community, one a Capuchin and the other a Josephite. The latter Father Liévin went to work as a miner at the moment when Father Boland was forced to leave his plant because of ill health. This experiment was met with sympathetic curiosity by the factory neighborhood, but the real impact of the O.V.P. was felt largely by other worker-priests and missionary apostolates to the proletariat. The O.V.P. became one worker-priest model "to carry the liberating message of the gospel to the working class, not by words, but by the witness of their life." Indeed the worker-priest mode of witness was endorsed enthusiastically by Boland's community. "The O.V.P. will earn their bread by their work," stated Father Reumont in one of his reports. "They will not be afraid of hard labor nor of tomorrow's uncertainties which the condition of worker brings with it, but they will consider these things as their proper pilgrimage of asceticism and renunciation."[44]

Some of the more traditional religious orders became involved in worker-priest ministries during this early period, thus laying the groundwork for further expansion at a later date. The Assumptionists and Franciscans were engaged in this activity only minimally. The former developed neighborhood experiments solely, while the latter sent merely one monk into the factories. However, the Capuchins were much more ambitious. At the request of Cardinal Suhard three of them were mandated to set up a community in proletarian Nanterre where they were "to create a working class Christendom in a natural milieu, outside of any existing parish." Father Césaire Dillaye was charged with directing this Capuchin group. He coordinated the daily and neighborhood activities of his tiny community, and he was responsible for the neighborhood chapel entrusted to his care. He and his colleagues worked intimately with Father Rétif's progressive parish at Colombes, and they met frequently with the Mission de Paris *équipe*. The other two priests were engaged in manual labor, because they felt that "factory work" was "indispensable" to their "total integration into the working class community."[45]

Their long interest in the social question predisposed the Jesuits to adopt the worker-priest model for a number of their clergy. In the summer of 1945 the Jesuit P.O.W. Georges Puységur joined a Mission de Paris community and began to toil at a Panhard Plant. His experience with brutal demeaning work and the courage of communist militants intensified his commitment to a mission involving the factory labor of priests. Within two years he was joined by Henri Perrin who had discovered his worker-priest vocation after much personal struggle. By the end of 1946 he was ready to give his life "totally for the working class," but he took some additional time contacting his own Jesuit Action Populaire and the Dominican-based Economie et Humanisme before he made his total plunge. It was the judgment of a socialist writer who defined "priests with white hands" as "renegades from the world of work" which prompted Perrin to take up factory toil when he did. In 1947 the Action Populaire and Cardinal Suhard collaborated to send six Jesuits into Paris' thirteenth arrondissement, a heavily working class district. Three of them were instructed to be links between parish and neighborhood, and the other three Fathers Puységur, Perrin and Rideau were mandated to take up factory work. In that same year two other Jesuits Fathers Magand and Galtier were engaged in manual labor in the Lyon area.[46]

The Dominicans were the first of the traditional religious orders to experiment with the worker-priest form of mission work. The impetus came from M.-R. (Jacques) Loew, the docker-priest of Marseille. Joseph Lebret, the director of the Economie et Humanisme team, charged his younger comrade with the task of writing a sociological study of the Marseille dockers. Loew was determined to utilize the participatory method of research so skillfully employed by Lebret when he studied the Breton fishermen. To accomplish this he went to work at the port as a common docker in 1941. He was the first full-time worker-priest. His witness on the docks, combined with his written testimonies, his neighborhood activities and his organizational skills as a parish priest, made him one of the most well-known of all the worker-priests.[47]

Soon other Dominicans adopted the stance of Father Loew. One such priest was Joseph Robert who began his worker-priest apostolate in the teeming ghettos of Paris' thirteenth arrondissement. There he worked with the Jesuit Henri Perrin, and they became fast friends. In a brief period of time this neighborhood was the locus of a wide variety of proletarian missions. Here could be found Dominicans and Jesuits, Jean-Marie Marzio and Jean Laudet of the Mission de Paris and the St. Hippolyte parish of the Mission de France with two of its own worker-priests. No other district of France had such a concentration of laboring clergy. Elsewhere the Dominicans had some priests doing factory labor in both Lille and Marseille.[48]

The Prado missionary order mandated a number of its priests and brothers to engage in factory labor. This was largely the work of its superior-general Alfred Ancel who was also an auxiliary bishop at Lyon. Initially he was critical of the worker-priest concept, but he was impressed with the efforts of the Mission de Paris. In 1945 he created a community in the midst of a Lyon proletarian district. He, another priest and a seminarian undertook the task of being an incarnational presence in their non-Christian neighborhood. Within two years Ancel was coming to accept the necessity for some clergy to engage in manual labor. Consequently he sent two of his priests into full-time factory employ, and he arranged for six others to work for brief periods of time. Alfred Ancel was moving slowly but progressively to that moment when he would become his church's first working-bishop.[49]

Thus by 1947 the worker priest ministries were in place. The Mission de Paris was established, and small clusters of secular priests were toiling in factories in Marseille, Lyon, Lille and elsewhere. Clergy in various religious orders were involved as well. The personal link behind all of this was Cardinal Suhard. From the vital missionary retreat at Tourette in early 1947 to the death of Suhard in the spring of 1949 the worker-priest movement began to expand quietly. The aging cardinal remained its most significant patron and defender, and he crowned his long career with a speech in honor of his laboring clergy. "There is a wall dividing the church and the masses," he told the crowd celebrating the fiftieth anniversary of his ordination, "a wall that must at any cost be battered down in order to bring back to Christ the multitudes who have lost him. That is why we are glad to entrust our Mission de Paris to certain of our priests, pioneers of the avant-garde." Within a few months he was dead, at the very moment when the worker-priests would begin a more rapid expansion and experimentation in controversial directions.[50]

The pioneer years had passed quietly for the worker-priests. *France, pays de mission?*, the Lisieux retreat, German war camps and the patronage of Cardinal Suhard had prepared the soil for their mission. Their own personal pilgrimages had played a significant part in leading them from the seminary to the factory gates. However, it was neither the theological reflections at Lisieux and Tourette nor the bold patronage of Cardinal Suhard which accounted for their growing militancy in the laboring apostolate. All that went before, from Albert de Mun to Henri Godin, did not create the worker-priests. It only set the stage for the mandate which would send them in that direction. Initially they stumbled about in the foreign land of the proletariat, hoping that their neighborhood programs would ingratiate them to their adopted working class. However, it was work itself which would make them worker-priests; the entry into manual labor would define them and shape their consciousness in the direction of a liberation *praxis*. They would continue to live in the neighborhoods and make their presence felt there, but work would be the key to their existence and make them citizens in the alien oppressive world of the proletariat. Suhard, Godin and their earlier experiences had prepared them for some form of mission to the poor; common toil to earn their bread would make them worker-priests.

VI

THE WORLD OF WORKER-PRIEST NATURALIZATION

"If the priests did as you, they would have the esteem of the working class."
—Marseille laborer to a worker-seminarian

Entry into the workplace to earn a living became the distinguishing mark of the entire worker-priest ministry. Indeed, the chief characteristic of proletarian existence was monotonous toil; if priests hoped to identify with workers, they would be forced to adopt this oppressive way of life. In doing so they embraced a world of privation and suffering, a world of daily injustice in the midst of the prosperity found in western industrial society. It did not take the worker-priests long to discover that manual toil was the very heart of their solidarity with the poor. Jacques Jaudon from Toulouse called it "the essence of our life"; André Piet, a Marseille Dominican, testified that it was "essential"; his Dominican brother from Paris, Joseph Robert described it as "a fundamental priority"; and Bernard Chauveau, a secular priest on the Renault assembly line, insisted that factory work was absolutely primary to his vocation.[1]

These opinions were by no means isolated. Instead they reflected a collective consensus which grew out of earlier experiences and long hours of passionate discussion. In a 1945 report to Jacques Hollande, the Ivry worker-priest Père du Mont suggested that "there be priests who work," who live their "entire priesthood at the factory." Such a cleric must "live his apostolate uniquely at the plant" with the kind of audacity that incorporates "the very depths of what factory life involves."[2] In less than a year, various rationales were being utilized to press the Mission de Paris in this direction.[3] By the late 1940s rapid agreement was being reached concerning the centrality of the prole-

75

tarian apostolate at the workplace. In a one-page note to Père Hollande, two of his priests put it this way: "It has appeared to us that it would be impossible to be effective without putting our life in a total community of destiny (*communauté de destin*) with the working class. . . . This is why we no longer accept any other means of life than our livelihood as a worker."[4] François Vidal of Marseille called factory labor "the decisive step," and Louis Flagothier, who entered a Liège metallurgical foundry in 1948, recalled that one "could not link up with the worker's world without sharing its work."[5] More specifically Father Henri Perrin called the entry into factory work "a necessary condition for reform and progress," a curb to clericalism, purification from a "caste mentality" and the rediscovery of a "*communauté de destin* with the working class."[6]

Père Jacques Loew echoed the *communauté de destin* motif, "an idea which was very strong at Economie et Humanisme," the équipe for which he worked. In the book he wrote about his first years of toil as a Marseille docker, this Dominican priest portrayed in some detail the logic which led him to the wharfs. Assigned to do a sociological study of this life by the Economie et Humanisme chief Joseph Lebret, Loew undertook the task, utilizing to the fullest the participatory sociology of his superior. The docker-priest thought that it was "impossible to make anything out of" this life "from the outside." Consequently, he concluded "that it was no good wasting time on paper theories: the thing to do was to buy some overalls on the old-clothes market, get a job like everyone else, and then, at the end of the day's work, go off and live with the very dregs of the population—the dockers on the port." Put bluntly, Loew's contention was this: "Dungarees, manual labor—prerequisites for the rediscovery and rescue of man."[7]

Although they expressed unanimity about the necessity of manual labor, the worker-priests entered the workplace at different times. Permission was not granted collectively but rather on a case-by-case basis by individual bishops and religious superiors. This clergy's sensing and discovery of a worker-priest mission through "praxis-reflection-praxis" sessions was not enough. Cautious prelates had to be convinced that such vocations should be mandated. After all, it had taken Charles Boland of Liège twenty-two years to convince his bishop to send him to work.[8] Cardinal Suhard, the worker-priests' most consistent patron, had to persuade both the Capuchin and Jesuit superiors to send members of their respective orders into Parisian factories.

This blend of caution and support for the worker-priest apostolate by members of the hierarchy is well illustrated by Cardinal Pierre-Marie Gerlier, the archbishop of Lyon. Robert Pacalet had been touched by working class life both in the Resistance and in his work as a J.O.C. chaplain. These experiences attracted him toward a worker-priest ministry. Such singlemindedness prompted him to turn down two prominent parishes proposed by his bishop. Pacalet recalls fondly the personal meeting with Gerlier in which the cardinal proffered his third suggestion. "I have a post to propose to you," he stated. "Do you know the Mission de Paris?" "Certainly, Eminence," came the response. "Well," continued Gerlier, "I intend to create for Lyon such common laborers. We need three priests. . . . I have chosen you for the third. Are you in accord?" Pacalet's affirmative response was the beginning of a worker-priest ministry which would continue under his bishop's mandate until the ill-fated condemnation of 1954.[9]

Gerlier was not as flexible when his auxiliary bishop Alfred Ancel requested a similar commission. Although he had supported the worker-priests with great caution, the superior of Prado became increasingly convinced that to know the working class meant becoming a part of it from the inside. Cardinal Gerlier hesitated for four years; it was not until 1953 that he was prepared to allow Ancel to do manual labor. Even then, he would not permit his auxiliary bishop to enter a factory. Ancel was forced to set up his own workshop at Gerland since Gerlier would permit him to engage in "only manual labor at home." The cardinal was not prepared to allow a bishop to enter the wider world of industry as a common laborer.[10]

Permission to engage in manual labor did not insure gainful employment for the mandated priest. In a number of instances getting a job proved difficult. Henri Perrin's initial confidence began to wane when he was not hired in his south Parisian neighborhood.[11] Others had difficulty finding employment simply because they were priests. A number of factory owners (*patrons*) and managers, mostly practicing Catholics, were embarrassed and hesitant when confronted with priests who wanted to work with their hands. Charles Pautet had a running battle with the employer at Renault. Hired as a turner, he had toiled barely three hours when he was told that he "could not be part of the work force 'because he . . . was a practicing priest.'" In fury he protested his position successfully to the management. "I wanted and still want . . . to share (*partager*) the destiny of all my working class brothers who, having no support, are placed by fate, be it good or bad, to earn their bread."[12] Father Pacalet faced similar problems in the Lyon area. When it was discovered that he was a priest, the management called a number of meetings to resolve this quandary. Unable to reach a decision, they called in the factory owner who agreed reluctantly that the priest should be allowed to work at his plant.[13]

Such instances, however, remained exceptional. Most of the worker-priests sought work in the fashion of men and women who required such mindless toil to put bread on the table. Like their laboring sisters and brothers they entered the work force as ciphers, as countless replaceable parts needed to keep the industrial system in motion. In this respect they were taking a significant step in identifying with the oppressive life of the working poor. Out of that experience would emerge their later militancy.

The reception they would receive from their fellow toilers was most critical for their entry into factory life. One worker-seminarian, André Deléage felt that this transition was so important that he wrote a report offering advice in this matter. He warned against superior airs and suggested that silence was the ideal approach until honesty compelled one to reveal his identity.[14] However, for most worker-priests, factory entry brought with it no preconceived strategy or game-plan. In his reminiscences Gabriel Genthiel put it bluntly, "Neither a strategy nor tactics; all this was foreign to us." His two teammates echoed this opinion. Father Henri Barreau spoke of entering the factory with "no precise goal," and Louis Bouyer, a working vicar, stated that he and his priestly comrade passed through the factory gates "with no preconceived ideas and with no desire to make conversions."[15]

Consequently, without any organized strategy or tactics, these priests found their first days of employment varied both in terms of their style of entry and of their reception. One worker-priest at Limoges informed his bishop that he had entered the factory "during the first days in his cassock" and that this had led his fellow toilers to conclude that he was there "to spy on the workers . . . or take them over."[16] This kind of reaction was not uncommon. When it was discovered that Jean Olhagaray was a priest the other workers regarded him with general suspicion, and Henri Barreau was told curtly that "priests come into the factory to combat the working class."[17] Given the standard anticlericalism of the French proletariat, such a reaction was not surprising. To avoid such initial judgments most of the worker-priests decided to enter the workplace incognito. The Dominican Jean Legendre told his comrades he was an unemployed philosopher, and Jean Cottin, a Le Havre worker-priest, recalled that his silence on the matter allowed him to be "a worker just like the others."[18] Henri Perrin spelled out this approach in detail in his notes:

> Only a few people from the outside knew that I was a priest.
> They ignored it in the factory, and I said nothing to anybody.
> For a number of reasons I had decided to live this experience

in silence. First of all, for myself, to be more simply one of them in their midst, to bring myself into their rhythm, their thoughts, their way of seeing things. . . . Then, to say without preparation that one is a priest is to risk strongly a provocation among the group of factitious attitudes like those that are taken against the church and the clergy.[19]

In spite of such precautions, their priestly identity was eventually discovered by their work comrades, and the stories surrounding such revelations form an integral part of the human tapestry of the worker-priests' incarnation. In his memoirs Roger Deliat of Renault recalled a conversation which went like this: "Are you married?" "No," responded Deliat. "Why not? Are you divorced?" "No!" "Ah, you don't make love to women?" Deliat: "That's right!" "Oh, they give you a hard time?" "No!" In exasperation, the worker exclaimed, "Perhaps you're impotent?" Again Deliat replied, "No!" "My word, surely you're not a priest?" "Yes, I am," said Deliat. "You're pulling my leg, old buddy; I don't believe it. I've never seen a priest at the factory. Maybe you're defrocked?" "No," was Deliat's response. Finally, his frustrated buddy exploded, "Tell me! I have the impression that you're fuckin' me over. You're pokin' fun at me, you know?" It took Deliat a number of days to finally convince his comrades that he was indeed a priest.[20]

At Marseille a report was sent to the bishop by a docker-priest describing the moment in which he revealed his identity. During a lunch break about fifteen of the men became involved in a heated exchange about the clergy. One worker called them "human pigs who exploit others," and an anarchist called Mustache said he knew a priest who was "a fat pig." Unable to contain himself, the docker-priest shouted, "Hey Mustache! Do you know the priest at Cabucelle?" "No," was his immediate reply. "Well, I'm that Cabucelle priest," uttered their comrade. A stunned silence followed. As the workers clustered around the priest, the trade union delegate and communist leader blurted out, "No, that's not possible! You're joking!" After some discussion, the priest informed the other men that he was on the docks "to earn his livelihood . . . and to . . . share (*partage*) the suffering of poor people just like Christ has done." The communist union leader raised a final question. "And Delay [the bishop], he agrees?" "Certainly," was the quick response of the docker-priest. "Without that we couldn't be commissioned." Another worker concluded the dialogue with a jovial note of acceptance of the church's *présence* on the docks, "Well, if Delay comes some day to run a winch, I will relieve him."[21]

All in all, the entry into work was a powerful and positive experience for the worker-priests. It enabled them to cross the wall which separated the church from the proletariat. In spite of some initial suspicions and accusations, they were welcomed by their work comrades. This led them to believe that their full naturalization into the proletariat had begun. "From that moment," testified one worker-priest, "we spoke man to man." Indeed, he felt that he had become "a militant . . . and no longer a parasite" in his comrades' eyes. Those with whom he worked echoed this conviction. "If the priests did like you," said one, "they would have the esteem of the working class." Another paid him the ultimate compliment: "Well, if I saw a worker-priest in the shit with me, I would tip my hat to him." At the metallurgical plants of Lorraine, the militants of the union told Father Michel Bordet: "You preach well at Mass; at the church you make good sermons. But the day when you came into the factory with us, that moment was the natural moment for the right to speak. Before, you didn't have the right to speak."[22] By becoming common toilers the worker-priests had won the respect of their fellow laborers. Incarnational identification had accomplished what almost seventy years of good intentions could never do.

Having achieved a successful entry into the workforce, the worker-priests set themselves to the lifetime task of earning a living by hard toil. Getting a job was just the doorway to their naturalization, to their incarnation into the proletariat. It was their day-to-day labor which would become the test and proof of that vocation.

The type of work that they undertook varied greatly. Most, however, toiled in heavy industry, especially the metallurgical trades. There they served as common laborers, though some, with the passage of time, learned a trade and became specialized workers such as turners, adjusters, machinists and electricians. A number of others remained at the more difficult chores, such as firemen at the large furnaces which produced molten steel.[23] Some worker-priests found employment on the docks of France's major ports, Marseille, Bordeaux, Le Havre and Dunkerque, while others toiled to construct large hydro-electric dams in the French hinterland. Francis Laval was a miner; Lucien Lacour became the chaplain of the Parisian firemen; Auguste Rosi ministered to prostitutes (though not for a salary); Jean Volot was a sailor; and Jacques Riousse labored as a technician in the movie industry. Finally, a number of worker-priests either performed artisanal work or toiled as sweated labor in small non-union workshops.[24]

This great variety of chores undertaken by the worker-priests is in stark contrast to the almost unanimous opinion that their work was brutal, unjust and alienating. In this respect, their identification with the industrial proletariat was total. Henri Barreau spoke for many of his priestly comrades when he drafted the following summary:

> We had experienced the factory atmosphere, the continual persecution, the lack of liberty, initiative and confidence, the scornful and condescending smiles of the foremen, the hush-money of the management, the penalties, the arbitrary firings, the lay-offs. We have experienced everything that hides behind the language of production needs: the sending away of those who are no longer young enough or lively enough and for others, infernal work, the cadence, the incessant march against the clock, the physical and nerve-wracking exhaustion, the nightmares while sleeping and the habitual deception on payday of ridiculously low wages.[25]

This oppressive atmosphere and work rhythm was characteristic of French industrial life, and the worker-priests discovered this reality by painful experience. The cycle of factory toil shaped their entire day as well as their sleep habits. At Lyon, Robert Pacalet rose at 5:00 a.m. to say Mass before being on the job at 6:00 a.m., and Henri Barreau was out of bed by 6:00 a.m. so he could bicycle about one-half hour in order to arrive at his plant by 7:00 a.m. At one point in his life André Depierre of Montreuil required two and one-half hours for the bus and subway rides to and from work. Often priestly chores, such as saying Mass and taking communion to the sick, required an even earlier rising. Shift work brought its own brand of physical and mental fatigue, and a number of the worker-priests testified to this ennui.[26] One worker-priest, Jean Wernier, captured the pain of shift work in these words:

> Midnight. I scarcely feel drowsy; this makes two weeks that I've not slept in the evenings. But now I must begin again to live during the day, to see again the sun's light, but tonight and the next nights others will be working; others will continue painfully while the whole world sleeps. I must never forget that across this shared (*partagé*) pain I am rediscovering the great pain of a suffering humanity and of Christ's body torn apart by sin.[27]

Added to these chronological deprivations of factory life was the relentless sameness and exhaustion of the work itself. Robert Pfaff and

Michel Bordet recalled the awful heat of the steel-producing furnaces, and André Piet remembered the physically numbing work of the turner, standing immobile at a machine doing the same thing hour after hour, day after day. One worker-priest confessed, "We are one of the factory wheels. Nothing can be done to get it to stop. . . . It keeps turning; we must turn with the rhythm which has been imposed upon us, neither faster nor slower." Echoing this assessment, a worker-seminarian called factory life a "regular and monotonous life rhythm" in which the laborer becomes "a prisoner of routine, a slave of physical fatigue, tedium, discouragement." "I was nothing else than an anonymous particle doing a job," he concluded. "Produce and shut up!"[28]

Danger from unsafe working conditions and job loss were two realistic fears faced by the worker-priests. Francis Vico recalled vividly the crushed hand of a Moroccan comrade, and Roger Deliat was so moved by accidents and deaths at his plant that he wrote the poem "La Mort d'un travailleur." Time and again, worker-priests were present at the factory to minister to dying *copains* and their families. Not surprisingly these laboring priests were not immune from tragedy themselves. In 1951 Father Michel Favreau was crushed by over a ton of wood on the docks of Bordeaux. Through his death, the worker-priests had joined what they considered the ranks of the working class martyrs. Indeed, many of them believed that the deaths of Jo Gouttebarge and Jo Lafontaine at relatively young ages were direct results of unhealthy working conditions.[29]

Further, the worker-priests faced the direct injustices of the workplace which arose from employer policies. Low wages was one such complaint that they often voiced. André Depierre and Bernard Cagne recalled that they received only "a living wage," which they defined as enough to purchase just "modest food." Fathers Riche, Olhagaray and Lepetit reported that the workers were "victims of insufficient wages," and Bernard Tiberghien was convinced that his 40F per hour wages at Citroën were "clearly insufficient in these days in the Parisian area to live in a human way." He called such wages "a thievery of the factory owners."[30] The ever-present fear of lay-off and unemployment, often prompted by direct management repression, was another tragedy that cast its shadow upon factory life. Time and time again worker-priests found themselves or their militant friends sacked because they had been involved in protest activities in defense of the workers. Robert Pfaff of Longwy was laid off with eleven other workers because he protested the use of police to aid "scabs" who sought to cross the picket line at his plant. In the Parisian area, Philbert Talé was given a choice by his boss, a technical job in England or a lay-off. The impetuous worker-priest retorted that his comrades were waiting at the door and would he like to repeat the offer so that they could hear. Unsurprisingly Talé was fired immediately. Joseph Gouttebarge of St. Etienne was harassed continually because of his union activities. He was given more difficult work, tied up in bureaucratic reporting and accused of irregular absences from the factory. For these reasons, he felt qualified to speak for his comrades: "Just like me, you wait for pay-day impatiently to see your paycheck . . . and you gasp angrily when you read it. . . . Just like me, perhaps, you have been . . . sent to a lower classification . . . seen your salary fall by 10,000F or more, and just like me, you are afraid to read 'that little note' which says 'we regret to inform you that we no longer need your services'."[31] It is not surprising that the accumulation of such experiences would push the worker-priests in more radical liberationist directions.

In spite of all this pain and injustice, the laboring clergy made another discovery at the workplace, the solidarity and camaraderie of the working class. André Piet described this as "one of the most beautiful things I have known," and Francis Laval remembered the solidarity of his comrades in the mine shafts as a friendship without obstacles or pretense. "Every race was there together," he reminisced. "There was no racism among us." Father Joseph Robert recalled the factory lunchbreak as "the good moment of the day" when the men talked and distributed union tracts.[32]

A number of incidents reported by worker-priests illustrate concretely the type of camaraderie which became emblazoned on their hearts. At Marseille a veteran molder and militant communist remarked to Father Piet, his younger comrade, in the presence of other workers: "I don't want a priest at my burial, but André, if you want to bring one of your colleagues, you can." In the same city at a sugar refinery a worker-priest was caught in a cross-fire discussion with two of his buddies. "You're right to work to gain our confidence," said one of the men, "but with your education you could be employed, at least, in office work, instead of sweating over this turbine with your chest and feet bare." The other comrade, who sensed the purpose of the worker-priest apostolate, responded curtly: "You don't understand a thing! Robert wants to live practically not theoretically. At an office they hide behind a good job. He [pointing to the worker-priest] wants to be in the shit just like us." Very quickly Georges Baudry at Limoges grew to admire the total life commitment of the factory militants, the almost priestly aura they had though many of them were communist activists. He spoke of one man who worked in an oven with a tubercular who would have lost his job if the management had been aware of his illness. When the healthy laborer was asked why he took such a risk, his response was immediate. "No one wants to work with him, but just the same, he's got to work to eat." Profoundly struck by such human acts, Father Baudry concluded: "For me the factory was a meeting place with God. I truly found God's presence in the reactions and attitudes of my comrades."[33] This growing propensity on the part of the worker-priests to find divine activity in the midst of human struggle presaged the later observations of liberation theology.

All of this—work, its rhythm, its brutality, its injustices, the fraternity which grew out of it—served to define these mission clergy and their world in a way they had never imagined previously. They were fast developing an outlook which was both outraged against industrial injustices and prepared to do something about it. This increasingly new vision emerged in the written memoirs of both the Jesuit Henri Perrin and the Dominican Jacques Loew. Perrin's toil stirred in him "a slow and progressive revolt against the capitalist world," a world in which he saw "the inhuman attitude of the manager who inspects the workers as one inspects a hall of machines." He felt disgusted by "this total factory atmosphere where for a century, the worker has felt bullied and exploited." He was convinced that the system's "blatant search for profit and money" created within the working class that "alienation and revolt" which brought to fruition "the proletariat's struggle for its liberation." In the Marseille ghettos Père Loew was overwhelmed by working class existence. "Poverty looms up so stark, so massive that one cannot see past it." To understand this impenetrable world of the docks, one must live it oneself, Loew concluded. Consequently, he lined up with the other dockers every morning to find work. This experience brought him a perspective which gave flesh and blood to his sociological research. "Later I shall return to figures and statistics," he said. "But then I shall know what lies behind each curve of the graph, because I have heard for myself the heavy step of the docker who, for lack of work, returns home barely two hours after he sets out." The daily oppression of this life led Loew, like Perrin, to condemn what he called "the drama of liberal capitalism." "I find the port divided into two sections," he wrote, "on the one hand, the men who enjoy all the profits and none of the risks and, on the other, those whose sole portion is the risks, in other words, the dockers." Having seen this class oppression with his own eyes, Loew concluded harshly that "the law of profit" was "the one ruling force in the harbor area."[34]

This incarnation into the daily oppression of manual labor had been a veritable baptism of fire for the worker-priests. They had entered into and been caught up by the relentless cycle of that life with all its injustices. So profoundly did this affect them that they experienced a powerful conversion which led them from a distant sympathy to the active life of labor militancy. Their initial stance of living "with" the poor had become living "as" the poor. The rage that grew out of that *praxis* would enable them to fight the battles "of" the poor. Their life of oppressive toil had come to convince them that full naturalization with the proletariat required entry into the revolutionary working class movement.

For the worker-priests, the most logical first step in this direction meant belonging to the union. Most chose to join the communist-dominated more militant Confédération Générale du Travail (C.G.T.) rather than the Christian-inspired Confédération Française des Travailleurs Chrétiens (C.F.T.C.) Their reasons for this decision varied. In many instances, worker-priests toiled at plants so dominated by the C.G.T. that the C.F.T.C. had, at best, only a marginal following there. In Jean Cottin's factory at Le Havre, the C.G.T. "was very much in the majority," and at Nancy in the Lorraine basin, "you had scarcely anything but the C.G.T. at the factory."[35] Coupled with this desire to be *présent* with grass-roots toilers was the worker-priest conviction that the C.F.T.C. was too ecclesiastical, too bourgeois or too reformist. This did not prevent a few of them from joining the Christian federation, but even these did so in the hope of radicalizing their union. Hence the worker-priests joined the union, not as an end in itself, but because they felt that it was a vital act of revolutionary justice.[36]

Therefore, the more Marxist oriented C.G.T. remained the conscious choice of the overwhelming majority of the worker-priests, even when this option was a most difficult one. Initially, Henri Perrin was distrusted by anticlerical militants of the C.G.T. At St. Etienne the C.G.T. local split over the entry of Joseph Gouttebarge into its ranks. Hostile voices were saying "what does a priest want with us?" or "he should enter the C.F.T.C." The impasse was resolved when the union secretary welcomed Gouttebarge. At times the difficulty involved an internal crisis of conscience for the worker-priest. Jean Olhagaray feared the Marxist partisanship of the C.G.T. leadership but joined nonetheless in the name of rank-and-file militancy. Bernard Tiberghien was certain that the C.G.T. pursued "the interests of the Communist Party more than those of the working class," but he was convinced that this union defended the proletariat better than the C.F.T.C. Consequently he joined the more Marxist union.[37] Finally, some worker-priests used the language of later liberation theology to justify their C.G.T. membership. Henri Barreau spoke for those men in one of his reports: "Because the proletariat is exploited, I am in solidarity with it for better or worse. Also, as a consequence of being a Christian, I am committed to take every means which I consider appropriate in this action of liberation. . . . These are the reasons . . . for joining the C.G.T."[38]

No matter what logic prompted their membership in this-or-that local or federation, their reasons for joining the working class movement in general were shared almost unanimously. Membership meant both full identity with the proletariat and total solidarity with its liberation struggle. Jacques Loew, who called his union papers "my identity card, my passport into the workers' world," believed that participation in worker battles was "action to build a better world, a kind of reason for living which can illuminate all the workers' life." This conviction that they were obligated as fellow toilers to eradicate injustices which grew out of the factory system was echoed again and again by the worker-priests. "Resignation" in the face of oppression was "an act of treason or at least a compromise," asserted one of these laboring clergy, while another affirmed: "We have become workers conscious of the necessity for class struggle, of the necessity for an organized struggle."[39] Even when their bishops did not permit them to join such militant unions the worker-priests assisted them actively as non-members. This was true with the Lille Dominicans Jacques Screppel and Jean Legendre as well as with the Belgian worker-priests Fathers Flagothier and Courtoy.[40]

The die had been cast. Union membership was openly partisan, and most established church leaders were troubled deeply by this unprecedented step. Their anxiety intensified as a sizable number of worker-priests assumed leadership positions in their union. Some of these clergy were sensitive to the potential problems raised by such prominence. This was the position held by Fathers Depierre and Tiberghien. On the Marseille docks, Jacques Loew was able to avoid leadership roles in spite of the effort of numerous militants to involve him in such tasks.[41] Others were unable to retain their grass-roots status within the union. Under the pressure of friends and comrades, a number of worker-priests accepted leadership posts. François Vidal of Marseille became a union delegate in such a way, and a few others became on-the-spot leaders by organizing exploited workers in non-union shops. In a Lille textile plant, Father Tiberghien was asked by desperate comrades who were being replaced by a machine to lead a protest in the name of protecting their jobs. Through his efforts a C.G.T. local was organized, and he was named as delegate to bargain with management. The Jesuit Charles Monier almost lost his job at a

Marseille soap factory because he organized a C.G.T. local to protest conditions at the plant.[42]

Many other worker-priests did not resist leadership positions. Indeed, they responded unequivocally to the pleas of their union comrades. For the most part, they were elected as delegates by the rank-and-file. Michel Lemonon from the Midi, Maurice Combe of St. Etienne, Robert Pacalet of Lyon, Roger Deliat at the Renault works, Philbert Talé of Paris, Jean Gray also of Paris, Yves Garnier of Caën and André Chauveneau of Limoges are examples of those who served in that capacity.[43] In addition, a number of the worker-priests rose to more prominent posts in their unions. Jo Lafontaine of Le Havre began his union career as a C.G.T. delegate and shortly thereafter was elected as his local's secretary, first for the plant section and then for the whole city. At Limoges Francis Vico started as a delegate, but he was soon a member of the C.G.T.'s executive commission for his entire trade.[44]

Perhaps the two most prominent union leaders among the worker-priests were Jo Gouttebarge and Henri Barreau. In late 1952, Gouttebarge was elected as a C.G.T. delegate for his steel plant. At this post he fought tenaciously against paternalism in the roll-shop and in defense of the persecuted North African workers. On the job he "organized the defense of eighty laid-off workers." In addition, he was in charge of his union section's newspaper. He used its pages to protest against injustices and to promote trade-union unity. Further, he was in his union's avant-garde through his leadership in the cause of ending colonial rule in French North Africa. At the very moment of the worker-priests' condemnation by the hierarchy, Father Gouttebarge became the C.G.T. secretary of his department's *comités d' entreprise*.[45]

Henri Barreau was one of the first worker-priests to become an active C.G.T. leader. By the late 1940s, he held a prominent post in his union at Montrouge and was so popular there that his comrades pressured him to seek full-time employment as secretary of the U.S.T. de la Seine, that C.G.T. metallurgical federation which was the largest and most militant in all of France. This move was so unprecedented that it caused ripples in both the union and ecclesiastical establishments. High-level communists were stunned. "A priest at the head of a C.G.T. section" posed a real problem "at the level of the central committee of the Communist Party." However, the young worker-priest's warm collaboration and grass-roots friendship with Montrouge communist militants influenced the elites of the Party. Barreau won the position and was welcomed by the Communist Party. His appointment troubled the church as well. While some ecclesiastical progressives saw his union activities "as a normal evolution of priestly witness," others judged that "this *engagement* should be reserved for laymen." Among the worker-priests themselves there was some debate, but the support of the Mission de Paris superior Père Hollande was instrumental in the church's willingness to accept Father Barreau's union leadership position.[46]

Most difficult for the church, however, was worker-priest militant participation in strike action. These clergy were convinced that true naturalization required a willingness to utilize this most well-known arm of proletarian activism. Jacques Loew, Jean Cottin, Bernard Chauveau, Louis Flagothier and Albert Courtoy recalled their involvement in strikes, and the Limoges worker-priests chastized the C.F.T.C. publicly for its refusal to remain in strike action with the C.G.T. Even though the Dominicans of the Nord, Fathers Screppel and Legendre, were not allowed to join the union, both men militated actively in a major strike as did the secular worker-priest Bernard Tiberghien. Father Screppel delivered a number of speeches to the strikers, and he advocated their cause to Cardinal Liénart. He joined Father Legendre in efforts to find food and provisions for the striking families. For his part, Father Tiberghien was a member of the strike committee. Earlier he had been involved deeply in a work stoppage at the Parisian Citroën plant.[47]

The nature and extent of worker-priest involvement in strikes varied, as a few detailed examples demonstrate amply. At Longwy, Michel Bordet's baptism of fire was unique. Initially, he was prepared to cross a picket line at his plant and go to work "as usual." He recalled: "At the factory gate, I encountered the strike pickets which stopped me and caused me to reflect upon the reasons why they were on strike." By the next day, he recalled, "I was a striker with them." Both Jo Gouttebarge and Henri Perrin assumed active leadership in strike action. In the St. Etienne area, Gouttebarge helped organize and maintain the great strikes of August 1953. He had called out the metallurgical workers in support of the striking railway workers. Although he had to organize the work stoppage by himself, he was able to accomplish eight days of strike with the support of all three trade union federations and to enlist almost one hundred percent of the work force in this action. One militant remembered that Father Gouttebarge had hidden over two hundred strikers in a church crypt when they were chased by the police.[48]

Henri Perrin's memoirs describe in detail his involvement in strike leadership at the large Tignes hydroelectric construction. Low wages, poor housing and dangerous work conditions set the stage for the forty-two day strike of 1952. When discussions with the management failed, Father Perrin was appointed secretary of the union's organizing committee as well as a member of the strike solidarity commission. He drew up bulletins for strike support and took charge of drafting daily communiqués on the progress of the work stoppage. Further, he ensured that the strike committee coordinated picketing, promoted discussion groups, organized the solidarity committee, provided for striking families' material needs, set up strike offices and published leaflets. Also he raised money and provided two meals daily for needy families in this difficult period. Finally, during the strike's fourth week, management was ready to talk. Soon thereafter enough agreement had been reached to allow the men to go back to work. The protesters had won the right to collective bargaining, new housing, better working conditions and improved salaries, and a worker-priest, Henri Perrin had been one of the central architects of that victory.[49]

These experiences on the protest line led many worker-priests to conclusions which would prove threatening to more conservative Catholic ideology and leadership. Father Robert Pfaff spoke for a large number of colleagues when he asserted the necessity of joining the workers' combat:

Another reason for struggle is this certitude that the working class cannot obtain any improvement whatsoever in its living conditions save by a strike, thus by violence. The great dates are strike dates. That's also a shame, but that has been their experience. Only the strike succeeds. Experience has proven and continues to prove daily that by struggling we make gains. . . . I no longer wish that we separate . . . politics from professional demands in order to determine a strike's legitimacy.[50]

From worker to militant worker, such was the pilgrimage of the worker-priests. They had found injustice at the workplace, but they had discovered also the resolve to fight that injustice through the revolutionary trade-union movement. They joined that struggle actively and came to share both the organized proletariat's outrage against oppression and its vision for a new and better tomorrow. Liberation theology was being discovered and practiced in the heart of western industrialized society years before it exploded from the barrios of Latin America.

Further, the worker-priests' increasing refusal to accept the reformist distinction between professional unionism and political causes (a distinction so critical to C.F.T.C. ideology) and their growing belief that a civilization of justice and harmony could be built with the assistance of a proletarian avant-garde convinced many worker-priests to join the peace movement (Mouvement de la Paix). Their presence in this struggle was less unanimous than their union participation but not by much. A number of them were sympathetic but cautious. Jacques Loew stands out in this respect. He was concerned about unwarranted publicity and partisanship. However, most of the others were prepared to be militants in the movement to end the cold war, to bring the troops home from Korea and Indochina, to ban the atomic bomb and to remove N.A.T.O. soldiers from European soil. It was recognized by these priests that the Communist Party was the organizing force behind the Mouvement de la Paix, but this did not prevent them from actively participating through their unions or in the neighborhoods. Some spoke on street corners or in factory yards; others distributed tracts in the same locales; and still others represented their local chapter at European congresses of the movement.[51]

A few examples illustrate this varied involvement. Francis Vico of Limoges was a peace activist very early because of the direct influence of Father Boulier, the most prominent priest in the entire movement. Boulier had been with Vico's father in the war-time deportation and through this solidarity had become a personal friend of the worker-priest's family. For Jo Gouttebarge war meant profits, indeed "the most scandalous of all profits," because it was gained "at the cost of . . . human blood." He utilized the columns of his C.G.T. newspaper to protest against N.A.T.O. and the Indochina War. Often his tiny one-room lodging was the scene of peace meetings of up to thirty people from the neighborhood. He organized street meetings as well. Friends recall that Jo would lead four or five men into the neighborhood square at about the time workers were coming home from the factories. There they would ring a tambourine, and after a crowd gathered both Gouttebarge and a local communist militant would address the gathering in the name of peace. For Henri Barreau the Mouvement de la paix was a bastion against the outbreak of another world war. Further, the Christian faith demanded such militancy, and the Biblical words "you shall not kill" and "blessed are the peacemakers" were proof of that as far as he was concerned. His commitment to end the Indochina conflict and to abolish N.A.T.O. from Europe was so strong that he joined the massive demonstration of May 28, 1952 against the entry of N.A.T.O. commander Matthew B. Ridgeway into Paris.[52]

In fact, it was this protest that catapulted the worker-priests into the public eye and incurred the wrath of the hierarchy upon their apostolate. The arrest of Fathers Louis Bouyer and Bernard Cagne in the wake of this march and the subsequent publicity it prompted was a turning point in the entire worker-priest movement. After their release from jail both men drafted a common report in which they described their experience in blunt terms. They began by promising their readers to speak of those "scoffed at, reviled, murdered in face and body, of our brothers in Christ, our companions of that street by the tobacco shop, of the truncheons and of prison." Then they proceeded to describe the demonstration which they felt was peaceful until the police began an unprovoked assault. In the midst of this mêlée the two worker-priests were arrested while trying to help a wounded comrade. At the jail they were beaten with fists and truncheons and left lying on a cellar floor. When the embarrassed police discovered that they had assaulted Catholic priests they tried to make amends, but the priests refused to be mollified. They spent the night in prison and there experienced both privation and solidarity with their comrades. Both men were interrogated the next morning, and recorded elements of police conversation with Father Cagne went this way:

Policeman: You're a priest! I'm a former seminarian, a Christian. You, you're a partisan of violence rather than fraternity. (Then he struck the priest with a placard holder.)

Cagne: I have never preached violence. But I understand my comrades when there is provocation.

Policeman: You haven't had enough, bastard, red priest. Your pope is at Moscow. Why don't you go see him? (Then he truncheoned Father Cagne a number of times.) I respect the priest but not the man.

Cagne: It is man that you must respect.

A civilian: But see, we are all brothers; you are our brother.

Cagne: That's right! My comrades of last night, we prove our fraternity daily, because I live with them, but since I've been with you, you've clubbed me. How can I believe in your fraternity? What makes me unhappy is that you call yourselves Christians, that you go doubtlessly to communion and that you hit me, a priest.

Policeman: I will write to Mgr. Feltin (Cagne's bishop).

Cagne: Go ahead! He will hear you but us as well.

Policemen: Communists!

Cagne: Yesterday I met many Christians who were not communists as well as other worker-priests.

Policeman: I used to admire the worker-priests, but now everywhere that I go, I will do all that I can against you. . . . Will you be seen with the Soviets?

Cagne: Since last night, I'm not afraid of them.[53]

After Father Bouyer was interrogated in a similar fashion, both men were released. For the moment, their ordeal was over, but within days their arrest and detention exploded into the public arena via the popular press. Prominent Catholics took opposing positions, and the worker-priests entered into that phase which would lead to their condemnation by the prelates of both the Vatican and French churches.

This life of militancy espoused increasingly by the worker-priests became a cause of concern for more cautious Catholics. These more timid believers found their thoughts dominated by the spectre of communism. More and more they came to fear the influence of Marxism upon the worker-priests, much as some conservative Christians today fear a similar impact upon liberation theologians.[54] Certainly, the worker-priests were not a clerical wing of the French Communist Party, nor did they rush out and join the party en masse. Nevertheless there can be no doubt that they were influenced deeply by Marxists and their views. Philbert Talé's comment that the best men he had met "were the militant communists" was a standard perception among worker-priests at the time.[55] Roughly the relationship between these clergy and communists passed through three phases.

Prior to their entry into manual labor, their attitudes reflected a wide variety of feelings ranging from mild hostility and suspicion to respect and acceptance. Some of them viewed communists as their most serious competitors for the affection of the working class. Father Boland, superior of the O.V.P. community near Liège, reflected this spirit and felt that weaning workers from communism was part of the missionary task. This crusade oriented approach was by no means unanimous. A number of clerical prisoners-of-war in Germany had come to regard communist fellow prisoners with respect and affection. They were called "the most energetic champions of the working class" by one priest-prisoner, and Henri Perrin, himself a P.O.W., felt that communism would be "an instrument" in the rediscovery of "the basics and perhaps the fervor of . . . Christianity." Others, such as Fathers Cagne, Pacalet, Vico and Depierre, formed bonds of solidarity with

Marxists in the domestic resistance movement. In some cases, humble origins and the experience of poverty's misery served to minimize any crusading mystique against Marxism that may have been part of their traditional priestly formation. This was the reality experienced by Jo Gouttebarge and Jacques Loew. In a very few cases, priests had been immersed in communism before their ordination. Charles Pautet was such an example.[56]

Their entry into proletarian neighborhoods and the workplace marked phase two of worker-priest rapport with the communists. This was characterized by the experience of daily contact. A camaraderie developed between many worker-priests and communists at the social level. Father Pfaff reported that he was not welcomed initially by his Marxist neighbors but that, in time, he had amicable ties with local communist leaders. Fondly, he described passing pleasant hours with youthful Marxist militants at the neighborhood café. Similar positive rapport was built up in mutual help activities through local groups and through civic organizations. The Arcueil team of the Mission de Paris helped communists transport fuel to needy families, and Father Depierre at Montreuil assisted his communist municipality in community health, family and leisure programs.[57]

However, it was chiefly at the workplace that these priestly toilers forged the solid links which bound them intimately with those communists who stood with them at the assembly lines day after day. When it was first discovered that these new employees were priests, it was often militant communists of the C.G.T. who came to their rescue. As time passed these clerics found themselves invited into the social and personal lives of many of their Marxist comrades. They passed hours together at local cafés and were adopted into communist families to spend holidays and celebrations with them.[58]

This growing intimacy could not obscure the fact that important differences still remained between the two. However, these divisions were asserted honestly and without rancor in a context of shared misery and struggle. Jacques Loew was perhaps the clearest example of this. He remained cautious toward the Communist Party and its militants throughout his sojourn on the Marseille quays. In spite of his good rapport with the communists, he was careful to avoid any charge of partisanship in their direction. Also his philosophical perspective led him, in principle, to oppose Marxism. His Economie et Humanisme experience and the mystical humanism of Gustave Thibon, Simone Weil and Madeleine Delbrêl influenced him heavily in this direction. This opposition, however, was not informed by a spirit of competition. Rather, for him, the issue was the integrity and relevance of his mission. The following conversation between Loew and the secretary of a local communist cell illustrates these concerns:

Communist: There's no way I can talk to Charlot (a J.O.C. militant).
Loew: Why?
Communist: He always wants to be right!
Loew: Why are you talking like this?
Communist: The elections! He doesn't want to vote communist. I told him that he will be playing the reactionary's game. He doesn't want to understand.
Loew: Pierre, old buddy, I've got to add-me too! I can't see my way clear to vote communist.
Communist: But you, you're a priest; that makes sense. You can't vote communist.
Loew: Do you think I'm talking like this because I've been given orders?
Communist: No, I know that you act according to your conscience. . . . But I'm also sure that if you weren't a priest, you would vote communist.
Loew: Ah, no! Don't you see how deceived you are. In the Party there are those things that I cannot accept. I know that it is the only working-class party, and that's why it breaks my heart not to be able to vote for it.[59]

Most of the other worker-priests were less hesitant and instead sought alliances at the workplace with their communist comrades. This meant neither an espousal of the Marxist weltanschauung nor a willingness to take out membership in the Party. Most of them avoided this scrupulously. Yet, in spite of this, many of the worker-priests discovered that their communist friends reflected the Christian mission and virtues better than many traditional Catholics. Maurice Combe called the Party members he knew "men who practiced the Gospel." One priest-docker stated his pro-communist bent: "At the docks, what hope does the church represent for the comrades? None! What does the communist delegate represent? Everything!"[60]

This second phase of daily contact with communists led invariably to the third and most controversial, namely that of militant *engagement* with grass-roots Marxists. The locus of these ties was primarily the

C.G.T. and secondarily the Mouvement de la Paix. Rapidly such activities led to greater publicity and opposition from more traditional ecclesiastical circles. As they came under increasing fire, the worker-priests defended themselves. They argued that defense of the poor necessitated links with the communists, precisely because these Marxists were "the influential elite of the working class." Father Deliat insisted that the struggle for human liberation demanded that the worker-priests march "arm in arm with the Communist Party," an argument developed years later by some prominent liberation theologians. At St. Etienne Jo Gouttebarge defended this position in a letter to his local Christian Democratic (M.R.P.) deputy. He argued that full incarnation necessitated solidarity with the communists who were "the soul of . . . the working class movement."[61] Henri Perrin adopted a similar position and added a theological dimension to it. He spoke of the church being caught between "a world on the verge of disappearing" and "new forces having an instinctual brutality." For him the former was capitalism, the latter Marxism. Then he described his assessment of the situation in a language akin to that employed by later Christian radicals in Latin America, the Philippines and elsewhere:

> It is not a government which is in the process of decline; rather it is the capitalist system which is built upon the freedom of profit. It is collapsing by its very excesses. . . . In opposition to this has been the rise of the proletariat with its decision to create a new order. Much more than during the era of the Roman Empire, the church seems to have stood on the side of the established order.
>
> In the fourth century, the church felt compelled to baptize the barbarians. Now we must baptize communism.[62]

Thus did the worker-priests evolve in their attitude toward and alliances with French communists and their organizations. It was not a set of theoretical propositions which led them in this direction. Rather it was their life experience within the laboring milieu and their increasing commitment to working class struggles which brought about a modus vivendi with party stalwarts. In most cases this proved to be a very satisfying experience. That Marxist analysis began to make increasing sense to some of them was chiefly a result of concrete privations and hopes shared in the industrial ghettos of France. A kind of Marxist reflection had emerged out of daily proletarian *praxis*.

Although the worker-priests found their lives increasingly dominated by the workplace and by the militant proletarian organizations

that grew out of this environment, they continued also to live and suffer like their comrades in the urban ghettos of the nation. There they
ate and slept, took their leisure, advocated for neighborhood causes,
developed worship patterns akin to their new life cycles, met with
other worker-priests and struggled to make sense of their contacts with
different sectors of the institutional church. As for the basic necessities
of life—food, clothing, shelter—theirs was the lot of their factory and
neighborhood (*quartier*) comrades.

Living conditions were most difficult for those worker-priests who
lived alone. They dwelt in working class neighborhoods alongside
their factory comrades, and there they endured the same squalor and
privation. Most of them lived in one room, and although some of them
felt this was adequate for their needs, others found their particular
setting exceedingly grim. Bernard Tiberghien recalled the pain of isolation, and Jean Cottin spoke of his room, with only a small sink, bed
and table, as "precarious lodging without comfort." Jean Gray remembered the contrast between his high rental cost and the privation of his
lodging, whereas Philbert Talé lived at a poor man's hotel in one room
with only a bed and a basin for washing. At St. Etienne, Jo Gouttebarge
found one-room lodging in the back of an alley "in the most disinherited neighborhood of the parish." The nature of Jean Volot's apostolate, the Mission de la Mer, necessitated its own unique form of
lodging. While on shore, this sailor-priest lived in the temporary makeshift hovels of the poorest sailors. At sea, he slept in the crowded grim
surroundings reserved for sailors who worked on Panamanian and
Liberian liners.[63]

However, it is to Jacques Loew that we owe the most detailed description of what it was like to live alone as a worker-priest. Having discovered that work and lodging were inexorably intertwined, he
concluded that "working with him [the docker] was not enough. At the
end of the day's work, instead of returning to the monastery, I should
be going back with him and living as a worker among the workers."
After some initial difficulty he joined some crowded families at an old
wooden barracks in a shanty town. Soon he was forced out of there by
German occupation troops. His tiny one room was equally grim and
confining. This reality and his day-by-day experience prompted him
to make this poignant observation:

> Smell, sight, touch—constantly irritated by parasites; hear-
> ing—continually assaulted by sudden outbreaks of quarrel-
> ing and children crying: the senses are put on severe trial. But
> can a house be certified as unsanitary on these grounds? Alas,

no! "Unsanitary—that which causes illness"; fire, ten times more quickly than elsewhere, but what statistics can convey the sound of these early morning catarrhal or tubercular coughs?[64]

He attacked the whole slum landlord system with its exorbitant rental structures, calling it "an institution exactly like that of ancient slavery."[65] Long before the liberation theologians spoke of these matters, Loew had discovered personally the intimate connection between poverty and injustice.

Worker-priests who lived together or with others had the advantage of a lodging situation equipped with weapons against the demons of loneliness and isolation. Nonetheless, this housing was often no better than the one-room hovels described above. Henri Perrin and other priests who toiled in dam construction found the barracks in which they lived to be overcrowded, dehumanizing and a violation of people's needs for privacy. In the Parisian area, some worker-priests lived in pairs closely situated to their factories. Still others lived in small Christian communities, both clerical and lay, which devoted themselves to the proletarian mission. Most well-known and oldest of these was the Montreuil *communauté* under the charismatic leadership of Father André Depierre. Initially, he and his comrades lived in an old house in "a very poor neighborhood." It had two rooms and a kitchen; Depierre himself lived in a "ramshackle room" of three metres by three metres with an old camp bed, a beat-up wardrobe and a simple desk. Also in the Parisian area was a Mission de France community led by Daniel Perrot, one of the Lisieux seminary's first professors. Under his charge were two worker-priests, Bernard Striffling who lived at the rectory and a priest-artisan who lived in "a very simple" ground-floor room.[66]

In the Lyon area there was a community similar to the one at Montreuil. It dwelt in a modest house "in the most working class neighborhood" of the city. One of the Lyon C.G.T. leaders Joseph Jacquet cherished the past years in which he belonged to this team (*équipe*) while he was a militant Jociste. There were twelve members altogether, eleven lay and one worker-priest. They held all goods in common much as the primitive Christian community, according to the New Testament, and welcomed others, including Lyon-based worker-priests, to break bread with them.[67]

A few worker-priests lived in parish rectories. François Vidal and Jacques Loew of Marseille are two such examples. Even in such instances, living conditions were modest at best. Father Loew's house was utilized in the following way. The sizable kitchen was employed both for cooking and receiving visitors, and the bedroom which slept three priests was also filled with bookshelves. A fourth priest lived in a crook of the house, and an old woodshed provided dwelling for a Spanish gypsy. The laundry and toilet facilities were opened to the public, and rectory land was used as a *boules* court for the neighborhood.[68]

Worker-priests from the religious orders lived habitually in *équipes* or in close proximity with each other. The Jesuit team of south Paris lived in a small house where a factory, a café and garage were its immediate neighbors. It had no gas, water or electricity. Three Paris Dominicans, including Joseph Robert, lived in comparable style. The Capuchin *équipe* of Nanterre lived in an old war barracks which its priests divided into a kitchen-dining section and sleep area. Alfred Ancel's Prado community at Gerland converted an old workshop into living quarters. In the Lille suburb of Hellemes the Dominican worker-priests lodged in an old working class bistro which they renovated to accommodate their needs. It had a large front room which was used for public activities; a small kitchen, toilet and courtyard; three upstairs rooms for sleeping; and a room which was converted into a chapel.[69]

Whatever their housing, privation and poverty were the common lot of all the worker-priests. This was their unanimous choice, a choice which demonstrated with crystal clarity their commitment to the oppressed. They were "content to live simply and in poverty in working class lodging desiring that their sole witness be that life of their neighbor with its problems." Such testimony by lifestyle prompted a Marseille slaughterhouse worker to say to his worker-priest neighbor: "Because you live in the same kind of house that we do, you are everybody's friend."[70]

Worker-priests adopted a similar approach to the clothes they wore and the food they ate. Although a few continued to don the clerical cassock from time to time, usually for specifically priestly functions, most abandoned it altogether. It came to be viewed as a garment of separation; so, they quickly put it aside to become priests in working class blue. Popular response in the neighborhoods was uniformly positive. Two comments recalled by Father Loew illustrate this. One man said, "I like you best when you're in ordinary workers' clothes," and another stated, "Come and see the priest; he's dressed like a man."[71]

The food they ate, how they ate it and where they ate it bore also the stamp of the working class with whom they identified. Father Dillaye recalled that his Capuchin team at Nanterre ate the common fare of workers which included soup, vegetables and some meat. Jacques

Screppel remembered that fried potatoes, soup, cheese and beer were the common staples of his team and the working class of the Nord. The priest-miner Francis Laval spoke of a diet consisting mostly of carbohydrates, such as potatoes with just a little bit of meat. The very nature of his work necessitated the consumption of much liquids, wine and water being the favorites. Those worker-priests who lived in communities or parish rectories ate more balanced and regular meals because there were people on hand to do the marketing and cooking.[72]

No such assurance awaited those worker-priests who lived alone. In these instances the eating patterns of working class bachelors predominated. Usually this meant a combination of meals at the workplace, at small neighborhood restaurants or cafés, at the homes of married comrades or alone in their rooms. For these men, their biggest and most nourishing meal was often eaten in conjunction with their work. This was especially true for those who had the good fortune to toil in plants that had lunch canteens. The food was very ordinary there, much like any cafeteria food, but it was reasonably balanced and filling. Where such facilities did not exist, the laboring priests would either bring a snack lunch or eat their major meal at a restaurant-café near the factory, either at lunch or immediately after work. Often this moment became for the worker-priests a high point of their day; the mixture of food and fellowship was a spring-board for further integration into proletarian life. In some instances, they would find places at the tables of their married comrades. At other times, their nourishment reflected their isolation, those moments when they ate alone. Philbert Talé's consumption of bread and milk and Bernard Cagne's eating of crackers and sardines in his hotel room are poignant testimony of the extent to which the worker-priests were willing to adopt the full life of the proletariat.[73]

No doubt the reality of full-time work, the daily goings and comings of life and the increasing commitment to militancy in working class struggles reduced leisure and intellectual pursuits to almost nothing for the worker-priests. However, the need for personal pleasure, repose and privacy made its presence felt to the extent that most of them found such moments, however rare. At the very least they needed time to relax away from the relentless cadence of their jobs. "The first necessity was to rest," recalled Bernard Chauveau, and Francis Laval insisted that the primary point of leisure was "very, very simple—breathe the air." Others were more active. Maurice Combe took long walks alone while many of his worker-priest comrades took Sunday trips with their friends to the mountains, the beaches or simply into the countryside. Movies, biking, skiing, rugby, camping and fishing were some of the varied leisure activities that appealed to the worker-priests, and in these respects they were not markedly different from their toiling comrades.[74]

For a number of the worker-priests, free time meant the pursuit of their deeply-felt intellectual needs. In some instances, these were met by those worker-priests who wrote for their trade union newspapers. André Depierre retained his philosophical and theological interests. In addition to reading the Bible and church fathers regularly, he wrote articles for prominent publications. He had personal contact with some of the church's progressive theologians, and Emmanuel Mounier was an intimate friend. Henri Perrin read regularly the Bible, the spiritual masters and the periodicals of the Catholic left such as *Témoignage Chrétien* and *Jeunesse de l'Eglise*. From the very beginning of his docker life, Jacques Loew was involved in intellectual pursuits. His *Les Dockers de Marseille* was the product of his mandate by Father Lebret's Economie et Humanisme team to study life at the quays of Marseille.[75]

Leisure had its more poignant side also. It could highlight the loneliness and isolation of worker-priest life. Philbert Talé provides such an example. He would rise late on Sundays and go to the vast and crowded Marché aux puces just to be around people and to chat with the newspaper vendors. "Solitude weighed down on me heavily," he recalled. He remembered seeing workers with their wives and children, and "I was alone" was his anguished thought. He felt the lack of his "comrades' care." "I had no one to love, no one to love me" was his final painful memory about the Sundays of his worker-priest life.[76]

Paralleling these leisure activities were the numerous ways in which the worker-priests viewed and experienced their *présence* in the neighborhood as a whole. For some there was very little involvement in *quartier* life. Work and trade union activities exhausted their expendable time. Others had a different experience. For them, the neighborhood was a source of personal contact and amicable relationships. Such warm camaraderie was precious to many of these priests precisely because it had been so difficult to attain. Jacques Loew's attempt to be part of his neighborhood was met with hostility in the initial stages. A deeply rooted popular anticlericalism greeted the docker-priest with such comments as "Hah! Someone will land him with a good kick in the pants! That'll teach him to come here." Nevertheless, Loew was persistent to the point that his neighbors came to accept him as one of them. In the communist *quartier* of Landrivaux Robert Pfaff was called "a putrid bastard," his pathway was blocked, and loud voices within his earshot hollered "Why's he coming to fuck around here?" Once again, persistence paid off. In time, Pfaff won over his neighbors. He would chat with them on the streets and drink with them in the cafés. His hard won acceptance was symbolized by the anticlerical woman who shouted to him one day "Come on in; have a cup of coffee with us; it's a long time since you passed by."[77]

Neighborhood involvement of the worker-priests was often collective as well. Clubs and *quartier* organizations were founded, and often these clergy joined in neighborhood carnivals and family celebrations. Also many worker-priests became embroiled in struggles for justice which involved the *quartier* directly. At Boulogne Roger Deliat joined his fellow apartment-dwellers by withholding his rent when the proprietor sought to impose a surcharge to cover the expense of electrical repairs. Jo Gouttebarge was instrumental in finding lodging for families displaced by the collapse of their substandard housing. Jacques Loew advocated a move away from acts of charity toward social reconstruction in the neighborhoods, and he insisted that this effort should, indeed must, come from the grass-roots.[78]

In this wide range of *quartier* activity, from personal intimacy to organized protest, can be seen one more facet of worker-priest incarnation. Whether at the workplace or in the neighborhood, these clergy had decided to identify fully with both the oppression and struggles of the French proletariat. By so doing they became a living paradigm of liberation *praxis* in the heartland of the industrial west.

In all this, work, union militancy, proletarian life and protest, one is hard-pressed to find any survival of the traditional priesthood. The clergy's normal duties of saying daily Mass, dispensing the sacraments and engaging in the classical style of spirituality seemed to be absent. What was left of that style of life which was the very essence of the traditional priesthood? It is in the areas of worship, religious practice, meetings among themselves and contacts with other ecclesiastical persons and structures that the worker-priests maintained some patterns of their religious past and training. But here, too, their new world, their incarnation into it and the demands it imposed promoted innovations which gave rise to fears and hostility within more conservative sectors of the church.

The worship and devotional patterns pursued by these toiling clergy were as varied as their multiple realities demanded. To be sure, a goodly number of worker-priests followed the traditional patterns of priestly worship and spiritual exercises. However, the very nature of proletarian life made such patterns increasingly burdensome. The Dominican Joseph Robert was forced to rise well before dawn to recite his daily Mass, and Father Depierre could not find the time to read his entire breviary. In spite of these difficulties many worker-priests sought to build a spiritual life around their work cadence. One put it this way: "I always had the possibility . . . at work on my machine, to consecrate three to four hours for prayer." Jacques Loew was especially creative while on the docks. At first, his supplications to God were for mere survival under the labor that fatigued him, but with the passage of time he developed a rule of contemplation surrounding the pile of sacks he had to load or unload. He would link his work burdens to the rosary prayers, the stations of the cross or the mysteries of Christ. In such ways many of the worker-priests tied their spiritual life to the concrete reality of their oppression.[79]

However, it was the increasing break with individual piety and the struggle for meaningful liturgical innovation which most characterized the worship life of these men. Participation in the Mass among the small militant Christian communities of which they were often a part was a frequent occurrence. Francis Laval described such worship as akin to that of "the first Christian church." André Depierre conducted simple Masses at his Montreuil community as did the Dominicans at Hellemes. At Mission de Paris meetings held every Tuesday at rue Ganneron, Père Hollande would bring a portable chapel and conduct a simple Eucharist. Some worker-priests, such as Yves Garnier, Jacques Loew and François Vidal, said Mass as part of their parish duties, and the Nanterre Capuchin *équipe* was charged with regular religious services at its neighborhood chapel. In addition, some of the worker-priests attended traditional meetings designed for spiritual refreshment such as retreats and recollections.[80]

Inevitably it was personal needs imposed by the reality of work and the expectations of the tiny militant Christian communities which were the most important factors that drove the worker-priests to seek liturgical reform. The Marseille worker-priests appealed to their bishop for a catechetical program tailored to proletarian reality, and Charles Pautet of the Mission de Paris charged that traditional religious exercises were obstacles to a "popular and missionary liturgy." André Depierre sympathized with this judgment and called for liturgical reform through house worship, dialogue Masses in both Latin and French, baptism in public places and the use of work tools as religious symbols during worship. The Mission de Paris itself adopted a number of these suggestions for its own religious services.[81]

No liturgical innovation was sought more seriously or publicized more widely than the evening Mass. This campaign was so well-organized that it included theologians, missionary parishes, Catholic Action groups, worker-priests and even some bishops. Toward that end, the Mission de Paris argued that the nature and times of factory work necessitated evening worship for Christian laborers both clergy and lay. The Jesuit Henri Perrin gave much time and energy to this campaign. He was convinced that evening Mass was the worship form most appropriate for the urban ghetto, "the factory and the high-rise." The appeal was successful. With the support of Cardinal Suhard, France's Assembly of Cardinals and Archbishops asked Rome to respond favorably. The Vatican replied cautiously but granted permission to use portable altars, to employ French in the earlier sections of the liturgy and to hold Mass in the evenings.[82]

Having gained the right to offer the Holy Sacrifice at this time the worker-priests began to adapt this to the needs of their milieu. The Jesuits and Dominicans of Paris' Avenue d'Italie held special Masses for neighborhood youth which combined traditional piety with the folklore and culture of the *quartier*. The Nanterre Capuchins employed similar patterns. Worker-priests organized evening Masses for their own Christian communities, and these left a profound impact on all who attended. One such Mass was described in a Jesuit journal. About twenty-five people attended, and they gathered around a shared table which served as an altar. Prayers would be organized around common needs, and the Mass would be read in French where permitted. Père Loew was especially touched by one of these Masses. He recalled the crowded room, the low ceiling almost touched by the elevated host and the flowers brought by the neighbors. "But more beautiful than any flowers," he stated "are the careful, if heavy, genuflections of this priest who has been working all day on the docks and whose movements evidence the weights he has been carrying."[83]

Certainly worker-priest meetings were the occasion for worship as well. There would be prayers, Bible readings, some meditation, and often Holy Communion would be shared. Nevertheless, it is important to describe these meetings in another context. They were chiefly the occasion for *recherche* in common, that activity half analytical, half visionary, in which the worker-priests among themselves would assess their apostolate critically. In fact, they were unwittingly precursors of the "*praxis*-reflection-*praxis*" sessions advocated by later liberation theologians. Beyond this there was a missionary and religious tone to these meetings, but the style and content were not traditional. They were informal and open as worker-priests sought to reflect upon their work and make it more meaningful to the proletarian milieu they had adopted. Over a period of time these meetings evolved steadily from small gatherings to larger units designed to coordinate regional groups. By the end of the epoch, the worker-priests had developed a clear national network.

Not surprisingly, those who worked in *équipes* met regularly and frequently with their teammates. The Lyon and St. Etienne worker-priests met about twice a month, often over lunch, whereas the Toulouse *équipe* shared evening meals about three times a week at a local bistro. There, an informal spontaneity and frankness characterized those occasions. In the Nancy area, Michel Bordet met practically every week "with the other worker-priests and the neighboring parish clergy." The Belgian worker-priests of Liège and Charleroi met regularly to discuss their lives, to eat together, to pray and to celebrate the Eucharist. At the Mission de la Mer, Jean Volot lived in a Dunkerque community of fellow members which "held their money in common," espoused a shared vision of the world and prayed and broke bread together. The Dominican teams included not only worker-priests but also other members of the order involved in proletarian missions. For example, Fathers Lebret and Desroches of Économie et Humanisme would meet frequently with the Avenue d'Italie community of Joseph Robert. Worker-priests assigned to parishes had meetings periodically with the clergy teams of which they were a part. Fathers Cagne and Bouyer were vicars at the famous missionary parish at Petit Colombes where they consulted regularly with their senior pastor Père Rétif. Jacques Loew organized his La Cabucelle parish at Marseille in such a way as to integrate the worker-priests with those clergy assigned strictly to parish duties.[84]

From the beginning the most organized of all the teams was the Mission de Paris, which included about a quarter of all the French worker-priests. They would gather practically every Tuesday at rue Ganneron where their superior Jacques Hollande lived. There they would pray, study, share meals and engage in what was called a *revision d'influence,* an activity that one report described as "a Christian judgment of facts experienced in the natural community of life." In addition to this weekly exercise, neighborhood *équipes* of the Mission de Paris would attend mutually supportive sector meetings. Less regularly, Père Hollande would organize four-day retreats for his priests that brought them into contact with such well-known Catholic progressives as M.-D. Chenu and Louis Augros of the Mission de France.[85]

It was not long, however, before the worker-priests began to coordinate their variegated experiences. Formerly isolated *équipes* began to meet more frequently with each other. In southern Paris, near avenue d'Italie, necessity and wisdom brought together the various worker-priest teams which resided there. Here the Jesuits, Dominicans, Mission de Paris priests and Daniel Perrot's Mission de France group collaborated in common neighborhood efforts. Independently of the Mission de Paris, the worker-priests attached to religious orders established their own forms of collaboration and coordination. For example, by the late 1940s the Dominicans, Jesuits, Capuchins and Franciscans were holding study weekends for their Parisian-based worker-priests. Soon meetings of the religious orders were expanded to the national level. Especially important was the 1949 meeting. Here Oblates, Assumptionists, Capuchins, Franciscans, Dominicans and Jesuits met to discuss together their respective proletarian missions. Père Hollande was an honored guest. The highlight of the meeting was the stance taken by the Jesuit Father Perrin and the Capuchin Father Rogatien, both of whom insisted that a working class mission necessitated priests doing factory labor.[86]

By 1950, the worker-priests throughout France and Belgium began to meet on a national basis. Initially, Père Hollande organized these gatherings. Themes for discussion and structure were decided by all the *équipes* via regular correspondence. Examples of such topics for reflection were "Where are we in our working class conscience?" and "What are the repercussions of our *engagements* upon our religious life?" Even when the budding national organization passed from Père Hollande's hands, the modus operandi remained roughly the same. Partly due to the crisis which led to the worker-priests' condemnation in 1953 and 1954, a national secretariat was set up with representatives elected from each worker-priest area. Jean-Marie Marzio was named national secretary, and the headquarters was his Parisian residence at rue Charenton. The secretariat would hold regular meetings between the annual general assemblies and was charged with the function of national coordination during this interim period. It collected dues, planned the yearly gatherings and facilitated regular communications, including reports, letters and newsletters between the different worker-priest teams. These herculean efforts were most impressive. From brief and informal contacts, the laboring priests had mounted an efficient and meaningful national network. However, the intervention of the church's leadership to modify their apostolate undermined these attempts at national organization. When the church condemned their movement in 1954, the worker-priests divided in their response, and the national secretariat became a shadow of its former self.[87]

During this missionary epoch, it was inevitable that the worker-priests would come into contact with other groups mandated by the church to present the gospel to the proletariat. The Lyon worker-priests had ties with Alfred Ancel, the superior of Prado, and a number of his order were involved in manual labor. Jacques Loew was a member of the Economie at Humanisme team, and Henri Perrin was in liaison with the Jesuit-based Action Populaire at Vanves. A few had some personal contacts with the leadership of the progressive Catholic press and Maurice Montuclard's Jeunesse de l'Eglise. The ties between the worker-priests and the Mission de France were quite intimate. Roughly one-fourth of these priests were trained at the Mission's seminary, and a large number of its students spent brief periods doing manual labor (*stages*) alongside of worker-priests in the field. Finally, most of these priests attended regular retreats at the Lisieux and later Limoges seminaries of the Mission de France.[88]

However, it was the older and larger apostolates that were most critical for the worker-priests, for these would be encountered most readily in their daily living. The parish of the working class ghetto whether it was traditional or missionary was the most important of these. Even prior to the factory entry of priests, there were passionate debates on the relationship between the proletarian mission and the parish. The issue was being aired before the inaugural retreat of the Mission de Paris at Lisieux. Henri Godin, author of *France, pays de mission?*, was advocating a break with the parish's notion of geographical territoriality and calling for mobile para-parishes, missionary in character and linked both to the parish and the social milieux of urban life. By the time the Mission de Paris was born, Cardinal Suhard had mandated that it be an apostolate outside of parish structures yet not hostile toward nor in competition with the parish. "We did not wish to create an antiparish," assured André Depierre. He felt that his Montreuil community was "a step toward the parish" and committed to "acting in accord with the parishes."[89]

However, Father Depierre's hopes and experiences could not be generalized. The day-by-day relationship between the worker-priest vanguard and traditional priests and churches was not always so idyllic. In a great number of cases contacts between the two were practically non-existent. Where they did exist, they were often occasional and superficial at best. At the other end of the spectrum were those worker-priests who were attached to particular parishes. François Vidal entered a Marseille factory in 1950 while still a parish priest, and Louis Bouyer and Bernard Cagne served as vicars at Sacre Coeur of Petit Colombes. The Nanterre Capuchins fulfilled the traditional priestly functions at a chapel which was connected to the same parish. Most well-known of all the laboring priests who also ran traditional ministries was the docker Jacques Loew. He was committed to developing an integration of the worker-priest form with the renovated parish, a model which he hoped could be utilized on a wider scale. He was convinced that this unity of traditional and worker priest would dispel the "impression that there are two parallel churches—that of the proletariat . . . and that of the well-to-do Christians," as well as bury the notion of the priest as "the man with white hands."[90]

Even where worker-priests had no specific parish duties or attachments good rapport existed often between the two. The relationships of the parish priests of southeastern Paris with the worker-priests there was exceptionally cooperative, and the Limoges *équipe* had intimate ties with the city's cathedral church and clergy. They would meet regularly "to study together the liaison problems between the parish and the proletarian mission." At Montceau-les-Mines Francis Laval stated that the "excellent rapport" he had with the local *curé* was explained by the fact that the latter was Louis Augros' uncle. Father Screppel recalled cordial relationships with the Hellemes priest, and Robert Pfaff described his *curé* as "a veritable brother with us."[91]

Equally frequent were cases of tension and hostility between the two parties. On occasion parish priests and their traditional advocates engaged in elaborate defenses to prevent the entry of missionary priests into their neighborhoods. Sometimes the conservative clergy would report worker-priest liturgical innovation to the bishops. Many of the worker-priests were critical as well. André Depierre reported that, in spite of few exceptions, "the Parisian parishes do not put anchor into this world of the masses . . . most are a kind of ghetto in their *quartier*." Even some laboring priests who served as parish *curés* became disenchanted with the latter chore. Yves Garnier at Caën is such a case in point. Such hostility between these two types of priests would erupt occasionally into conflict. Both Charles Pautet and Michel Lemonon clashed with parish priests because the two men dressed in working class blue refused to wear clerical garb. Lemonon remarked that his detractor was offended because the worker-priest wore "a patched blue work-suit spotted with concrete and cement." He concluded angrily, "It is clear that he would be indignant with the Son of God who devoted himself to his own trade."[92]

In spite of efforts to the contrary, suspicions between the two groups were too prevalent, contacts too rare and traditional patterns too deeply rooted for significant changes to occur in so short a time. When the news came from Rome that the worker-priest experience was to be terminated, the whole gamut of parish-worker-priest relationships was exposed with full force to the public eye.

Similar confusion surrounded the ties between the laboring priests and those specialized Catholic Action movements which were mandated to missionize the proletariat. They were interrelated from the start by virtue of the fact that most of the visionaries behind the birth of the Mission de Paris and many of the original worker-priests had been active in the Jeunesse Ouvrière Chrétienne. Further, the clandestine P.O.W. priests in Germany found themselves in intimate working rapport with the Jocistes of the S.T.O. So interlocked was the J.O.C. to the new missionary spirits that a debate was in the air even before the Mission de Paris was born. Henri Godin was warned by J.O.C. chaplains that his priests should be wary of trying to supplant "the rights of the laity in the working class movement." Godin sought to assure his Catholic Action colleagues that he was not intent on usurping their functions, but he suggested that, to be effective, the J.O.C. would have to be "adapted to the masses and therefore less adapted to parish life." Toward this end he called for organizational links between the Mission de Paris and the J.O.C.[93]

However, the issues were not resolved as easily as that. Beyond the Lisieux retreat of 1943 and throughout the following decade the debate continued. Both sides were ready to acknowledge the right of the other to exist, but habitually each would seek to defend the priority of his own apostolate. A number of Catholic Action clergy sought to limit the worker-priests for fear that the role of lay Catholic militants would be minimized. These J.O.C. and A.C.O. priests felt that clergy should be at the factory only "to discover militants and animate a Catholic Action laity." In addition, Catholic Action chaplains were willing to accept the idea of priests engaging in manual labor as long as this served a merely educational purpose. Canon Cardijn, the international Jociste chaplain, summarized tersely the anxieties of his apostolate: "There is a danger to wish to substitute a priestly for a lay apostolate. A priest, no matter what he does, will never be a worker. In spite of everything, he will always be merely a substitute for a worker, because he is a priest."[94]

Increasingly the worker-priests and their supporters grew critical of Catholic Action approaches. The Dominican theologian M.-D. Chenu acknowledged the pioneer role of this lay apostolate, but he was convinced that its ties to the parish rendered it less effective than the Mission de Paris. For its part, Hollande's organization believed that the J.O.C. was concerned chiefly with its own survival and expansion within an ecclesiastical milieu rather than with a genuine incarnation into proletarian life.

The drama of these continuing divisions was played out in the field as well. Often the two groups clashed. On the factory floor, Jocistes would view the worker-priests as either misplaced intellectuals or representatives of a "leftist clericalism." Worker-priests were equally critical. Louis Bouyer stated that working class Catholic Action "didn't understand very well what we were doing,"[95] and André Depierre felt that it divided the proletariat by its competitiveness. For him, the Mission de Paris notion of *présence* was superior to Jociste *conquête*. Other worker-priests were not so gentle. For example, the Limoges *équipe* offered this blunt conclusion: "The Catholic Action movements have never succeeded in planting themselves within the proletariat but are always on the fringes because they want to safeguard the ideal family morality at any price, instead of attacking resolutely the revolution in working conditions."[96]

Good relationships existed as well. *Masses Ouvrières*, a monthly journal for Catholic Action chaplains, would pay tribute occasionally to the worker-priest ministry, and at times, some of the laboring priests would write articles for this periodical. However, it was at the grassroots level where the best rapport existed. René Boudot, a militant Jociste, was an intimate friend of Robert Pfaff at Longwy; Louisette Blanquart of the Jocistes' feminine auxiliary worked with Fathers Loew, Depierre and Besnard; and Joseph Jacquet of the J.O.C. lived in a community which contained worker-priests. The leadership of both groups sought to promote such cooperation and held joint meetings to that effect. Unfortunately such noble sentiments could not be imposed automatically on existing conditions. The more complex realities of some collaboration, some suspicion and even some open conflicts would continue and heighten with the passions of the worker-priest cause célèbre which rocked the church in the early 1950s.[97]

Most critical of all relationships between the worker-priests and the institutional church was the one they held with their bishops and abbots. After all, it had been the hierarchy which had mandated their apostolate in the first place, and it was this episcopal support which would continue to legitimize their activities. Since the war, leadership in the French hierarchy had passed to the progressives who lifted their voices in support of the missionary apostolates to the proletariat. Most important of these prelates were the cardinals Emmanuel Suhard and Maurice Feltin of Paris, Achille Liénart of Lille, Pierre-Marie Gerlier of Lyon and Jules-Géraud Saliège of Toulouse.[98]

However, such endorsement was no guarantee of smooth communication between these prelates and those priests they mandated to enter the factories. To be sure, some good rapport did exist. Jean Cottin remembers fondly the cordial relationship between his Le Havre *équipe* and the archbishop of Rouen, and Jacques Loew had virtually no conflict with either Mgr. Delay of Marseille or his Dominican superior. Jacques Jaudon lauded Cardinal Saliège both for his support of the Toulouse worker-priests and for his empathy toward striking workers. The overwhelming almost universal regard that these laboring clergy had for Cardinal Suhard is the clearest example of the positive side of worker-priest hierarchical relationships.[99]

Yet there were important nuances which demonstrated that communication between the two groups was not as stable as first appearances might suggest. Often a prudent distance was maintained which could lead to misunderstandings. Louis Bouyer described the rapport of his colleagues with the hierarchy as "episcopal" in tone. This aloofness is illustrated by a brief encounter between Bernard Cagne and Mgr. Veuillot, Cardinal Feltin's coadjutor bishop. Cagne was at the archbishopric for a celebration, and he was wearing civilian clothes. Veuillot had some difficulty in accepting the fact that this man without a cassock was indeed a priest. At Longwy, Fathers Pfaff and Bordet had strained relationships with their bishop. Pfaff reached this sorrowful conclusion after a painful encounter with Bishop Lallier of Nancy. "Bishops and priests still feel incompatible with the priest who does manual work. For them, the worker's condition and struggle are considered to be Marxism. One cannot conduct a strike and have faith. They do not see the convergence of work and faith." Also the perceptions of the nature of the relationship between the two groups was not exactly the same. Even Cardinal Suhard insisted that such rapport be characterized by loyalty to church tradition and obedience to episcopal authority. Conversely, the worker-priests felt that bishops "should remember that they were created not to dominate but rather to serve."[100]

Some of this confusion and ambivalence was manifested in the personal encounters between the worker-priests and their religious superiors. Cardinal Suhard remained the perennial favorite, and his Mission de Paris priests remember affectionately his informality, his visits in the neighborhoods and his sympathy with their mission. Feelings were more mixed toward his successor Maurice Feltin. André Depierre and Philbert Talé recalled him fondly, but Jean Olhagaray and Emile Poulat were more critical. Olhagaray was convinced that Feltin was not the man for his job, and Poulat felt that he did not have the temperament to back up the positive attitude he had toward his worker-priests. A similar ambivalence was shared with regard to Cardinal Gerlier of Lyon. Robert Pacalet remembered warmly the support that Gerlier gave him upon his entry into a worker-priest ministry. Others praised his neighborhood visits, and still others lauded his appearance at the funeral of three men who had been killed accidently at their factory. However, not all the Lyon-area worker-priests were so positively inclined. Maurice Combe recalled being isolated by the cardinal at a protest meeting, and Jean Tarby saw his archbishop as a medieval man who had supported Philippe Pétain. Although many Parisian worker-priests regarded Achille Liénart as cold and distant, his own worker-priests remembered his warmth and support of their mission.[101]

Much like the secular hierarchy, the superiors of religious orders maintained a liaison with their worker-priests which was both interested and distant. Père Loew was comfortable in his relationship with the Dominican superiors. Such was not the case with Henri Perrin who felt increasingly restricted in the Jesuit order. Consequently he won permission to leave and become a secular worker-priest.[102]

Perhaps this strain between many of the laboring clergy and their religious authorities can best be explained by the radically different worlds in which the two parties worked and ministered. The worker-priests had become part of the oppressed proletariat whereas their bishops moved in civic and ecclesiastical circles. The wall which divided the church from the proletariat had become a barrier between the worker-priests and the church's hierarchy as well. Possibly in calmer hours the goodwill of both parties would have allowed the time to resolve their differences concerning the nature of church authority. However, the issues and tensions of the epoch intervened to prevent this. By the beginning of 1954 the worker-priests would be allowed only two options—remain at the workplace or abandon their posts in obedience to the bishops.

In less than a decade the worker-priests had entered fully into the world of an oppressed industrial work force—so fully, in fact, that their lives were altered at their very essence. They had become naturalized into an existence foreign to the experience of the church. They had crossed over the wall which existed between that church and the working class, between the prosperous west and its seamy underbelly. Now they were on the other side, totally accepted by their toiling comrades but alien to the very church and world which had sent them. Factory work, union militancy and a proletarian life day in and day out reshaped their previous notions and values. Just as their experience in this social milieu evolved, so did their ideas. They had entered the workforce with a mélange of concepts ranging from social paternalism to militant radicalism. Having lived and fought within this social setting, they came to adopt the revolutionary values later associated with liberation theology.

VII

THE WORLD OF WORKER-PRIEST
REFLECTION

"I have not preached the gospel to the poor;
it is the poor who have preached the gospel to me."
—Joseph Robert, Dominican worker-priest

It would be simplistic to describe the worker-priests as "doers" and not "thinkers." That would be a half-truth at best. Certainly they were not professional theologians nor were they interested in creating unified systems of thought. But think they did, for a number of them were avid readers and given to intellectual pursuits in what leisure time they had. André Depierre and Henri Perrin serve as two reminders that some worker-priests were active in the Catholic intellectual renaissance that coincided with the missionary explosion of the 1940s and early 1950s. Indeed, worker-priests were kept abreast of these developments through study days and retreats which brought them into contact with the writings and personalities of French avant-garde theology. Quite frequently they encountered these men and ideas at the Mission de France seminary.

At the heart of this intellectual explosion was the Dominican order. Joseph Lebret, director of the Economie et Humanisme *équipe*, was frequently an active participant at strategy sessions designed to assist the various missionary apostolates. However, his most direct impact upon the worker-priest movement was his personal influence over his colleague Jacques Loew. H.-M. Feret and the noted ecumenist Yves Congar were two other Dominican theologians met by worker-priests at Mission de France study retreats. Congar maintained close ties with the Dominican worker-priests of Paris, and he was known personally by André Depierre. Maurice Montuclard, founder of the Jeunesse de l'Eglise movement, attracted some worker-priests to his radical views. Maurice Combe of St. Etienne was one such priest. During his ministry he was "in a relationship" with Montuclard's *équipe* where he discovered ideas designed to bring Christians out of their bourgeois ghetto.[1]

However, it was the name of Marie-Dominique Chenu that was on the lips of the worker-priests most frequently. Not only did he join them in their planning sessions; also he maintained regular correspondence with Père Hollande. Chenu sided with the worker-priests openly in their conflicts with Catholic Action, and he defended them with a controversial article on the relevancy of their priesthood. He led retreats for them at Lisieux, and his presence at their frequent meetings, both on Avenue d'Italie (Paris 13ᵉ) and at rue Ganneron, left a lasting impact on these pioneer priests. Chenu would listen without interruption, raise a few questions and reflect on their experiences. After these discussions he would integrate what he had learned there with his theological training and use it to link the worker-priests' innovative witness to the long history and tradition of the church. For this he would retain the lasting gratitude of the worker-priests.[2]

The ideas of some of the other French Catholic progressive theologians were known to a few of the worker-priests. The Jesuits Henri de Lubac and Jean Daniélou were two of these. Daniélou himself was one of the church's important theological voices calling for a radical missionary stance toward the proletariat. Emmanuel Mounier was probably the most renowned lay theologian to impact upon the worker-priests. The critical link was André Depierre, a personal friend of Mounier and his *Esprit* team.[3]

However, it would be false to assume that the worker-priests were chiefly recipients of the theological wisdom of all these masters. It was more mutual than that. To be sure, they learned from these avant-garde thinkers, but these priests were also a prime source of inspiration for the advanced thought of the day. Their experience supplied much of the raw data for theological reflection among men such as Congar, Montuclard, Mounier, Chenu and others. Also it must be remembered that the very life-style of the worker-priests militated against their values originating primarily from the books and ideas of prominent theologians. The worker-priests had little time for reading and intellectual pursuits. Their ideas and reflections emerged largely from the encounter of their personal religious heritage with the factories and industrial ghettos of France and Belgium. Their thoughts grew out of their daily existence of oppression. They learned their radical values via a process similar to the one used by Paulo Freire in Brazil years later.[4]

Proletarian existence prompted and guided their reflections. They were not system-builders. In fact, they were the very opposite of ivory-tower theologians. In the midst of the working class they saw, heard, smelled, tasted and felt. All their senses were learning, and this sensual awareness was turned into ideas which helped them adapt more effectively to their milieu. This process of discovery and value development the worker-priests called *recherche*, a word which is best translated to include the double notions of "inquiry" and "quest." In a report to Father Hollande in 1949 Jean-Marie Marzio described *recherche* as a "discovery" of his neighborhood, "not in the sense of a speculative awareness but in a far greater comprehension of this mass which is our district." Father Jean-Claude Poulain of the Mission de Paris explained to his new archbishop Maurice Feltin that *recherche* was the discovery of "this new world" called the proletariat, a discovery which caused the priests to "become assimilated with it [the working class] by endeavoring to become reborn within it." For Jean Volot of the Mission de la Mer *recherche* was the very heart of his apostolate. He called it reflection or the posing of questions "in the face of reality." It was not intellectual discussion but rather the raising of issues which "emerged from concrete experience." Further it was a community activity much like the practice of "the primitive church."[5]

Clearly then *recherche* was much more a process than a simply defined concept. A 1951 Mission de Paris report stated that the *équipe's* mission was "always in the process of *recherche*." In 1953 Father Jean Gray stated, "We are along the route, and it is a long *recherche*—hard, often obscure." Its pattern followed the older Jociste methodology of "see-judge-act" (*voir-juger-agir*) and presaged the later "praxis-reflection-praxis" of liberation theology. Philbert Talé recalled the instructions given to him upon his entry into the Mission de Paris. "First of all you don't bring something . . . you look for something," he was told. "First of all, you don't teach . . . rather you learn." Thus *recherche* was neither a concept nor a methodology conceived in advance. It grew out of both the daily life of these priests and the regular meetings they held to reflect on these events. "We spoke of our days, our work and our life . . . as workers," recalled Father André Piet of Marseille, and Father Charles Pautet echoed such a concrete definition by decrying any form of *recherche* based upon "a priori techniques and methods." Father Henri Barreau described this process by portraying concretely a Mission de Paris meeting at rue Ganneron. "We ate together often," stated Barreau, "and then we stayed together until 11:00 p.m. or midnight. All of us were present . . . and we debated our problems."[6]

This was *recherche* as it was practiced, a quest for the discovery of Christ and one's mission in the working class. It was a highly experiential process far from books, theologians and classrooms. Rather it occurred at rue Ganneron, among *équipes* in the field, on the assembly line, at the local café, in trade union struggles and at the hovels that passed for working class lodging. It was not found in philosophical tomes nor in theological treatises; instead *recherche* took its written form as reports, notes, letters, petitions, trade-union tracts and the poignant poetry which emerged from heart-wrenching experiences. In a word *recherche* was the articulated reflection of life experience designed to chart the worker-priests along their daily path.

In this quest, the central guiding conviction was that of Christ's incarnation and how that was manifest in the worker-priests' mission. Throughout the years of their apostolate, the notion of incarnation was the thread which joined together the evolving strands of their tortuous and varied pilgrimages. A large number of the missionary apostolates and their supporters advocated a crusading proselytizing notion of incarnation which they called *conquête* (conquest). They were out to win over the proletariat from paganism, materialism and Marxism. Such was the conception of the Jeunesse Ouvrière Chrétienne and its episcopal supporters. Even the Lisieux retreat, which gave birth to the Mission de Paris, and Father Godin were caught up in these triumphalist ideas.[7]

However, the worker-priest commitment to incarnation was markedly different. Certainly some aspects of the *conquête* spirit survived, but they were soon dissipated in the light of concrete reality. The task was solely that incarnational reality "to be *présent* ("present") among the poor . . . simply to be *présent* . . . in a proletarian milieu." François Vidal of Marseille called it "an incarnation in the working class world," becoming "an indigenous member" of that civilization, and Jean Gray remarked that incarnation meant becoming "a worker among the other workers" just as an alien becomes a naturalized citizen in his adopted country. Father Jacques Riousse, working in the film trades, spoke of it as being "in the real life of the workers, people with no other resources than the force of their labor." André Depierre described this incarnational spirit in greater detail in a 1949 report to Father Hollande. He stated that the task was "to discover this fatherland [the proletariat] which became ours by the will of the church . . . to do nothing but listen to it and there to become naturalized by communing more and more in its profound life." Yet, he continued, incarnation reaches deeper than that. We must "work with these new brothers, suffer, struggle, hope and love with them. Consequently we must place our heart, our conscience and our intelligence on the same 'wavelength' as their heart, their conscience and their intelligence."[8]

To be sure, the worker-priests believed that their incarnation was tied to the redemptive plan of God. "Incarnation should never become an end in itself," asserted Jean-Claude Poulain. "Always it is only the indispensable means of becoming redemptive." The hope was to give "birth to the church in a grass-roots milieu by an incarnation which shares everything except sin . . . to incarnate the church into all of human life, family, economics and politics." Father Jean-Marie Lepetit put it this way: "I think that my *présence* solely as a poor man among the poor, as a man among men, taking upon myself the whole of their lives, has already a sense and a significance of the church . . . for by my priesthood, Christ and the church assume the life of this people who do not recognize God." With such views it is not surprising that the worker-priests found Biblical language to help them express their points. They described the milieu in which they were operating as "the lump" which they hoped to ferment in a Christian way by their *présence* there. They called themselves "the leaven in the lump" reminiscent of the brief parable uttered by Jesus in the Gospels of Matthew (13:33) and Luke (13:20–21). "The masses want their destinies regulated from the inside in their own natural communities," stated one Mission de Paris report. "We must be like leaven in the lump (*levain dans la pâte*)." In criticizing the *conquête* mentality of the J.O.C., the Belgian Father Boland advocated the more hidden approach of placing "the eternal intimately within the temporal, the spiritual within the material, the leaven in the lump." As a leaven, he concluded, "we must give it the time to do its work."[9]

Just as this Biblical symbol became standard vocabulary to portray the worker-priest incarnational style, so also did they employ certain descriptive phrases to clarify that mode of life more fully. One such explanation was *d'être avec* ("to be with") or *vivre avec* ("to live with"). The Dominican Joseph Robert described his apostolic task as an incarnation "in order to live with (*vivre avec*) the people." "We were with them, present with them," recalled the Capuchin Césaire Dillaye, and he was convinced that his *équipe* was marked most by its life "with them (*avec eux*)." A Limoges worker-priest report spelled this out in greater detail. "To live (*vivre*) in daily contact with the poor and the miserable" was the stated task of these priests. "So that they may come to us, we must live the same life (*vivre la même vie*); we must live in the sadness and torments of life; we must espouse their condition with exactitude."[10]

The notion of a total sharing (*partage*) of proletarian life was another way in which the worker-priests characterized their incarnation. Both Maurice Combe and François Vidal recalled the necessity of sharing (*partager*) "the life of the people." André Chavanneau recalled a similar conviction when he labored at Limoges, and Father Yves Garnier felt that "sharing (*partage*) the workers' lives" led him to discover the "profound riches" of the proletariat that he had never known. Father Depierre summarized this position by stating that the Mission de Paris' new brand of priesthood involved "living in their [workers'] milieu (*vivant au milieu d'eux*) . . . in order to share (*partager*) with them . . . the insecurity of their life."[11] Such a *partage* could not be superficial. It had to be a sharing "from the inside (*dedans*)," or it was not a true incarnation. In a report to Father Hollande the worker-priest René Besnard came to the following conclusion: "There is a new world to be baptized. We must be on the inside (*dedans*). To exclude ourselves would be a grave error which would retard the march of humanity toward God." Robert Pacalet of Lyon used similar language to defend his active participation in working class militancy. "I think that the issue for the church is to place itself on the inside (*dedans*) of this immense movement," was his passionate plea.[12]

Finally, a number of the worker-priests used the term "community of destiny" (*communauté de destin*) when they spoke of their incarnation into proletarian life. This notion was articulated most thoroughly by the Economie et Humanisme research team. There Jacques Loew used the concepts developed earlier by Simone Weil and Gustave Thibon to describe his incarnational destiny on the Marseille docks. To be in a *communauté de destin* with others, he explained, was to find oneself wrapped up in the same life determinisms and values of an adopted family, group, social class or community. "For me," he elaborated, "the issue was to work in a factory or on the Marseille docks, above all, to enter into a *communauté de destin* with these men." This meant "being happy together" with them, being "unhappy together"; it demanded being "attacked and wounded by the same reality" and earning "one's bread by his own work." A number of other worker-priests employed this terminology as well. Loew's Dominican comrade near Lille Jacques Screppel felt that this apostolate required "a total rupture with bourgeois life" so that he could enter into "an absolutely total *communauté de destin* . . . with the workers' life." René Besnard spoke of his "*communauté de destin* with the poor," and another Mission de Paris priest Pierre Riche used this phrase as a synonym for his naturalization into the proletariat.[13]

No matter what language they employed, it was the concrete reality of their life in factory and neighborhood which defined their full plummet into the proletariat. Their priority option for the poor was radical—a total identification with working class existence. Incarnation was a natural, almost spontaneous, way to express that life, and Christ's own adoption of human flesh came readily to their minds. Msgr. Alfred Ancel believed that "to be a worker like the others" was to mirror Christ who "for thirty years became a man like the others." Henri Barreau called his proletarian life "the recommencement of Christ's incarnation," and the Belgian Damien Reumont claimed that he had become a factory worker "just as Christ himself became man . . . in order to save men."[14] This worker-priest identification with Christ's human life and death was expressed most poignantly in a public statement designed to defend this unprecedented ministry:

> When we aren't hired, when our body is broken with fatigue, we are with Christ, who could have been a prince or doctor, but who chose, until he was thirty years old, this working class life and who continues to be humiliated, exploited and who suffers in his very flesh which is that of the poor and exploited construction workers. . . . The priest who endures this world fulfills in his body that which marks the suffering of Christ. Christ's witness cannot be the word only but also blood. We live the passion of Christ with our worker brothers.[15]

Most graphic of all was the personal language and intensity with which these priests described their incarnation. In rich and varied forms they moved beyond the vocabulary and thought of classic theology into the arena of working class oppression and the individual witness (*témoignage*) which grew out of it. Three examples suffice to show how deeply they felt about their immersion into the proletariat. Roger Deliat articulated his incarnation in the terminology of a religious conversion:

> In spite of the isolation of eight years of seminary and seven years as a vicar, in spite of all the deformed qualities within the working class, the C.G.T., the Communist Party, the strikes, the revolutionary ideas which I gulped down during these fifteen years in "church" society, I found my working class stripes at one blow. Injustices, I saw them; abuses, I felt them. The cover-ups by the authorities shocked me. No need for grand discourses on class struggle; one had only to look around and live in a factory . . . to understand that this strug-

gle is first of all a fact for those who use the workers for their own personal interests.[16]

Joseph Gouttebarge, a priest-metallurgist from St. Etienne, integrated the cruel and heartrending experiences of proletarian life into the already sensitive soul of a poet. He was wounded deeply by the agony of his incarnation into the working class, and he turned to verse to cry out his pain. In a poem called "Cafard" ("Tedium") he poured out the anguish of what it meant to share (*partager*) the life of the common laborer from the inside (*dedans*):

Lord, you have suggested that you would send me into the
    world of the poor,
But you did not tell me of all the companions waiting for me
    there.

But Lord, I don't know where to find this monster called
    Tedium. He clings like an octopus, like the night, like a mist.
He penetrates your very being; he clings to you at every
    moment.
His lightest gesture becomes infinitely heavy . . .

    He is inside. . . .
    He swallows us. . . .
    We cannot escape . . . EVER!
    "Oh, if I had only known . . ."

Tomorrow, we must pay the grocer, the baker.
Tomorrow, the gas and electricity as well.
Tomorrow, maybe a baby, and my cheque hasn't come.
Tomorrow, we must go to work—eat, sleep, only to begin again.
But that, that's nothing, if tomorrow I no longer had that
    undefined monster, faithful as my shadow—Tedium!

Is this God among the poor?
If I understood your Incarnation, Lord . . .
    it is nothing to be poor,
    it is nothing to rot and perish,
    it is nothing to give everything,
    to love 'til the very end
And to begin again when we are crushed.

But to live the Tedium of the poor?
And this is necessary or I fail my mission.[17]

Finally, the contrast between the ecclesiastical milieu and the proletarian mission field into which the worker-priests were sent prompted Henri Barreau to pen the following words describing his incarnation. He chose consciously to use the format of a priestly vow made to Christ:

> I commit my life and offer all that I am . . . to become and to be a true worker while, at the same time, a priest among the workers, just as you have been a man, God among men.
>
> To take up and carry in my priestly heart their entire life, work, poverty, struggles, sufferings and hopes, the humiliations of their most base conditions . . . their temptations, just as you took up our flesh and carried our sins.
>
> To place my destiny with their destiny and my life with their life and to be in communion with all their aspirations, as you Father have given your Son to the world in order to understand and to save this world.[18]

Father Barreau's vow, Jo Gouttebarge's poetry and Roger Deliat's spiritual transformation were not concepts. They were a profound articulation of the concrete reality of working class oppression. They were incarnation itself, lived daily, felt daily, reflected upon daily in the very midst of proletarian life. It was the worker-priests' very *recherche*, their life and their contemplation, their quest and their inquiry. Incarnation dominated their meetings, their retreats and their reports, and as time passed, they became convinced more and more that their *partage* would never be total unless they too earned their bread by the sweat of their brow. Manual toil itself would be at the very heart of their notions of incarnation.

Thus, it was the entry into wage labor that marked the first critical point of their missionary venture after they had penetrated the working class world. The *recherche* surrounding this issue allowed these men to articulate more ably the decision which transformed them from priests for the workers into worker-priests. A rationale for clergy to engage in factory labor began early, albeit sporadically, among the members of the Mission de Paris. Its first laboring cleric felt that his entry into gainful employment would help to dispel the proletariat's conceptions that "the church was the most materialistic institution of all" and that its priests were under capitalistic and bourgeois control.

For André Depierre "work in a factory" meant "a rediscovery of [his] priesthood . . . painfully day by day." In fact, he concluded, "the fundamental and most important path for the worker-priests" was "to be at work."[19]

For the Mission de Paris and for other priests mandated for service in the proletarian mission, wage labor was an incarnational choice that grew out of personal and communal *recherche*. One by one these clerics sought permission to enter the workplace as full-time laborers. The hierarchy responded positively to these case-by-case requests. However, by 1947, a collective apologetic had been developed by the Mission de Paris and others to justify this almost unprecedented form of ministry. Father Hollande's *équipe* framed an inclusive list of its arguments as early as 1946. First of all they adopted the "imitatio Christi" or Nazareth viewpoint which was based upon the quiet years of Jesus' labor as a carpenter. Further, Hollande's clerics suggested that priests working full-time were living testimony of the church's commitment to "the virtues of work." Finally, they were convinced that a priestly *présence* at the factory extended "the offering, the mediation, the intercession and the expiation" of the Mass "into the work milieu." To these arguments the Mission de Paris added what it called "apostolic reasons." These included the idea of the church's supernatural incarnation at the workplace and the notion that the proletariat must be encountered where it was, "above all, at work." "We must be the leaven in the lump," the list concluded.[20]

Among the worker-priests it was largely the Belgian O.V.P. community which systematized an apologetic for the manual labor of priests. It developed this in response to opposition raised against this clerical form. Its priests sought to allay fears by reminding their more cautious Catholic brothers and sisters that the hierarchy was mandating these clerics and that the church could not be present anywhere in its fullness without the priesthood. Finally, they tried to calm anxieties by insisting that priests operating in this unusual capacity required the kind of special training offered by the Mission de France.[21]

After describing the varied forms and results of this ministry, the O.V.P. undertook the task of providing a theology for this sacerdotal mode. Although they acknowledged that work was not a priestly function in and of itself, they maintained, nonetheless, that a sacerdotal character could be given to it if taken up by mandated clergy. Indeed, manual toil itself had received God's highest blessing. "Christ our priest, from the moment of his incarnation . . . was a worker . . ." argued the O.V.P. "He had calloused hands; he did not belong to the rich and powerful clan." Father Boland chose to elaborate the Nazareth argument in his defense of priestly labor. "The young man Jesus passed his time in common (*vulgaire*) work, in a common workshop (*atelier vulgaire*)," asserted Boland. "We believe firmly that this manual labor was not simply a pastime until he reached his thirtieth year . . . but instead had its own importance, much like the cross, in that it was in line with the redeeming and setting right of humanity." "Yes," summarized Boland, "Christ awaited his full development as God-man by practicing this pure manual work." The O.V.P. was as good as its word. Father Damien Reumont committed the Liège team to the practice it espoused by the following vow: "The O.V.P. will earn their bread by their work. . . . They will not be afraid of hard labor nor of tomorrow's uncertainties which the condition of worker brings with it, but they will consider these things as their proper pilgrimage of asceticism and renunciation."[22]

Although the other worker-priests did not take the time to systematize their reflections in the same way as their Belgian brothers, nevertheless their own *recherche* led them to similar conclusions. Father Bernard Lacroix of the Fils de la Charité order called "manual work" a "solidarity with the most crushed," and the priest-fireman Lucien Lacour referred to labor as "a listening post" or "a radio band for both receiving and emitting." Père Loew and his fellow Dominicans at Marseille spelled out their rationale for the worker-priesthood in a report to their bishop. "The vital center of the working class world is actually the plant," they argued. "There the worker thinks and speaks. There he is in contact with the trade union, political instructions and propaganda. Soon enough he goes home, harassed, needing peace and quiet, and those moments of relaxation at home, all for the purpose of going back to work, will not be determinative in his formation." Like it or not, pleaded these Dominicans, "it remains true that it is at work that the worker receives what we can call his culture, his vision of the world and his principles of judgment." For these reasons Father Loew felt that the Marseille missionary *équipe* should "earn its bread by manual labor, in the same manner as St. Paul" had done. The Dominican Jean Legendre, the Jesuit Henri Perrin and the Capuchin Father Rogatien defended their industrial toil utilizing the same logic. Father Legendre spoke for all of them when he affirmed, "Factory work is an indispensable condition to know the workers . . . to be known and accepted by them."[23]

By the late 1940s the worker-priests had adopted a nearly unanimous opinion concerning their unique ministry of manual labor. Work with one's hands, toil to earn one's livelihood may not have been necessary for the priesthood per se, but it was absolutely essential for those clergy who strove to be a manifestation of Christ's incarnation in the working class. Without the naturalization of fatigue and calloused hands, those priests would have been marginalized and would have remained alien to the proletariat. *Recherche* had demonstrated to them that sharing the neighborhood poverty of this social class was not enough. In addition, they had to work for their bread just like all the others. The fact that Jesus had worked too served to justify this; the priestly task of continuing his incarnation demanded it.

Massive entry by clergy into full-time labor by the late 1940s had been highly controversial while the debate raged, but it paled before the next turning point in the worker-priests' quest (*recherche*) for a more authentic incarnation. For the most part, they had convinced the church's leading prelates that manual work was necessary for their specific apostolate. They were notably less successful in pursuading these same bishops and abbots that worker-priests should become *militant* workers. However, these laboring clerics were touched deeply by the injustices they saw at the factories and on the docks. They became aware rather quickly that the trade union was the source of hope and integrity for the toiling masses. This realization, combined with their participation in union life, convinced the worker-priests that "to be with (*d'être avec*)" their comrades in a less than militant sense would not suffice. Naturalization required that they be with them also in that *engagement* found in the workers' movement which strove to build a better world. By such an unprecedented step they moved beyond more traditional modes of passive poverty into the dangerous activism advocated by later liberation theologians.

Joseph Gouttebarge, himself a trade-union leader, defined this incarnation of priestly militancy in the following way: "We are involved actively (*engagés*) in the midst of the proletariat or with it in combat. Combat has made us discover and live a real and efficacious fraternity. It's made us see imperfectly what this fraternity will be in a more just society." He was convinced that *engagement* meant that the worker-priests should "struggle against the abusive and criminal exploitation that the ruling class creates through values and pseudovalues such as authority, respect for the established order, fidelity to tradition . . . passive obedience, simplistic submission" and "the resignation which keeps the laboring classes in an enslaved situation."[24]

Similar to their commitment to manual labor, the worker-priests came to endorse *engagement* because of what they found through their *recherche* in the midst of life. Bernard Chauveau called it "a revelation" received along "his journey" within the proletariat. It grew out of his "relationship with the working class," and it involved an identification with "its struggles and its combats." André Depierre was discovering this as early as 1945, and the Marseille *équipe* concluded that "a conscious worker cannot stay outside this struggle." Henri Barreau internalized the battles of the proletariat he had entered. Within us, he declared, "was born their [workers'] class consciousness. . . . More and more each day we were brought shoulder to shoulder with all our comrades, to participate sincerely in their daily struggle against their exploiters and to aspire with them to a society where human beings are no longer ravenous animals in the eyes of others but rather where the products of labor belong entirely to the workers."[25]

Such a novel and controversial notion of priestly incarnation precipitated an inevitable controversy. By 1952 a debate within the missionary apostolates, as well as within the entire institutional church, was in full swing. This compelled the worker-priests to defend their *engagement.* They justified it in the name of incarnational "solidarity with the working class." One of their reports argued that being workers made them subject to the injustices felt by that class; likewise being workers stirred them to militate actively in proletarian combat to remove these outrages. They felt that non-participation in the working class struggle was a form of the heresy called angelism. Finally, they insisted that charity demanded that priests assume positions of union leadership which frequently made one vulnerable to lay-offs or other forms of management persecution. "The priest does not have the right to refuse a dangerous post where a family man might be sent," the report concluded. In a letter to a Catholic M.R.P. deputy in the French parliament,[26] Father Gouttebarge went so far as to suggest that *engagement* was demanded by the very reality of evangelization:

> Basically the church would like us to enter the factories but without active involvement (*engagement*) in the working class movement. We cannot accept this position.
>
> Why? Because the working class movement, including politics and trade union activity, is the soul of the working class world, and our essential spiritual mission consists in baptizing a soul. We cannot marry a body without the soul. How can we baptize this soul without knowing it, without vibrating in the rhythms of its most profound and authentic aspirations?[27]

Between these militant views and the notion of class struggle was a very thin gap. For the most part, the worker-priests crossed that distance with relative ease. This too came as a personal revelation from their concrete *recherche* in the midst of industrial life rather than through the academic mediation of theology, sociology or political science. "I discovered another vision of the world," testified Father Bernard Striffling, "and I discovered it through class struggle, through the practice of class struggle." For "Gabby" Genthial, *engagement* meant "an entry into class struggle . . . into the world of class struggle," and the Marseille worker-priest Albert Gauche reported, "Class struggle was never presented to me as a philosophical conclusion of the communists. I have found class struggle along the way, just like every worker. . . . This struggle," he asserted, "is not the fruit of a social theory . . . but rather the normal consequence of the exploitation of the many by a few privileged for their personal profit."[28]

Nevertheless, this living daily experience of class struggle forced the worker-priests to reflect upon it in consciously theological ways similar to the subsequent analysis of many liberation thinkers. Henri Barreau turned to religious logic when he was confronted with his class struggle position. To a factory director who accused him of taking sides in a dispute, Barreau asserted, "We cannot serve two masters at the same time, God and Mammon." He did not deny that a priest was obligated to love people in opposite camps, but he was convinced, just as strongly, that there could be no real wholeness until the destruction of "the capitalist sin." Father Barreau and his worker-priest brothers knew that traditional Catholic social doctrine was opposed in principle to class struggle. Instead the position of class collaboration was advocated. In spite of this official stance the worker-priests had discovered a reality which contradicted this view radically. Thus they found themselves in opposition to the traditional positions of the church. This vulnerability vis-à-vis official Catholicism forced them to develop apologies for their unpopular stance. One such defense was offered by Robert Pfaff at Longwy. He denied that his acceptance of class analysis was Marxist, but he regretted that his church had "condemned the communists without ever condemning the capitalists." After all, elaborated Pfaff, "capitalism is atheistic in its very structure . . . [and] . . . comportment, a spirit of insatiable cupidity, avarice and domination." This reality forced him to note, "Class struggle is perhaps sad, but it exists."[29] His final denunciation of capitalism was an attempt to explain the reality of class struggle to his Catholic detractors:

There are two camps facing each other: on one side, the bourgeoisie, whose houses have no resemblance to the houses in our worker cities . . . those who command and those who profit. On the other side are the workers, those whose total life is in submission to the factory, those who obey and those who are exploited. . . . Externally, only the working class world seems to conduct this struggle. It seems to have the monopoly on violence. The workers threaten, rant and cry out injustice. . . . The bosses' world justifies itself very politely, and very rarely is a manager seen acting menacingly in an overt way. He is much too cunning for that, and he has other means of pressure than these. The bosses' world is even ready to make propositions for unity; one sees this scarcely on the workers' side. They know very well that this would serve for nothing or, at least, that it would go no further than a sentimental unity, never in any case, a financial unity.[30]

More conservative Catholics were unprepared to see such oppression in the midst of their own comforts. Instead they were obsessed with how closely Father Pfaff's language was echoed by the militants of the French Communist Party. It was feared that, wittingly or unwittingly, the worker-priests were being seduced by the philosophy and ambience of Marxism. It was true that these missionary clergy had begun slowly and increasingly to form bonds of friendship and cooperation with grass-roots communist militants. This did not mean, however, that they had become converts to the tenets of Marxism as their foes suspected. Yet, it did insure that the worker-priests would never again view the communists from the narrow and negative perceptions in which their traditional faith had trained them. Their daily contact with real communists promoted a different form of *recherche* and reflection.

Most of them had come to the conclusion that the Marxist workers were the avant-garde of the entire proletariat, the source of its struggle against injustice and for a better world. The Limoges *équipe* reported that it was Karl Marx who gave to the working class both its vision and its will to combat unjust conditions. These priests were convinced that the only way Catholics could establish credibility among the workers was to join Marxists in the "social revolution." This alliance would prompt not only the discovery of "many verities in Marxism" but also the strengthening of a genuine resistance to "the errors of Marxism." Both Bernard Cagne and Maurice Combe insisted that worker-priest *engagement,* in its most effective form, gave priority to its work with the Marxist vanguard and not the unorganized subproletariat. Robert Pfaff echoed this conviction when he made this missionary observation: "It is no longer the proletariat in its sad sub-civilization that one thinks of baptizing but a civilization which is coming to be which is opened up by the Marxists."[31]

Such analyses foreshadowed the attraction of some liberation theologians to Marxist perceptions, and like these later radicals, the worker-priests too faced formidable opposition from the traditional Catholic anticommunism which was so powerful. Matters came to a head in 1949 when both the Vatican and French cardinals condemned communism totally and all collaboration with its militants. Henri Perrin and the other worker-priests of his neighborhood met to reflect upon these anti-Marxist pronouncements. They were afraid that the hierarchical position would undermine the ministry they had worked so hard to establish. Their conclusion was that communist-Christian cooperation was absolutely essential to their entire missionary endeavor. Perrin himself felt that "freedom of option should be given at the grass-roots level" so that Christians could work with communists in their youth organizations, in the C.G.T. and in the Mouvement de la Paix.[32]

The other worker-priests shared the anxieties of their brothers in Paris 13[e]. They were angered at the Vatican's anti-Soviet foreign policy and its ostracism of communists. There was no denial of the errors of communism, but these men found the hierarchical document simplistic and inflexible. Its spirit of anathema, they felt, favored "a political or social orientation contrary to the interests of the working class." "Whether one deplores it or not," asserted the angry worker-priests, "communism is, in fact, the major expression of the militant working class." Further, they hastened to add that the militant Christians' struggles against injustice and colonialism and for peace and a more just socio-economic system linked them in an inevitable alliance with the Communist Party. Against the more juridical approach of the hierarchy statement, they called for a "missionary strategy" involving philosophical dialogue between Christians and Marxists, objective study of communism at the seminaries and a clear distinction between totalitarianism and "a collectivist and planned economy." In this way the worker-priests felt that the road would be cleared for Communist-Catholic collaboration.[33]

Not all the laboring priests were this optimistic nor have all liberation thinkers been prepared to use Marxist analysis. The hesitations of Jacques Loew have been noted earlier. However, even Loew refused to identify with the crusading anticommunism espoused by most conservative Catholics. His anticapitalistic credentials were impeccable, and on the docks, he learned "that class struggle was an historic fact." He condemned the factory owners' inhumanity and praised the zeal and integrity of his many communist friends. However, he wavered at the point of what he felt to be a rigid social imperialism in the class struggle doctrine of classical Marxism, and he was critical of "communism under its Stalinist form." Finally, his anticommunist arguments were based upon his own personal religious convictions, convictions that combined a Gandhian pacifism with the traditional Catholic notion of a religion that transcends social classes.[34]

No doubt, this position was more theoretically amenable to traditional Catholic sensibilities, but in the hostile atmosphere of social tension and Cold War, it was no more useful in promoting a working compromise on the issue of Marxist-Christian cooperation. The worker-priests continued to struggle among themselves in this *recherche*, but external pressures within the church and social conflict rendered an acceptable compromise practically impossible. The debate lingered on, growing more and more acrimonious, until the hierarchy brought the worker-priest experiment to a halt.

Out of the controversy surrounding *engagement*, class struggle and Marxism grew broader notions of ecclesiology and mission. The construction of a more just society in the name of the church was not a conviction born of liberation theology. It was part of the collective hope shared by the worker-priests years earlier. They spoke constantly of a new world being born outside of the church, and for them, this was the society being built by the industrial proletariat. In all of this the church's task was to baptize this new humanity rather than bring more individual members into the ecclesiastical apparatus. André Depierre elaborated this position in a 1949 Mission de Paris report. He stated the church was foreign to the new world being born by the collective action of the working class. The proletariat, he asserted, was the only collectivity "conscious of its real rights, of the justice which is its due . . . and of that mission to transform humanity which falls upon it." And the Christians, what must they do? Just this, concluded Depierre: "Our proletarians will exact of us that we be Christians in all things or nothing, that we baptize all this world or none of it, that we render God, Christ and the church *présente* in toto or not at all."[35]

This position was affirmed by the Mission de Paris as early as 1946. It called the proletariat's "hunger and thirst for justice, its sense of human dignity . . . [and] . . . its capacity for giving itself totally to the building of a better world . . . building blocks for a new Christianity." In this light Hollande's priests called for the church to be "really *présente* in this new civilization, as it knew how to be *présente* in other epochs, in the Roman world and in the barbarian world . . . so that its divinity might be perceivable." Father Besnard, one of these Parisian laboring clergy, summarized this entire point of view succinctly: "There is a new world to be baptized. We must be on the inside (*de-dans*). To exclude ourselves would be a grave error which could retard the march of humanity toward God."[36]

Not surprisingly, these burning convictions were intensified and radicalized when confronted with the increasing opposition of a more traditional church. Gradually the substantive differences between the ecclesiastical world which sent them and the world into which they were naturalized began to exact their toll. Caution and suspicion grew between the worker-priests and more conservative Catholics; by the 1950s fear and conflict came to dominate. A deep disappointment over the state of the church began to permeate the consciousness of this pioneer clergy. Much like the class which they had entered, they felt alienated from the institutional church which had mandated their mission. André Depierre criticized what he perceived to be its "bourgeois humanism," its "medieval appearance" and its "individualistic morals and spirituality." Others spoke more harshly. Jean Gray called it an adversary of the working class, a body committed to a "bourgeois and conservative world," and Father Jean-Marie Lepetit labelled it treasonous to the gospel mission. Robert Pfaff was convinced that the church was "no longer of their [workers'] class." "We are compromised with those who have exploited them." The Longwy worker-priest was saddened by the conclusion he felt compelled to make when he was asked if the church was still of the people. "In doctrine, yes," he stated, "certainly also in desire. In fact, no!" Jacques Screppel was equally critical of his own Dominican order. In spite of its mandating of several worker-priests like himself, the fiery Hellemes monk lamented, "Isn't it regrettable that the living forces . . . of the Order . . . are almost totally absorbed in the service of established Christian communities?"[37]

More and more the disgruntled worker-priests turned to their own teams (*équipes*) as a model for the church life they advocated. They were opting for a more communitarian and collegial style in place of the hierarchical and bureaucratic pattern they felt was stifling the church's life. However, they would be forced to wait until Vatican II and third world grass-roots communities brought these dreams to fruition. In the meantime, the worker-priests were not advocating any formal break with the church leadership. Theirs was not a spirit of revolt. They were interested rather in breathing new life into the institution. Fathers Riche, Olhagaray and Lepetit of the Mission de Paris called for "a team approach (*en équipe*)" so that the church could learn to live "in a communitarian way," and Father Pfaff at Longwy believed that his mission required a coordination of *équipes* from the parish, neighborhood and factory.[38]

This form of ministry was practiced by Jacques Loew in Marseille and by André Depierre from his Montreuil base near Paris. Loew was convinced that priests and laity involved in the proletarian mission "should be attached to a community" which practiced the apostolic poverty and lifestyle of the primitive Christian church. This would connect it authentically to "the workers' milieu." Links with the parish would place it within the institutional church's framework. At Montreuil Father Depierre advocated and lived this *équipe* style for over thirty years. He insisted that the missionary "must have an *équipe*, a community" which involves "a totally communitarian life." Without this new form of lifestyle Depierre was certain that the Christian could not be engaged fully in the proletarian *communauté de destin*.[39]

Not only had hard work, proletarian life and militant *engagement* reshaped worker-priest ideas. So too had their experience of Christian community. This *équipe* style of Christian life encouraged the *recherche* mode of inquiry to thrive, another reality characteristic of later grass-roots communities found in Latin America and elsewhere. Having applied it to their new worlds of wage labor and proletarian militancy, the worker-priests turned it with effectiveness toward analysis of their own priesthood and the religious life. This led to some marked departures from the traditional doctrines and practices of the church.

Every major unprecedented step taken by these laboring clergy into the proletarian world brought with it a corresponding shift away from the more orthodox perceptions of the priesthood. The standard notion of the priest as the holy and separate one, distinct from the people and the living embodiment of a higher more spiritual world was challenged deeply by the worker-priests' plummet into the proletariat. Afterwards they put this challenge into words. Their view of the priesthood was thoroughly incarnational. "The priest is not a separated one but rather a consecrated one," stated one Mission de Paris report. He was "to live in the midst of the world" making himself "like others in every way (except for sin)." Such total immersion in proletarian life marked him as "the conscience of God in the midst of his comrades." This new brand of priest had to place himself "at the call of this world" where he would become the "one for others" by "rendering Christ *présent* at the very heart of life." He would become one with the workers, "sharing their life, living in their midst."[40] Joseph Robert penned the following summary description in 1949:

> It is neither the clothes nor the lifestyle, nor the capacity for contemplation or intellectual work which defines the priesthood but rather the relationship of the priest to God and man. . . . It is not in being the minister of a cult nor the director or inspiration for a parish activity separated from the milieu, but rather being one of them, sharing (*partageant*) all their sufferings and all their human hopes, all their efforts of charity, justice and liberty . . . in the name of a deeper inspiration and for a wider horizon.[41]

As incarnation came to include both manual labor and militant activism in proletarian causes, so did worker-priest views of the sacerdotal life evolve accordingly. Even in 1945 one Mission de Paris clergyman called for the "priest-worker, living his entire priesthood at the factory, going forth for trade union and other needs and in this way, exercising his apostolate solely at the factory." However, it was the Nanterre Capuchins who portrayed most graphically this integration of manual labor and the priesthood. "Our life at the factory is not . . . an addition," protested one of these friars. "Rather it is the manner whereby we realize our priesthood." The priest, he continued, is "a consecrator of work . . . by the witness of his *présence* . . . not by some juridical fiction but by his *présence* even in this world of work." This consecrated life was likened to Christ's high priestly status on the cross, thus linking Bethlehem with Golgotha. "Christ is the witness before the Father's face of the terrible human condition," and in his laboring priest is combined "incarnation, redemption, sacrificial oblation and revelation."[42]

Tension began to develop most acutely in the arena of class militancy. It was felt by many that involvement in partisan issues of any kind compromised the universal essence of the priesthood. By this argument, *engagement* was a direct threat to catholicity. Even some worker-priests were inclined to feel this way. Among these was Father Loew of Marseille. Most others, however, were prepared to defend a class-conscious priesthood, but they did so in the name of the church's universality. "We cannot adduce a priori what is the unity of the unique priesthood of Christ . . . or the practical conduct of the priest," stated one apology written by a number of Mission de Paris clergy. Instead the church's priests are always part of "a given humanity," and when that humanity involves a mission field, the "primary law" of the priesthood is "naturalization." No, concluded the document, "the priesthood is not linked inexorably with races, classes or social conditions," but it is indigenous, colored at its "grassroots level . . . by the condition of those very ones to whom we are sent and whom we love just as they are."[43]

This was the reality of their doctrine of the priesthood, an evolution kindled by the proletarian milieu in which they lived. It was a priesthood shaped by a break with one world and an adoption of another. Roger Deliat described it in this way. "Through the years I did priestly ministerial acts . . . but less and less. Little by little the obstacles placed in our way in the parishes . . . and our ruptures with past forms . . . made me foreign to the clerical milieu." In contrast to this, he spoke of his new "priesthood on the inside (*dedans*)" of the working class. "To be *présent*, to work in and for this world led by atheists toward an economic, social and human order which is more just, more favorable to the lowly . . . that is the drama of the priest and Christian involved militantly (*engagés*) in the working class."[44]

One area within the classical notion of priesthood that dominated worker-priest *recherche* was the traditional idea of sacerdotal poverty. For centuries this had been regarded as among the most noble of virtues. Members of religious orders and most secular priests were required to make a vow of poverty. However, it was common knowledge that this practice of evangelical privation was often honored in the breach. Over the centuries many priests had come to live comfortably, if not extravagantly, even though they owned nothing per se. The worker-priests were appalled by the lie of this theoretical poverty. Using a combination of traditional Catholic doctrine and their own proletarian immersion, they sought to give to the notion of priesthood a poverty for which the Catholic Church could be justifiably proud. The Nanterre Capuchins, under the inspiration of Francis of Assisi, strove to live an "effective poverty, presented under a form understood by the working class world." For them, this meant that such a poor priest "should work to earn his bread." "Besides," they concluded, "this is how St. Francis understood poverty." Henri Barreau viewed the poor life as "a sign of priestly mediation," "a privilege" and "a condition of the kingdom of God." However, this had to be the special poverty of the proletariat, a poverty "in solidarity with his class brothers." "I am poor with the poor by force of circumstance," was his testimony."[45]

Meanwhile the poverty of the worker-priest demanded more than this voluntary solidarity. A deeper renunciation, even repentance, was required. The former system of priestly "culture and privileges" had to be repudiated. The "absence of power" and a life of "solitude and uselessness" were mantles that had to be worn daily by the worker-priests, or true poverty could never be theirs. In short, poverty could only be a gift from the proletariat given to those willing to embrace its full incarnation. To Jo Gouttebarge's poignant question, "Have we loved the poor in the form of the militant workers rather than in the fashion of good church ladies doing benevolent deeds?" the Limoges *équipe* gave the following response: "It is only because I live in the midst of the poor and of those who hunger and thirst for justice that I might be given perhaps the opportunity to live a life of priestly poverty."[46]

By these redefined values and by their lifestyle the worker-priests had turned their backs on the idea of poverty as a virtue in and of itself. Instead they had linked it to their total incarnation, wage labor and the militant struggle against injustice. Thus they adopted both the classical notion of priestly poverty and the liberationist principle of "the priority option for the poor." In the name of the former, they took up the privation of the oppressed; in the name of the latter, they fought the cause of the oppressed. Their understanding of priestly spirituality would demand a similar overhaul. Questions and anxieties concerning the classical religious life assaulted these laboring clergy. Was not the priest a man of prayer? Was he not a meditative man, a contemplative who practiced the spiritual rhythms which had become so characteristic of the western Latin church? Just as the twin realities of manual toil and *engagement* had compelled the worker-priest to reshape the patterns of his worship and devotional life, so also did it cause him to rethink his very perceptions of spirituality itself.

Not so surprisingly the worker-priest linked his spiritual life to his incarnation within the proletarian world. This was especially true in the *recherche* of the religious orders who sent priests into the factories. Père André of the Nanterre Capuchins called for "a worker spirituality for . . . the working class masses," a spirituality "proper to the worker-priests." This would be a *via dolorosa* of being "a poor man in the midst of others," of enduring "honestly the agonies of the workers' life" and of a search "for God via a path acceptable to the worker." Jacques Screppel of Hellemes and the Belgian O.V.P. *équipe* made similar observations. Even the secular worker-priests were aware of the need for this special spirituality. "We must search for (*rechercher*) a new rhythm of prayer," asserted Father Jean-Claude Poulain of the Mission de Paris. "We must experiment with different colorations of the spiritual life." The worker-priests, in light of such assessments, were prompted to ask, "What is life's time-table? What are those religious exercises of priests most devoted to the particular services of the workers?"[47]

These questions were answered largely by the development of a spirituality around the work cadence. Worker-priests created a religious rhythm in accord with their monotonous toil. The O.V.P. suggested that "the worker-priest should be a contemplative in his work," using his very toil to honor "the total life of Christ." The Dominican Joseph Robert was convinced that the "roughness, disciplines, humiliations and pains of work" gave it "an ascetic aspect" not "always found in classical asceticism." Thus, summarized Father Robert, "factory life, accepted voluntarily, should maintain and deepen the priest in a state of permanent charity toward his brothers for whom he carries their suffering and joys, their sins and efforts, their griefs and their hopes." So important was this adapted spirituality that special instructions to employ it were developed for seminarians about to undertake common toil. They were told to adopt "the life of Jesus of Nazareth, a life of prayer and manual work, a life of charity, a life humble and hidden." "At Nazareth," the document stated, "Jesus had no apostolate. He prepared himself for public life by being in communion with the life of the workers, by taking upon himself their miseries and sins, by offering his prayer, his work and his suffering for their redemption."[48]

It was an easy step for the worker-priests to take when they identified their toil with Christ's Passion, with his road to the cross. "I achieved the redemption of this world by my work pains, fatigue, cold . . . monotony," stated Father Boland of the O.V.P., and one theological supporter of these clergy made the following testimony at a public meeting: "In Savoy this winter, the worker-priest who worked on construction in −25° weather had his priestly and apostolic suffering joined to that of Christ in his oblation as the divine victim." The martyr death of the docker-priest Michel Favreau became the most costly example of this Passion *imitatio*. His earlier observations on the religious life he employed on the Bordeaux docks were a heartrending prophecy of the final testimony of his lifeblood. "Prayer is much easier than in the mish-mash of fairs and meetings. When one carries bags or boxes in the shadow of the crossbeams, which are shaped in a cruciform fashion, it is easy to unite oneself to the crucified Christ. Every day is Good Friday." It was this daily inhuman monotony of toil which revived Golgotha most vividly in the hearts of the worker-priests. This was put so poignantly by one of the Limoges laboring clergy: "I have seen the priest who lives with me coming home in the evening from his work and opening the Bible and placing himself before God like Isaiah's suffering servant or the Passion of Our Savior. The comrades go back home also worn out, just as he is, but when they go home, they find crying kids or their fatigued wife."[49]

Even in their controversial *engagement* the worker-priests found soil in which to plant their work spiritually. Father Robert made this clear when he stated that there was "a contemplative resource attached to manual work, and this work is deployed more and more in those struggles of the working class movement which will restore a more natural, a more human rhythm." For Henri Barreau entry into the proletariat was a "conversion," "a metamorphosis" into "the very substance of the priesthood" that he had desired. "I had become a worker," he exclaimed with joy, and that included his participation in the movement for the construction of a new and better world. Concerning his union ties he had this to say: "Just like Christ, who by his death has separated religion from all political castes and from all cowardly conformism, I refuse all political subterfuge which could be only a source of division and sterility. Just as Christ places himself in total solidarity with the people of his time and all time, and more particularly with the victims of the eternal egoism of the powerful, so also I place myself in solidarity with the world of the workers." Charles Boland went so far as to say that the labor activism of the worker-priest was his "cross par excellence," his "most supreme testimony to gospel virtues."[50]

Prayer itself, in so many ways the antithesis of activity, was also an integral part of the life chosen by the worker-priests. They felt the need to communicate with God in the midst of assembly-line toil. "My work and its orientation have given to me my interior life," testified one Capuchin worker-priest, and the Pradosien Jean Fulchiron stated, "My work . . . its course, its walkways and alleys . . . favored personal prayer. I had grand moments of silence and calm."[51] The following diary entry by another worker-priest is especially graphic in this description of prayer life on the factory floor:

> This morning, with a buddy, I discovered a new aspect of life's drama. In the midst of the machines, absent-mindedly looking over our work, I heard in the name of Christ the drama of a human life, a life parallelling that of others, but nevertheless so different. Then, there is the work which continues, the machine which collapses . . . the motor which burns out, the machine which fuses, the transmission currents which blow out, the drudgery, the mixture of smells from the sacs on the pallets, the sweat which pours out. It's all a new prayer.[52]

The religious life of the worker-priests is proof positive that no simple label can be applied to them. Any notion that they had become militant activists who had lost all sense of their religious vocation was an invention of their foes or of those who were too afraid to understand them. Their deep spirituality exposed such a fallacious position. They were neither activists nor contemplatives, neither "doers" nor "thinkers." Indeed, they were all of these, integrated into one whole, shaped profoundly by the working class milieu and the collective reflections which grew out of it. Theirs was a *recherche,* a quest for gospel action and thought in a world alien to the church. They had integrated their faith and religious life into their own evolving proletarian existence and consciousness, only to find that they too had become foreigners in the eyes of those who had sent them. Misunderstanding soon led to open disputes until tensions could no longer be resolved. By 1952 the worker-priests were at the brink of ecclesiastical anathema. Their apostolate had entered the rocky road of public conflict.

VIII

THE WORLD OF WORKER-PRIEST
CONFLICT

"We called for a different vision of the priesthood."
—André Depierre, Montreuil worker-priest

Controversy had dogged the worker-priests' pilgrimage from the very beginning of their apostolate, but by 1952 it had reached dangerous proportions. Prior to this, conflict and disagreement, in a more positive sense, had been part and parcel of the notion and practice of *recherche*. The worker-priests had struggled and continued to wrestle within themselves concerning the nature and practice of their mission. Should their efforts be concentrated in the neighborhood or at the workplace? Did the reality of *présence* and incarnation necessitate a stance of *engagement* and militancy? Further, the increasing involvement in trade unionism and the Mouvement de la Paix brought with it that strife which the worker-priests labelled increasingly as class struggle. Strike actions and arrests in peace demonstrations were conflictual to a high degree but were viewed by these clergy as necessary actions for the liberation of the laboring classes.

Finally, there existed misunderstandings between the worker-priests and members of the hierarchy. Relations had not always been cordial between these laboring priests and certain bishops, and as tensions increased, so did division and strife intensify even among the worker-priests themselves. Also the workers and their trade unions could not escape this atmosphere of polarization. However, it was the rifts with the church leadership that would evolve and explode into mutual recriminations and irresolvable division, a division which would culminate in the hierarchical decision to ban the worker-priest experiment.

Although these battles would move to their denouement rapidly after the controversial arrests of Fathers Bouyer and Cagne in the anti-

Ridgway protest of May, 1952, the seeds of caution and suspicion were present at Rome as early as the mid-1940s. In November, 1946 both Louis Augros of the Mission de France and Jacques Hollande visited Rome in order to report their missionary efforts to the Holy See and win its continued approval. In many respects the Roman trip was quite positive. The two were received in audiences by powerful curial figures, and many of these had words of encouragement for the Frenchmen. Msgr. Montini, the future Paul VI, was impressed by the bold efforts of the Mission de Paris. He was reported to have said: "The worker-priests, the stakes are worth the risk. Then we cannot reproach ourselves for having done nothing." Other cardinals were notably more cautious. Msgr. Tardini of the Vatican Secretariat struck both Hollande and Augros as limited in outlook, and they found a similar caution in Msgr. Ottaviani of the Holy Office.[1]

Of course, their most important audience was with the Holy Father himself. They were most elated by what they felt to be his support for their apostolic efforts. However, their written summary of the meeting with Pius XII contains a conversational section which is more equivocal than the optimism they heralded. The interchange was reported like this:

Pius XII: But you have begun already, haven't you? You have results already, some successes, some hopes?

Response: Yes, but it will be very long and difficult.

Pius XII: Yes, but you are confident?

Hollande: Yes, we are confident, but it is necessary that these priests live truly in the midst of the workers, the pagans and that some be even factory workers.

Pius XII: Yes, but they must be very prudent, very prudent, because there is a danger for their vocation.[2]

Upon their return to France both Augros and Hollande announced the more positive results of the trip. This was understandable, but the details of the report to the Mission de Paris had noted a more equivocal reaction at Rome.[3] In short, the worker-priest ministry was not endorsed heartily. It was allowed to continue, but a note of caution had been present. The first Roman visit had produced a respite for the worker-priests rather than a victory.

For the next few years the worker-priests reflected the Vatican's appeal for prudence by maintaining a low profile. With very few exceptions their activities remained little known to a wider Catholic or non-Catholic public. Events of the year 1949 changed this markedly.

The worker-priests were drawn into the public eye by a number of sensationalist newspaper articles published about them by sectors of the popular press. During the summer of that year *Témoignage Chrétien*, *France-Soir*, *Paris-Presse-Intransigeant* and *Match* printed material about the worker-priests which produced a negative reaction in important Catholic circles.

Especially offensive were the articles which appeared respectively in the tabloids *France-Soir* and *Paris-Presse-Intransigeant* under the titles "Commandos de l'église" and "Chrétiens de choc." In light of these stories Father Hollande felt constrained to defend the Mission de Paris to members of the hierarchy. He reminded Msgr. Ancel that his missionary team had "made a resolution not to publish newspaper articles . . . and to refuse all interviews," and he sought to assure the Prado leader that the appearance of yellow journalism on the worker-priests did not reflect a change in that policy. Instead, he elaborated, his priests were avoiding journalists as much as they could. Hollande pointed out instances of fabricated stories and distortions of factual information in the controversial articles, thereby hoping to quiet Ancel's anxieties. Before the French episcopate could respond negatively to these press accounts, Father Hollande sent a similar letter to its secretary Msgr. Chapoullie. In it, he stated bluntly, "I tell you precisely that none of these journalists had been received at rue Ganneron in spite of their repeated demands." To assure the bishops of his sincerity Hollande issued a public statement in which he lauded his clergy's "ties to their hierarchy" and their "will for silence" to be maintained in their work.[4]

In addition, many worker-priests were angered by what they felt to be a yellow journalism which jeopardized their mission. Especially furious was Father Henri Perrin. He accused Jean Balensi of *Paris-Presse* of betraying all the rules of journalistic conduct. He felt that Balensi had misrepresented himself and had taken advantage of his [Perrin's] goodwill by creating a series of sensationalist articles about the worker-priests. Perrin was convinced that he had been used for anti-communistic "red" baiting; consequently he appealed to Balensi to publish no more articles in the series. The Jesuit worker-priest reserved his praise in this affair solely for *Témoignage Chrétien*, which he believed wrote an honest article designed to correct the sensationalist press.[5]

In spite of these efforts to calm troubled waters, conflict continued to boil with the appearance of the Holy Office's decree against communism that same summer. The troubled and negative reaction to this by the worker-priests exposed the hitherto hidden divisions which existed between these clergy and their hierarchical leaders. Joining with a number of their supporters numerous worker-priests published a statement which challenged the values and strategies of both the Vatican's and French cardinalate's documents against communism. In order to preserve peace between the priests and their bishops, Fathers Hollande, Laporte and Depierre of the Mission de Paris met with Msgr. Chapoullie that same month. When they left that encounter they felt that a modus vivendi had been reached, that Msgr. Chappoulie had come to understand the importance of being sensitive to proletarian attitudes toward the church. They were even convinced that the hierarchical statements did permit some *engagement* with the communists under certain circumstances, circumstances which they described as a "temporary collaboration on limited goals." For specific examples of this, the three men referred to trade-union alliances, membership in the C.G.T., personal friendships, mass action in the peace movement and a presence in paracommunist groups.[6]

However, the issue was by no means settled. In less than a year the conflict erupted again at Lyon. There the worker-priests clashed with Msgr. Alfred Ancel, one of Cardinal Gerlier's auxiliary bishops. Ancel was so disturbed by a meeting with some local worker-priests at his Prado house that he wrote them a lengthy letter in order to build a bridge between the contending parties. He spelled out several concerns. First of all, he appealed for open communication and mutual understanding. Then he turned to his deepest concerns, the meaning of the priesthood and the form of its *présence* in the working class. He insisted that he had a "sole difficulty" with his worker-priests, namely their "participation . . . in the temporal activity of the proletariat." His contention was that the very catholicity and transcendence of the priesthood demanded that these ordained apostles eschew all trade union membership and strike activity.[7]

Ancel had stated the issue clearly. Should a priest adopt a partisan stance and become involved in temporal *engagement?* His unequivocal answer was "No!" and that opinion was shared by the French church's episcopal leadership. Indeed, it is still echoed by the highest ecclesiastical authorities with respect to priests holding public office. Papal objection to clergy in the Nicaraguan government is perhaps the most widely publicized example of this objection. In order to resolve this accelerating tension between the bishops and their worker-priests, the church hierarchy mandated the preparation of a *Directoire*. This manual of instruction was to be used to guide the conduct of all priests who embarked on a *présence* of factory work. Mention was made of "difficulties . . . from this unprecedented form of priestly life," and it was maintained that the *Directoire* was published to address these. Dialogue was called for by appealing to the worker-priests to offer suggested revisions to the draft document, but it was clear that the nature of the episcopal paper was disciplinary. The *Directoire*'s purpose was to circumscribe the worker-priests in those particular areas where the bishops felt most uncomfortable.[8]

First of all, the document insisted that priests "must remain submissive" to their bishops; for the worker-priests this meant participation only in those forms of ministry mandated by their hierarchical leaders. Secondly, the worker-priests were reminded of the priority of their spiritual duties. They were "sent into the proletariat to evangelize it and not to direct its terrestrial effort of liberation." Objections to liberationist interpretations of the gospel thus predated similar conflicts in post-Medellín Latin America. Along the same lines, the *Directoire* insisted that the distinction between the priest and laity must be maintained strictly. The priest was to be "a simple *présence*" and thus avoid a particular "temporal option." Instead of militant *engagement*, he was to coordinate his activities with Catholic Action and missionary parishes. Finally the bishops' document made provision for the continuing "theological, social and pastoral formation" of both worker-priests in the field and those priests mandated for this particular form of ministry. Especially important was the need to protect these clergy from falling under the influence of the Marxist and Stalinist milieu in which they lived. This fear of communism was a most significant roadblock to understanding between the bishops and their more radical clergy.[9]

Anticipating a negative response from the worker-priests led some prelates to make personal appeals for support to their own laboring clergy. Both Msgr. Delay of Marseille and Cardinal Gerlier of Lyon made such pleas, but they were to no avail. Conflict did erupt and was precipitated by an eighteen-page document sent to the worker-priests by Alfred Ancel. Much of it was a recap of earlier anxieties, and its content was largely an expansion of the points listed in the *Directoire*. These parallels made it a quasi-official commentary on the hierarchical document. In it, Ancel accused the worker-priests of abandoning "the traditional forms of the priestly life" for a relativistic notion of adaptation. He reminded them that Christ "never regarded manual work as a priestly function," and he insisted that "the worker-priest should not play the role of a militant . . . neither in the C.G.T. nor in the C.F.T.C." Also Ancel warned against what he felt to be a false distinction between the true church and its institutional forms. His final caveat concerned the "Marxist ambience" that he believed was seducing the worker-priests through a wind of "collective autosuggestion." Consequently, he insisted upon caution and prudence, especially when it involved any *engagement* with "the C.G.T. and all para-communist organizations."[10]

Rather than cool tempers the Ancel document caused an explosion which rippled throughout the worker-priest communities. In a letter to Msgr. Veuillot at Paris, Jacques Hollande pleaded that a *Directoire* was premature for the worker-priests at that particular moment; he suggested that Msgr. Ancel seemed to be playing the role of negative harbinger for a coming condemnation. Other responses were not as kind. One unsigned report stated that worker-priests were "alone . . . competent" enough to ratify a *Directoire* governing their missionary *présence*. Robert Pfaff of Longwy was offended by both the *Directoire* and Ancel's response to it. He felt that these papers were too juridical and that they failed to understand the practical requirements of worker-priest life. Another statement suggested that no easy separation could be maintained between preaching the gospel to the proletariat and joining in its temporal liberation. To accept Msgr. Ancel's judgment, stated this worker-priest document, would be to allow the "amputation" of the church's working class mission. Not all clergy involved in manual toil opposed the *Directoire*. Jacques Loew was its most noted worker-priest supporter, but his voice was that of a tiny minority among his toiling brothers.[11]

For the most part, this growing strife remained internal. The wider French public was unaware of the intensifying tension among the worker-priests and between them and the French hierarchy. Disputes about the *Directoire* were not resolved. The basic issues, similar to those of today's debates surrounding liberation theology, remained as a source of conflict between the contending parties. Indeed, a wide gulf was growing between them. Within six months events would once again catapult the worker-priests into the public eye. Unlike the press campaigns of 1949 this publicity would lead to their condemnation by the Vatican and the French episcopate.

The incident precipitating this final series of conflicts was the arrest and police maltreatment of Fathers Bouyer and Cagne in the anti-Ridgway demonstration of May 28, 1952. Not only did sectors of the popular press report this incident; also the two priests made public their own account of the matter. Catholic members of the governing Mouvement Républicain Populaire were mostly horrified over the matter, but some militants of the M.R.P.'s progressive wing defended the worker-priests against what they felt to be excessive police brutality. The progressive Dominicans who published *Vie Intellectuelle* articulated a similar position, but they were more critical of worker-priest involvement in acts which could subject them to Marxist influence. *La Quinzaine*, a leftist Catholic bi-monthly, supported Fathers Bouyer and Cagne unequivocally.[12]

However, the two clergy were most delighted with the endorsement received from their parish Sacré Coeur de Petit Colombes and its pastor Louis Retif. At a parish meeting both proletarian and bourgeois members upheld the action of their clergy, and Father Retif told his flock that his two vicars had demonstrated an authentic faith throughout the ordeal. Further, he wrote a public letter to the police which he had printed in *Témoignage Chrétien*. In it, he denounced both the police violence of the arrests and the arrogant assumption that these officers had so acted because of their Christian faith. However, it was Maurice Cardinal Feltin, the archbishop of Paris, who would have the last word in the matter. His public communiqué condemned the police's treatment of his priests, but it was less than supportive of the two men's peace activism. In fact, a decided ambivalence toward worker-priest *engagement* could be noted.[13]

It is within this context of worker-priest militancy that a growing polarization was manifest between these clerics and their bishops. The anti-Ridgway protest and the arrests of Bouyer and Cagne did not create these divisions, but it did cause them to surface to the point where they could be ignored no longer. The strife over the *Directoire* and the worker-priests' increasing militancy in unions and the peace movement intensified papal and episcopal wishes to curb the autonomy of their controversial clergy. This is not to suggest that a cordial relationship did not exist between the two groups. In fact, the love and affection of worker-priests for Cardinal Suhard became an unblemished memory after his death, and those bishops, who allowed worker-priests in their dioceses, were uniformly friendly to this form of sacerdotal *présence*.[14]

Nevertheless, hostilities grew with the passage of time. From the *Directoire* until the Vatican ordered a shutdown of this experience in November, 1953, the involved bishops struggled with the worker-priests to reach a working compromise on the issues which divided them. On March 11, 1952 a first official joint meeting was held between worker-priests and members of the French hierarchy. Eighteen bishops, Jacques Hollande and three worker-priests were present. The three laboring clerics gave a moving testimony of their work, but the bishops were troubled by what they felt to be the worker-priests' excessive concern "for the temporal liberation of the workers' world."

They stated their concern succinctly: "It is the bishop who has the right to decide, in each case, if an *engagement* is compatible or not with the proper priestly mission of the worker-priests."[15]

Soon the French episcopate turned from words to deeds, and the casualty was the Mission de France seminary. In the spring of 1952 Cardinal Liénart insisted that the seminary preserve the traditional forms of the priesthood and that Louis Augros submit his resignation as director. Shortly thereafter it relocated at Limoges, and there the students became increasingly attracted to the worker-priest form of ministry. Nineteen of them, in fact, refused to accept ordination unless they could become worker-priests. This crisis prompted an investigatory visit from Rome, and the report that grew out of this was deeply critical of the avant-garde seminary. Cardinal Pizzardo, the Vatican prefect in charge of seminaries, forbade students to do any factory work, and within a year (August, 1953) the Holy See had closed this Mission de France institution until further notice.[16]

More directly a number of bishops began to intervene in ways that would limit their worker-priests' *engagement*. These clerics were not invited to send representatives to the February, 1953 meeting of the nation's cardinals and archbishops, and within a month Cardinal Feltin imposed upon Jacques Hollande the unhappy task of forbidding some of his priests from exercising open leadership in both the C.G.T. and the Mouvement de la Paix. Caught between the cross-fire of his own priests and Feltin, Hollande was barely able to hold the contending parties together.[17] It was, however, in Marseille that the episcopal-worker-priest tension exploded into an irresolvable conflict. The issue erupted via a letter addressed by Msgr. Delay to his Action Catholique Ouvrière diocesan committee. In it he raised the issue of Christian membership in the Communist Party and concluded unequivocally: "The presence of a Christian on the inside of the Communist Party is actually impossible." Following this missive the worker-priests André Piet, Charles Monier and Albert Gauche heard that Msgr. Delay was preparing to dismantle their *équipe*. They fired off an advance protest on May 5 in which they refused "to abandon that post entrusted to us by . . . our comrades in the combat." Their bishop was undaunted. On May 27 he informed them that their team was indeed to be terminated because of their temporal *engagements* and their adoption of Marxist values. The three worker-priests refused to comply, arguing that their incarnational vocation demanded that they remain at the workplace. Throughout the summer both positions hardened, and soon other bishops were drawn into the conflict. Cardinal Feltin made some especially valiant efforts to heal the chasm that was developing throughout the nation between the two groups. He called meetings, met with worker-priests privately and continued to defend them publicly.[18]

All this was to no avail. Rome had decided already to intervene against the worker-priests. Word of the coming interdiction had been passed to select members of the French hierarchy as early as June 29. By the end of August the Roman Congregation of Religious had commanded that the superiors of all religious orders recall their worker-priests. At the end of his three-week tour in France, Cardinal Piazza, prefect of the Roman Consistorial Congregation, demanded a report from the French bishops on ways they could act to resolve the growing crisis. Finally, on September 23, the new papal nuncio Msgr. Marella summoned twenty-six bishops, prelates and superiors of religious orders to inform them of the Vatican's decision to terminate the worker-priests. In addition, the nuncio instructed the French bishops to inaugurate the unpleasant chore themselves. "The measures should be taken as if they come from you," stated Msgr. Marella. Episcopal response was mixed. Msgr. Delay felt that his previous decision had been vindicated, but others were shocked. Cardinal Liénart announced that this decision was "a catastrophe for the French church and for the workers' world." Cardinal Feltin forced back tears as he pleaded with his fellow bishops: "Rome must take into account that after this the church will appear definitively linked to capitalism. . . . We must go to Rome to explain that to the Holy Father and propose a statute to him." The meeting ended without compromise. The nuncio had a message to deliver: the worker-priests were to be condemned, and the French bishops were commanded to announce the bad news.[19]

Most likely it was Cardinal Feltin's resolution to tell his worker-priests privately about the Roman decision which led them to make a final attempt to convince the hierarchy to save their apostolate. On October 5 they handed to Feltin what came to be called "The Green Paper." In it, they argued that incarnation meant not only the adoption of the material standards of a class but also its "human consciousness." This demanded full *engagement* with the proletariat, and they stated this bluntly and with clarity in language which anticipated the principles of liberation theology:

> . . . we could do no other than opt for the active liberation of the working class of which we had become members, in collaboration with its most conscious and organized elements, in whom each day the workers put their trust. . . . It is due simply to our conditions of life and work, to our sharing the whole of our lives with our comrades, to meeting at all levels

with conscious militants—particularly those of the C.G.T. and the Communist Party.[20]

Further, they insisted that "class struggle" was not "a metaphysical idea" but rather "a brutal fact thrust upon the working class." Although they acknowledged that they had committed errors along the way, they felt that the church's institutional apparatus was linked willy-nilly to capitalism. This convinced them even more strongly that their vocational task was to link together Christ and "the proletarian revolution."[21] The "Green Paper" was stillborn. It changed nothing. The bishops refused to meet with the worker-priests in spite of appeals, but it was too late even for the French hierarchy. The October 13 meeting planned for all bishops who had worker-priests in their dioceses was cancelled without further notice, and Cardinals Feltin, Liénart and Gerlier were invited to Rome to receive the Vatican's definitive judgment on the issue.[22]

Meanwhile all was not well among the worker-priests themselves. Existing disagreements within their own ranks were exacerbated by the massive external assaults which threatened to destroy them. Their national meeting in Paris toward the end of 1952 reflected these tensions as they attempted to address the accusation: "You are workers; you are no longer priests." It was their feeling that the statement was a distortion of reality, that, in fact, they could "belong totally to the working class with its misery, its hope, its struggle and its future" as well as belonging equally "to Christ." They were convinced that they had made a necessary break with the traditional and classical priesthood to become bearers of Christ in that "future church" which had opted "in favor of the 'excluded,' the rejected . . . the oppressed." "We cannot," they confessed, "be guardians of an established order which is not that of the people among whom we live."[23] Through these ideas, seeds were being sown which would bear concrete fruit in the form of grassroots Christian Communities in the third world.

Nevertheless, in spite of this virtual unanimity on major concerns, the year 1953 marked the intensification of discord among the worker-priests within the National Secretariat. Not surprisingly, much of the open argumentation transpired among the Parisian worker-priests, but because of the Secretariat's network, these divisions were recorded in reports and letters and then circulated among the *équipes* located throughout the nation. One such report was compiled by Father Jean Gray. His concern was to resolve tensions among the worker-priests so that they betrayed neither their "comrades, the working class" nor "the mission that the church" had "entrusted" to them. He defended worker-priest *engagement* and insisted that this demanded "a long *recherche*" on their "mission . . . priestly role" and "attachment to the church."[24]

However, a number of more militant worker-priests were becoming increasingly disenchanted not only with the organized church but also with the traditional notion of the priesthood. In a letter, Father Emile Poulat confessed that he was troubled with the lack of analysis in the Gray report. He felt that the role of the Communist Party in "worker solidarity" had been avoided and that the views of the priesthood contained therein were too "Sulpician" and "too clerical." Others used even stronger language to critique the moderates in their ranks. One spoke of the "truly intolerable clericalism" he found in their *équipe* meetings, and he was convinced that their very group structure encouraged this "unhealthy atmosphere." Many others were restless with their limited *engagement* and sought to intensify it. Bernard Chauveau defended increased contacts with Marxists, and René Besnard sympathized with those worker-priests who wanted to join the Communist Party.[25]

On the other side of the spectrum were Mission de Paris clergy and those worker-priests more cautious and traditional than Father Gray and the other moderates. Yvan Daniel, member of the Mission de Paris but no factory worker, found much of the "Gray Report" acceptable, but he felt that its view of the priesthood was too indistinguishable from the tasks of the laity. Unlike the Poulat group Daniel wondered if their meetings had any spiritual content. "I ask myself if one could say that our meetings are even meetings of priests." Not surprisingly Daniel challenged his comrades' *engagement* as well: "We are an *équipe* of priests; it seems to me that we should make judgments like priests and not primarily as trade union or political militants." Jacques Loew shared similar anxieties, and among all the worker-priests, it was he who most reflected the hierarchy's misgivings. Uncomfortable with worker-priest *engagement,* he advocated more discipline, hierarchical control and training of clergy designed for such avant-garde mission work. In fact, these anxieties concerning his laboring brothers' militancy led Loew to leave the work force earlier than the other worker-priests.[26]

The year 1953 was also a time of polarization within the trade union movement. In these conflicts the worker-priests, by a large majority, took a sharply critical stance against the Confédération Française des Travailleurs Chrétiens. February of that year marked what could be called the Desgrand Case. In one of its regional publications the C.F.T.C. challenged Father Desgrand's role as a militant leader in the C.G.T. When he was summarily dismissed by his employer, the local C.F.T.C. felt that he had been dropped for legitimate reasons. Beyond this the pro-Catholic union attacked the whole notion of worker-priest *engagement:* "We believe that it is impossible for these priests to be involved actively as directors or partisans in trade union or political movements." Worker-priests of the Lyon-St. Etienne area rallied to the defense of the beleaguered Desgrand. They accused the C.F.T.C. of a pro-capitalistic partisanship and challenged "the presumption" that its position was "*the* Christian one."[27]

At Limoges that same year the worker-priest *équipe* attacked the C.F.T.C.'s behavior in a local strike action, behavior in which the Christian-inspired union had instructed its members to go back to work. In response to this tactic, the Limoges worker-priests judged that the C.F.T.C. had "betrayed the immediate interests of the working class." They felt that "the fidelity of the C.G.T. to the real interests of the proletariat" was in marked contrast to the treason of the C.F.T.C. A parallel document was published in the Parisian area in the wake of the August strike wave. In this instance, all the worker-priests of this area, both secular and religious, chastised the C.F.T.C. for breaking strike unity by signing "a separate accord with the government." They called this unilateral action "an unconditional capitulation . . . of the vital interests of the workers in struggle."[28]

This continuing acrimony between the C.F.T.C. leadership and many of the worker-priests was deeply irritating to the aging Gaston Tessier, the Catholic trade union federation's long-time general secretary. On April 24, 1953 he brought charges against eighteen of these clergy before the archdiocesan tribunal. It was his contention that these men were guilty of defaming his character and that he was approaching the church's court for reparation of damages. He was especially humiliated because their public statement of August had appeared in the Communist daily *L'Humanité*. Both parties stood resolutely behind their respective positions the day they came before the ecclesiastical tribunal. The worker-priest representatives Henri Barreau and Jean-Claude Poulain drafted a twenty-two page document defending their brothers against the Tessier charges. In essence, they claimed that their critique of Tessier was not aimed at his person but rather at his position as a trade union leader. We do "not question his dishonest conduct as a private person," stated their defense, "but rather the dishonesty of his policies as a trade union director." Tessier's lawyer argued that the worker-priests had violated the value of union pluralism and had trampled upon the canonical law governing defamation of character. By the time the archdiocesan court had decided against the worker-priests (March 24, 1954) the issue had become irrelevant. Both the Vatican and French bishops had already condemned the worker-priests publicly. The Tessier verdict had proven anticlimactic.[29]

The stage had been set throughout 1953. The dénouement of the worker-priests was in the air. Acrimonious conflict had ruptured the already thin lines which had linked the church's ecclesiastical leadership to the worker-priests. Divisions had grown apace both within their own ranks and from external sources. The reality of cold war and the strike waves of August helped to poison further the already festering wounds between the worker-priests and the C.F.T.C. leadership, further convincing the beleaguered clergy that they were under fire by the minions of big business. Suspicion was rife; the chasm could not be bridged. Rome's condemnation of the worker-priests was the tragic climax of a strife-ridden year.[30]

On November 4, 1953 France's three most prominent cardinals Maurice Feltin of Paris, Achille Liénart of Lille and Pierre-Marie Gerlier of Lyon travelled to Rome to receive the harsh judgment from the direct hands of the Holy Father. There was no room for negotiations; they were there to receive instructions. Pius XII was prepared to let these priests continue some type of "apostolate in the midst of the workers' milieu," but it was abundantly clear that the old idea of worker-priest would not be tolerated. The pope insisted on five major changes in their ministry: (1) These missionary priests had to "be chosen especially by their bishop." (2) They would be required to receive a specialized doctrinal and spiritual formation. (3) The extent of their manual labor would be limited to safeguard "all the exigencies of their priestly state," and (4) They were to abandon all "temporal *engagement*" which included "trade union and other responsibilities." (5) Finally, they were to have clearly defined links with other priests and the parish.[31]

The Roman decree wreaked havoc with the already strained relationships existing between the worker-priests and their ecclesiastical superiors. From this moment until the bishop's ultimatum in 1954, all attempts to breach this chasm ended in bitterness and failure. Cardinal Feltin called together the worker-priests under his charge in order to inform them of the Vatican's decision in as positive a light as possible. It was to no avail. The worker-priests were wounded deeply and remembered with chagrin the treatment they received that day. They continued their attempts to meet with Feltin as a group, but he consented to see them only on a person-to-person basis. It was Feltin's contention that the time of obedience was at hand. Rome had spoken, and the worker-priests were justifiably expected to leave the "deleterious and poisoned milieu" of the proletariat. The worker-priests' judgment on Feltin's logic was harsh. "It appears to us to be profoundly unjust," they said, "to denigrate the working class dignity and human values and to accuse it of a radically spiritual misery in order to justify your judgment on the quality of our priestly life." Efforts continued to bridge the chasm, but it was too late. The lines had been drawn too sharply. Archbishop Feltin and his worker-priests were polarized hopelessly as the new year approached.[32]

At Lille and Lyon the situation moved toward a similar denouement. Cardinal Liénart's earlier and consistent support of the worker-priests led many of them to believe that they might expect him to be one of their open defenders. These hopes were dashed precipitously in early January 1954. In a declaration published in his diocesan weekly he upheld the papal position with the following words: "To be a priest and to be a worker are two functions, two different states of life, and it is not possible to unite them in the same person without altering the notion of the priesthood." At Lyon the situation deteriorated as well. All the difficulties raised previously by Alfred Ancel were intensified by the papal ultimatum delivered at the hands of Cardinal Gerlier. Some worker-priests felt abandoned by their archbishop by virtue of his incapacity to understand the world in which they lived; others were moved deeply by the pain he felt as the bearer of bad news. All of them, however, were shocked and angered by the content of his message.[33]

Meanwhile under this increasing hierarchical pressure the worker-priests strove mightily to maintain their internal solidarity, but it was not easy. Jacques Hollande was increasingly anxious that his Mission de Paris priests were moving toward open revolt against the official leadership of the church. In a letter to Jean-Marie Marzio (December, 1953) he posed a pointed rhetorical question. "Who is responsible before God and the church for the worker-priests, the archbishop or an *équipe* without a mandate?" Georges Suffert, a Catholic journalist, recalled a lunch meeting he had with André Depierre. He described a fatigued Father Depierre, exhausted by hours of dispute with Fathers Henri Barreau and Jean-Claude Poulain. It seems that the Montreuil worker-priest was appealing to his two comrades to be more open to a continuing dialogue with the hierarchy. Even in the midst of this strain a remarkable solidarity was sustained. "We had the same opinion," Depierre remembered. "We wrote the same things, signed the same things in the face of those decisions which menaced us."[34]

By 1954 tensions had reached the breaking point between the

bishops and the worker-priests. The main problem was not a lack of will to communicate. It was the Roman decision that made discussion impossible. The issue for the new year was which side would capitulate to the other. The Vatican had sent non-negotiable instructions to both parties. Time for dialogue had run out as far as Pius XII was concerned. The worker-priests begged for more time to debate the issues and resolve them collegially, but under papal pressure the bishops were saying in effect: obey now and then we will work out an apostolate together within the Vatican's framework.

This episcopal stance was made clear in a collective letter dated January 19, 1954. All bishops with worker-priests under their charge authored this communiqué jointly. After references to the mutual anguish of both parties, the prelates referred to the Vatican demands as presented by the three cardinals the previous November. "You have all the essential directives," they wrote. "Our purpose now is simply to give you some detailed guidance on putting the statement into practical effect." The bishops pointed out that manual labor by priests would be limited to "no more than three hours a day" and that worker-priests would be expected "to resign from all temporal responsibilities to which the trust of [their] comrades may have called [them]." This latter prohibition included rank-and-file union membership as well. Finally, the prelates insisted that these instructions be obeyed fully no later than March 1, 1954. The worker-priests were ordered to disband their national network and attach themselves to priestly communities under their respective bishops. Then and only then could the threads of the dialogue be joined again. Until that moment, only one road was permitted—"loyal and filial submission."[35]

The worker-priest response was also collective. On February 2, seventy-three of these men (later the total increased to seventy-eight) issued a communiqué in answer to the bishops' ultimatum. It began by stating that the episcopal demands had to be set in the context of a massive assault against the nation's militant proletariat. "We cannot see," affirmed these clergy, "how priests can be forbidden, in the name of the Gospel, to share the conditions of millions of oppressed humanity or to be on their side in their struggles."[36] In light of this the worker-priests reaffirmed their commitment to stand by the proletarian cause. This resounding manifesto would be echoed by the credos of liberation theology which emerged out of similar oppressions in the third world:

> It [is] impossible for us to accept any compromise consisting
> in a pretention of remaining working-class without doing a

normal day's work and without undertaking the commitments and responsibilities of the workers. The working class
has no need of people who 'condescend to its misery.' It needs
men who share its struggles and its hopes.

Consequently we declare that our decisions will be taken
in a spirit of total respect for the working-class state and for
the struggle waged by the workers for their liberation.[37]

In these brief months similar action had been taken against those
worker-priests belonging to religious orders. Both the Jesuit and Capuchin communities responded obediently and quietly to the papal directives. The Dominican situation was more complex and tragic.
Jacques Loew submitted to the papal wishes immediately, but not all
the Dominican worker-priests followed his initiative. In the Nord
Jacques Screppel and others protested, and André Piet of Marseille
sought laicization in order to remain with the workers. Even the order's avant-garde theologians were made to feel the full weight of Roman ire. Maurice Montuclard's Jeunesse de l'église movement was
condemned, and the pro-worker-priest thinkers Fathers Boisselot,
Feret, Congar and Chenu were exiled from Paris by their order's superior. Defending the worker-priests and their views had become
costly as well.[38]

In the remaining weeks before the March 1 deadline, both sides
sought to justify the positions they had taken already. The letter of
Msgr. de Provenchères, the archbishop of Aix-en-Provence, became
for the French bishops a quasi-official apology directed against the
worker-priests' February 2 communiqué. First of all he assured his
readers that the episcopal disciplining of the priests did not constitute
an "abandoning of the working class" but rather was solely a shift in
strategy. The worker-priests were praised for their devotion to a noble
task, but they had fallen into errors which necessitated a religious cor-
rection.[39] The heart of the archbishop's letter was stated as follows:

The object of the Pope and the Bishops was to save the mission . . . and to safeguard the sacerdotal life and the sacerdotal apostolate of the priests sent as missionaires to the
working class.[40]

More specifically this meant the removal of two deviations from
their midst, namely "temporal commitments in trade unions and other
movements" and a decline of the traditional priestly spiritual life.[41]

Throughout France a number of worker-priest *équipes* made final efforts to bridge the gap to their bishops before the sun set on March 1. Those clergy toiling on the large hydroelectric projects of the French hinterland informed *Témoignage Chrétien* that their incarnation demanded that they be "construction workers" in their "body . . . heart . . . lifestyle . . . and reflexes." At Toulouse and Limoges the worker-priest teams wrote apologetic reports to their respective bishops Cardinal Saliège and Msgr. Rastouil. In both instances the worker-priests defended their evolving priesthood in light of incarnational exigencies, and they subjected the institutional church to some scathing critiques.[42]

Meanwhile other bishops echoed the rationale developed at length in the letter by Msgr. de Provenchères. The archbishop of Bordeaux Msgr. Richaud insisted that "ministers of the gospel are not to put themselves at the head of a combat," especially if such action would involve collaboration with Marxists. At Nancy Msgr. Lallier argued that the struggle for proletarian justice was legitimate, but it belonged in lay not clerical hands.[43]

In the Parisian basin thirty-one worker-priests made one final attempt to explain their opposition to the episcopal decision. Emile Poulat drafted the document which they sent to Cardinal Feltin. Their loyalty to the church and its hierarchy was reaffirmed, but they insisted that their official mandate was "to live the full life of the proletariat." These thirty-one men acknowledged that "the novelty of the problems" raised by their "way of life" had caused some significant setbacks, but they were convinced that dialogue could resolve these differences.[44] They made a last passionate plea:

> We have been told that a mission means setting forth without possibility of return and necessarily means making a break with the past, with a particular training, mentality, culture and sociological environment. . . . We believed in what we were asked for and have lived accordingly. . . . We do ask you to respect the roots we have grown. We do ask you not to stifle in us Christ's call to share the lot of our brethren in labor. . . . We ask you not to betray the missionary endeavor of France.[45]

Cardinal Feltin's last communication with his worker-priests before the March 1 deadline reminded them that the church's intervention was "neither a condemnation nor a suppression but rather a management" of their apostolate. The archbishop of Paris fell back on traditional definitions of the sacerdotal life to critique his clergy's notion of "temporal *engagement*."[46] Nothing new had been said; the old rhetoric was repeated again and again by both parties. March 1 was approaching rapidly, and neither side had budged.

After this exchange the worker-priests waxed silent. They turned inward upon themselves as they struggled to respond to the rapidly approaching March 1 terminus. On February 20 they met for the last time as a national *équipe* at a café in the Parisian working class suburb of Villejuif. For two days the worker-priests wrestled with their impossible choice in a spirit of painful collegiality. Discussion was passionate as the men struggled to overcome an atmosphere of sadness. The priestly pioneers were unable to reach unanimity. They discussed the three possibilities of submission, remaining at work or continuing the effort to convince the bishops that their form of priesthood was necessary. After much debate they agreed that dialogue with the hierarchy could not be abandoned no matter what other choices they made. Further, they remained united in the conviction that the church and working class must still be brought together. At this point the agreement ended. They split into two groups, those who would obey their bishops and leave the factories (the *soumis*) and those who would remain on the job with the attendant religious sanctions that choice would bring (the *restés au travail* or *insoumis*). Both groups met separately the following day to decide how they would approach March 1, 1954.[47]

The first of March came and passed quietly, without incident and without public display. However, the division of the worker-priests into two groups at Villejuif and the continuing polarization which followed has made this date a watershed. From an official ecclesiastical point of view the worker-priests had passed into history, and a totally new phase of the apostolate would open. Of the original one hundred about two-thirds chose to remain at work living under the sanctions of the church. The remaining one-third laid down their tools in obedience to their bishops in the hope that a dialogue would produce some form of proletarian mission acceptable to both parties. The drama of the worker-priests continued after March 1, 1954; indeed, it continues still. However, with this date, the pioneer phase was definitively over.[48]

Different reasons had been advanced for their condemnation both by the bishops and by the worker-priests. They had divided over their perceptions of mission, the priesthood, *engagement* and cooperation with Marxists. Yet behind all this lay a deeper conflict based upon the incapacity of two different worlds to understand each other. Limoges worker-priests were right: "We cannot understand each other's speech. These are the problems of the proletariat, Monseigneur." It was never a question of good versus evil men. Both worker-priests and bishops were committed to the church's mission to the proletariat. Yet they had come to view this from different sides of a wide gulf. Perhaps the last word on the matter belongs to Cardinal Suhard whose haunting prophetic words five years after his death still described the tragedy of March 1, 1954. "There is a wall between the church and the working class." Rome had intervened to break the fragile bridge which the worker-priests had been erecting between Catholicism and the proletariat, or so it seemed. One hundred priests were forced to make an impossible choice, but it did not end there. Their unprecedented *présence* in the factories and proletarian ghettos of France and Belgium produced a profound impact upon their church and society that could not be reversed, an impact which has continued to the present day not only for the third world but for the industrial west as well.[49]

IX

THE IMPACT OF THE WORKER-PRIESTS

"The worker-priests were sundered in their living flesh . . .
assailed at the very root of their religious existence."
—Emile Poulat

The story of the worker-priests did not come to an end with the hierarchical condemnation of 1953 and 1954. That brief interlude of roughly four months merely brought to a close one chapter of their witness. It marked the end of the pioneer phase of their unique ministry. Certainly March 1, 1954 was a watershed, and although it intensified existing divisions and hurts, it could not erase the impact of the worker-priests—either at that time or in the years to come. Their witness and life was too profound for that. Not only did they stir the hearts of their contemporaries both in France and abroad; also they survived the events of 1953–1954 and a subsequent Vatican condemnation to become an acceptable mode of priesthood throughout the world in a post-Vatican II church. Today worker-priests, including a few of the pioneers, still toil at manual labor and, by so doing, provide for Christianity one paradigm of a liberating gospel for the industrial west.

Even initially the condemnation of the early 1950s could not obliterate their impact. The internal tension and conflict between the worker-priests and their bishops was never solely a private ecclesiastical battle. These clergy were already a public *présence* among those for whom they had dedicated their lives. From this perspective alone the route of silence could not be pursued if the church hierarchy recalled its apostles from their working class life. At the very least, the worker-priests had impacted upon the thousands of fellow laborers who shared their life of oppression. They could not slip quietly away into the night from the solidarity they had embraced.

However, it was not the proletariat's outcry that made the worker-priests a cause célèbre. The groundswell of protest came largely to the public eye through Catholic channels and through the secular mass media. Both the Vatican and French hierarchy proved incapable of damming the flow of protest from Catholic ranks. Initially the most overwhelming impact of the worker-priests was the massive support they received from the church's militant rank-and-file. This was most notable in the other missionary apostolates mandated by the church to penetrate the proletariat. Of course, there was no unanimity in their attitude toward the worker-priests. After all, for almost a decade there had been tension and conflict between a number of these laboring clergy and the other priests and laity they encountered in their daily life, whether from neighborhood parishes or from local units of the Jeunesse Ouvrière Chrétienne and Action Catholique Ouvrière. Consequently, one could expect this friction to emerge publicly in the wave of papal and episcopal censures.

The J.O.C. leadership, especially its chaplains, had been concerned from the beginning that the worker-priests were confusing the sacerdotal and lay mandates. Nevertheless, communication was maintained throughout the period between Catholic Action and the worker-priest apostolate. Information about their novel form of ministry would appear in Catholic Action reviews, and clergy engaging in manual labor would write occasional articles for these periodicals as well. Finally, official leaders of the various proletarian apostolates met from time to time for the express purpose of mutual understanding and cooperation.[1]

Nonetheless, these groups had not had sufficient time to resolve their divisions before the hierarchical interventions. As a result the J.O.C. leadership welcomed the church's decisions against the worker-priests but did so in light of the critiques it had offered earlier. In November, 1953 *Masses Ouvrières* published an editorial on the matter, warning that "the priest . . . even as a worker, remains a 'separated one': *segregatus!*" The implications for this were clear: "The *engagement* of the priest, no matter how profound it is, should never compromise the church's laity whose responsibility in this order is primary and irreplaceable." Officially, the Jeunesse Ouvrière Chrétienne made its position public by a twelve-page document which appeared in a special supplement of *Lettre aux Fédéraux* (March, 1954). In it, the controversy was outlined and the hierarchical rationale was quoted and defended. Beyond this, the J.O.C.'s national secretariat had sent a circular to all its federations with the January 19 episcopal letter attached.[2]

The very persistence of the J.O.C. executive in upholding the church's position is one indicator of how deeply much of its rank-and-file was committed to the worker-priests. One example of such Jociste support was a letter written by thirteen members from Saint-Brieuc. They felt that, as "Christians and militant workers" who toiled with both Marxists and worker-priests, they were in a good position to assess "the consequences of these . . . measures taken by the church." They suggested that attacking the worker-priests for their *engagement* was tantamount to undermining Jociste militants who were "*engagés* in the revolutionary syndicalism of the C.G.T." "Class struggle" was "one of the realities of our workers' life," they affirmed, and they were deeply critical of the church's panicked fear of "atheistic communism." Finally, they concluded that "the leaders of the church" condemned the worker-priests through "an ignorance of working class reality." J.O.C. militants throughout the industrial centers of France responded in kind, demonstrating that those who toiled directly with the worker-priests were usually their most enthusiastic supporters.[3]

The Action Catholique Ouvrière responded in much the same way as its younger counterpart. Its official position showed complete solidarity with the Vatican and episcopal decisions. In February, 1954 the A.C.O. National Office issued a letter to all its members on the matter. It stated the A.C.O.'s awareness of the agony caused by "the church's decision to recall the worker-priests," but it reminded its militants that the A.C.O. for a few years had cautioned against "certain forms of worker-priest *engagement*." Like the J.O.C. position, the A.C.O. executive warned that the respective missionary tasks of both clergy and laity dare not be confused. In spite of this united stance some of the A.C.O. leadership indicated overt support for the worker-priests. Its popular chaplain Maxime Hua was an open friend of these clergy and their activities. He admitted that excesses had been committed, but he insisted that "the worker-priests have never abandoned their missionary task for other so-called 'temporal' tasks." Some chaplains expressed their endorsement more strongly than Hua. Father Genelot, a Grenoble chaplain, applauded the laboring clerics for demonstrating "a new way to live the priesthood in a workers' way."[4] Another offered his praise in the following manner:

> I am an A.C.O. chaplain. With all my being I believe in the witness of these [A.C.O.] militants, of these neighborhood cells, but also I believe that the presence of priests sharing the workers' life is an indispensable sign of the church's affection for the workers.[5]

Within the A.C.O. it is much more difficult to determine the full extent to which the rank-and-file militants felt a solidarity with the worker-priests. Nevertheless, all indicators point to overwhelming support for these condemned clergy. The very anxiety of the organization's leadership with respect to its grass-roots response suggests that the A.C.O. masses were inclined to view the hierarchical anathema negatively. In addition, hundreds of militant workers took the time to send individually written testimonies to church leaders in frank support of the worker-priest ministry. Many of these labor activists criticized both the A.C.O. and the C.F.T.C. for their refusal to join the peace movement and cooperate with communists.[6] Their commitment to the worker-priest apostolate was stated bluntly as this one example demonstrates:

> Our Christian militant workers cannot make up for the absence of the priest from work. . . . It is necessary that the clergy come to discover again the working class where it exists: in the neighborhoods but also in the factories. To visit the factories does not constitute a sufficient opening. Equally it is necessary that, at least, the priest can have a union card in his pocket when he works.[7]

In some instances entire A.C.O. groups would publish documents, write letters or issue statements in solidarity with the worker-priests. The Christian workers of Montarello announced that "worker-priests" were necessary "in the working class" and that their "suppression" was public proof "that the church denies the workers' condition." At a public meeting held in Paris (February, 1954) an audience of largely Catholic proletarians assured the worker-priests that they could "count on [their] complete solidarity," and a communiqué by two hundred Catholic workers had this to say: "The worker-priests share our struggle; that is why the decision taken against them attacks each one of us deeply."[8] Although the leadership of specialized Catholic Action tended to echo the hierarchical opinion, the rank-and-file remained some of the most ardent defenders of this radical ministry.

The response of parish clergy to the worker-priest condemnation was mixed, but the missionary parishes found in the industrialized areas of France were quite often prepared to defend their colleagues employed in manual labor. Once again, it was those most intimately linked to the worker-priests and their lifestyle who rallied to their defense. Clergy from such diverse industrial concentrations as Grenoble, Lille, Longwy, Roubaix, Marseille and Dunkerque upheld the worker-priests before their bishops. Not surprisingly, priests from Paris and its red suburbs were quite vocal in expressing their solidarity with their condemned brothers. The well-known Daniel Pezeril and Louis Retif of Sacré-Coeur de Colombes were among their most noted parish supporters.[9]

At Marseille, a sizable number of parish clergy reacted with hostility when Msgr. Jean Delay closed the local worker-priest *équipe* in 1953. One suggested that "to suppress the worker-priests is to cut off the church from the working class," and the St. Louis sacerdotal team told their bishop: "We would like you to permit us to tell you how much we deplore this massacre which will deprive us . . . of incontestable links and enrichments." Jean Clairefond, the *curé* of Notre-Dame de Jerusalem, had this to say about the worker-priests: "I am a witness of their poor and sparse life, of their priestly dignity. I have for them a profound esteem and great friendship. Your position with respect to them cannot leave me without a reaction."[10]

Often support for worker-priests by parish clergy took the form of praise for their avant-garde ministry at the expense of the more traditional mode. They spoke of the "unbridgeable chasm" between the parish and the proletariat, and they lamented the "bourgeois culture" of its clergy. To combat this they advocated a worker-priest form of ministry. Paul Collet, a Toulouse *curé,* insisted that both the parish and the A.C.O. demanded the support of clerics who performed manual labor, and another traditional priest stated unequivocally that "the parish priest is vividly aware that many cannot be evangelized without the worker-priests." Certainly there were numerous *curés* who welcomed the hierarchy's actions against their more radical colleagues. Some of these had always been hostile to these avant-garde pioneers, but it is a testimony to the worker-priests' positive impact in their neighborhoods that so many of the parish priests with whom they worked mourned their passing and fought for their return.[11]

Echoes of solidarity were heard from other missionary apostolates as well. The Mission de France had always endorsed and participated in the worker-priest experience, and the Jesuit-based Action Populaire, though significantly more cautious, had commendable words for the controversial priestly pioneers. Jean Villain, the director of this apostolate for years, defended the hierarchical judgment, but he also expressed his hopes for some continuation of the worker-priest movement. Even the non-proletarian apostolates could not remain untouched by the conflicts surrounding the working clerics. *Jeunes Forces Rurales,* the periodical of the Jeunesse Agricole Chrétienne, published an article on the issues, and Catholic Action's student branch, the Jeunesse Etudiante Chrétienne, praised the worker-priests openly.[12]

Beyond the masses of all these missionary apostolates, the worker-priests were able to win the hearts of the most articulate and avant-garde thinkers found within the Catholic intelligentsia. This was especially true with respect to the noted progressive Dominican theologians. Both Yves Congar, and the director of Jeunesse de l'Eglise Maurice Montuclard were avid apologists of the worker-priests. The more cautious Congar was prepared to acknowledge the correctness of the hierarchical critique, but he insisted that "the church was with the workers" because of its avant-garde clergy. Montuclard was far less equivocal since the views he was publishing paralleled those the worker-priests lived. However, it was Marie-Dominique Chenu who was most affected by these men. From the beginning he had been one of their important vocal advocates. At the height of the public controversy he wrote an article in *Vie Intellectuelle* defending their priesthood. He argued that the hierarchical critique was too narrowly based upon classical models of the ordained ministry, models that were inapplicable to a missionary situation. "We refuse to limit the priesthood to these sacramental and cultic functions," he asserted, because these tasks apply only to an already established church. However, in a mission land the mandate was "to bring to this non-Christian world the witness (*témoignage*) of faith." That, he was convinced, was exactly what the worker-priests were doing. These voices of Dominican protest would pay a heavy price for their dissent; before the dust of controversy had settled, they would feel the disciplinary action of Rome.[13]

The world-renowned review of progressive Catholic thought *Esprit* manifested a position clearly in favor of the worker-priests. Jean-Marie Domenach, one of its editors, remembered fondly that he was "profoundly sympathetic" with their ministry. In retrospect, he called this solidarity "one of the greatest moments of my life." He had praised the beaten and arrested priests at the anti-Ridgway demonstration, and he was convinced that their ministry had "become a symbol for many of the world's Christians" who could not accept a god who served as "an emblem for one strategic and economic system." However, it was the prominent Catholic Jean Lacroix and the review's editor Albert Beguin who developed *Esprit's* apology for the worker-priests. Lacroix was prepared to acknowledge as valid some of the episcopal anxieties, but he insisted that "the existence of the worker-priests was necessary for the catholicity of the church." "Without them," he argued, "its universality would risk remaining abstract." Beguin was more blunt. For him, the removal of the worker-priests was "a pure and simple suppression of the worker mission" of which these clergy were the "archetypes."[14]

Other Catholic intellectuals felt constrained to offer their analyses as well. A Belgian priest Josse Alain wrote an essay in 1953 called *Jésus Incognito* which he described as a "support for the worker-priests being total workers while remaining totally priests." H. Daniel-Rops, a noted Catholic historian in France, defended the bishops but praised the clergy toilers as well. In a collection of articles written by prominent progressive Catholics, Jean-Robert Hennion wrote a piece in which he sought to see both sides of the controversy. Nonetheless, he was obviously sympathetic toward the worker-priests. Even many of their more conservative critics did not repudiate the basic form and intent of their mission. A case in point is Pierre Andreu. His *Grandeurs et erreurs des prêtres-ouvriers,* published in 1955, is a pointed critique of what he considered to be worker-priest excesses, but he retained his sympathy for the effort itself. "In its conception their mission was just," he concluded. "In its realization, it was a failure."[15]

In some instances Catholic intellectuals manifested group solidarity for the beleaguered worker-priests by going public with their protests. Two weeks before the March 1 deadline, a number of them participated in a mass meeting held at the Salle des Agriculteurs in Paris. Jean-Marie Domenach was one of the featured speakers. Out of this event came an open appeal asking the bishops to reconsider their decision in light of the negative effect such a condemnation would have on the church's proletarian mission. On their own, a group of mostly Catholic thinkers produced a manifesto which was printed in the great Parisian daily *Le Monde.* Included among the signators were J.-M. Domenach, Albert Béguin, the Lacroix brothers and the widow of Emmanuel Mounier.[16]

Many of these intellectuals were journalists by profession, and it was through their newspapers that the public was often informed about the worker-priests. The Catholic press was an absolutely critical means whereby the condemned clergy were brought to the attention of a wider audience. Georges Hourdin, perhaps France's most important Catholic journalist, used his newspapers to publish stories about this controversial clergy. In addition, he had fraternal ties with the Dominican worker-priests and had met with Henri Perrin on a number of occasions. However, the direct ties of his publishing house to the church prevented him from endorsing the worker-priests openly after they had been censured officially by the hierarchy. Nevertheless, he did write an article in the book *Problèmes du catholicisme Français* which praised them for their "sharing in the suffering of the world."[17]

Far less cautious in their enthusiasm for the worker-priests were the press organs of the Catholic left. The most unequivocal of these was the bimonthly *La Quinzaine*. Though a lay publication it utilized theological advisors, the most famous of these being M.-D. Chenu. However, this did little to enhance its credibility with ecclesiastical leadership. Since 1952 the leading prelates of France had regarded it with suspicion, and by mid-March, 1954 it had fallen under the anathema of the Vatican. Quite likely its condemnation can be linked to its solidarity with the worker-priests. As early as January, 1952 *La Quinzaine* was describing these clergy as "a silent *présence* of Christ in the world that he loved above all, that of the poor." This support continued for the next two years, culminating in a January 15, 1954 article called "Les Prêtres-ouvriers et la classe ouvrière." In it the following conclusion was reached: "Today the working class considers the worker-priests as a sign of sincerity in its regard. Upon their maintenance or their removal depends, in large measure, its openess to the . . . apostolic effort of the church."[18]

Though more cautious, the weekly *Témoignage Chrétien* was also an advocate of the worker-priests. This social democratic newspaper had been one of the few periodicals to print material about them before the controversy, and these were uniformly favorable. However, when the situation polarized in 1953 *Témoignage Chrétien* sought to take a mediating position. It published documents from both sides of the issue, but its own sympathies were displayed cautiously in the newspaper's editorials. Its almost 50,000 readers were reminded that "for millions of people the decisions made by the hierarchy with respect to the worker-priests are a source of scandal." Hence, summarized the same article, "we must say that the witness brought to people and particularly to Christians by the action of the worker-priests must not be lost."[19]

Somewhat surprising was the relatively positive attitude of *La Croix*. French Catholicism's quasi-official and most influential daily, with its circulation of more than 100,000, followed the strict episcopal line throughout the conflict, but it did not conceal the respect and affection it felt toward the worker-priests. Joseph Folliet, one of the church's well-known progressives, called them "an integral part, an essential element" of the church's mission to the proletariat. To be sure, the Catholic daily's editorials took an openly pro-hierarchical line, but the paper never degenerated into anti-worker-priest polemics as such. Émile Gabel, its editor-in-chief, wrote of the necessity for the church to act as it did, but he also asserted that the condemned clergy were "a hope" and "a symbol" for "the evangelizing of the workers' world." *La Croix* had come a long way from its conservative, even reactionary, heritage. Since the war, it had opened the door to some progressive voices, and in spite of its loyalty to the episcopal decisions, this new stance was most apparent in its public affection for the worker-priests.[20]

Finally, the conservative Catholic press addressed the issue as well. The weekly *France Catholique*, with a circulation comparable to *Témoignage Chrétien*, was the most important newspaper in this group. Chastened by its overt sympathies with Pétain's Vichy, it had abandoned its earlier reactionary shrillness for a more moderate rightist stance. It acknowledged that "the apostolate of the worker-priests" was "a grand undertaking" but reminded its readers that the hierarchy had "the last word" on these matters. Behind this support of the church's leaders, however, lay *France Catholique*'s own deep anxieties about communism. Anti-Marxism was the prism through which the Catholic right critiqued the worker-priests. There were, of course, other Catholic or Catholic-inspired newspapers more openly integrist and hostile to these priests, but with few exceptions, they had minimal circulations and had been rendered suspect by their collaborationist activities during the war. Although most of the specifically Catholic press was sympathetic to the experience and plight of the worker-priests, the extent of that endorsement varied from newspaper to newspaper. Regardless of the stance taken by this or that Catholic periodical, one fact could not be denied. The worker-priest apostolate and the controversy surrounding it was no longer a private issue. It had captured the attention of the general Catholic public, and this was in no small measure due to the efforts of the Catholic press.[21]

However, the impact of the worker-priests in France was far broader than that felt by the nation's Catholics. The hierarchy's decision could not be reduced to simply an internal church matter. It had become an issue for large numbers of militant workers and their organizations as well. Not surprisingly the French Communist Party had its own public opinion concerning the worker-priests and the cause célèbre surrounding them, an opinion fraught with ambiguity. At first, the Party was highly suspicious. Jeannette Vermeersch, wife of Party Secretary Maurice Thorez, suggested that the worker-priests were prepared to use proletarian rhetoric to divide the working class and lead it from revolutionary goals into reformist "bread-and-butter" issues. By the time of the hierarchical offensive the Parti Communiste had changed its tune. *L'Humanité*, the Party's daily, charged that the Vatican was dismantling its experiment because of the worker-priests' class solidarity against the capitalistic preferences of the church's prelates. Thus the Communists were able to combine their growing affection toward these clergy with their anti-Vatican cold war politics.[22]

Most importantly, it was the role played by the worker-priests in the C.G.T. at the militant grass-roots level which led the Party's leadership to laud and defend them. On occasion their protests against the C.F.T.C. and F.O. unions would be published in communist newspapers. Pressure from the C.G.T. rank-and-file had forced union and party leaders to take the worker-priests seriously, and when they did, they came to respect and trust them. That scenario was played out when Father Henri Barreau was elected secretary of the influential Union départementale de la Seine, one of the C.G.T.'s largest federations. Lucien Trilles, a militant communist and cégétiste, recalled a similar evolution in his native Midi. Jean Bratteau, a C.G.T. *permanent* in Paris since the late 1950s and a communist since his youth, spoke of his "excellent relationship" with the worker-priests whom he felt to be "an enrichment for the trade union movement."[23]

Most impressive, however, was the extent to which grass-roots workers themselves responded to the church's condemnation. Not only had they cleared the way for communist and C.G.T. acceptance of the worker-priests; also they had risen in large numbers to defend their clerical comrades during the dark years of 1953 and 1954. The solidarity demonstrated by Catholic workers, especially by militants in the A.C.O., has been noted already. Beyond this, hundreds of non-Christian proletarians went on record to join their Christian brothers and sisters in the name of the harassed worker-priests. A few examples demonstrate the poignancy of their pleas. "The worker-priests are the only ones [clergy] who are truly of our blood," said a Dunkerque worker, and two others called these clerics their "friends" and "brothers." A group of twenty-two proletarian mothers wrote the following passionate words to Cardinal Feltin: "We have two priests on our street who have shared our life for several years. They have come into our homes; they are true friends of ours. In seeing them struggle beside our husbands, we have come to believe that a greater justice and a durable peace are more accessible. . . . Also we know that this is the message which Christ came on earth to bring." No, the worker-priests were not on a lark. They had not taken a stroll through the proletariat. They had plummeted its very depths, beyond the safety of ecclesiastical boundaries, beyond formal Christian-Marxist dialogue and beyond the original forays of the 1940s, and in this *d'être avec* with proletarian life, both worker-priests and their newly discovered comrades touched each other deeply. The laboring clergy had left their mark upon the nation's workforce.[24]

Even the walls of the proletariat could not contain the full impact of the worker-priests after the Vatican had decided to condemn them.

Their cause reached the very halls of government. François Mauriac, a devout Catholic, a literary figure and frequent columnist for the great Parisian daily *Le Figaro,* was affected so profoundly by the worker-priests' condemnation that he stirred the public waters by suggesting a new concordat between France and the Holy See. His words, in addition to a growing public outcry, led to political debates on the propriety of the nuncio's intervening in French internal affairs. Pressure was put on the Foreign Ministry to protest the matter. Then Foreign Minister Georges Bidault recalled that he had no hand in the Vatican's decision, though he sympathized with it. The Communists were not convinced. They saw the condemnation of the worker-priests in the light of a broadly based cold war policy involving the United States, the Vatican and Bidault's governing M.R.P. However, until the necessary documents are made available to researchers, the role of the government in this affair will remain shrouded in mystery.[25]

Nonetheless, it was the mass media which made the worker-priests a national cause célèbre for the general public. In the year of the controversy alone almost nine hundred articles were published about them throughout France. Distortions were rampant, sensationalism was the order of the day, and partisan stances were taken by one and all. The fact remains, however, that the worker-priests had caught the press' attention, and that alone guaranteed that their experience and sorrow would become one of the great events of the day. Comments were made and articles written in such diverse papers as *L'Espoir* and *La Tribune* in St. Etienne, the Protestant newspaper, *Réforme, Rivarol, Le Populaire, Le Canard Enchaîné, L'Express, Samedi-Soir* and many others. Add to these the great Parisian dailies *l'Aurore, Combat, Le Figaro, Le Monde, Paris-Presse, La Croix* and *l'Humanité,* and one can see the full breadth of coverage given to the worker-priests in their hour of trial.[26]

By way of example *Le Monde* was favorable to these avant-garde clergy. It would follow the conflict from event to event, but its sympathy for the condemned men led it to suggest that behind the hierarchy's public rationale were unpublished fears emanating from the Vatican. The more conservative *l'Aurore* was hostile to the beleaguered priests. They were accused of giving "unwitting aid to Marxism" and of reducing their priesthood to partisan activism. For its part *Le Figaro* entrusted the worker-priest pilgrimage to François Mauriac. As a loyal and conservative Catholic this man of letters was prepared to accept the hierarchy's judgment, but he could not help but sing the praises of the worker-priests. "They are our pride," he stated, "and, to tell the truth, we cannot imagine a day in which they would be no longer."[27]

The world of fictional literature was also captivated by the worker-priests, both in France and abroad. To be sure this mode of expression led to some factual distortion, and doubtlessly most of these authors romanticized an experience which did not need it. Nevertheless, these works represent a powerful impact upon one societal sector often impervious to both ecclesiastical and proletarian issues. Beyond that, this literary output brought the worker-priest story into contact with a wider public. In the twenty-year period from 1943 to 1963 twelve novels were written on the subject as well as four plays, and a number of them were translated into several languages. Alain Jansen's *Il n'y aura qu'un visage* was a novel of a worker-priest caught in a bind similar to the actual crisis of 1954, and Daniel Pézeril's *Rue Notre Dame* told the story of an aging canon who found his entire ministry called into question by his encounter with a worker-priest. However, it was Gilbert Cesbron's best-selling novel about a worker-priest *Les Saints vont en enfer* which most captured the reading public. Published in 1952, it has sold almost 800,000 copies and has been translated into Spanish, Dutch, Italian, Portuguese, German and English. Among the plays written about the worker-priests are Fritz Hochwälder's *Sur la terre comme au ciel* (1952) and Costa du Rels' *Les Etendards du roi* (1956).[28]

Literary output was hardly the sole, let alone the most important, means whereby the worker-priests became known throughout the entire western world. Their novel missionary life had become a symbol and an issue for a wider public through religious and secular media as well. In the two decade period beginning in 1943, fully seventy-eight works were written about the worker-priests. These included twelve biographies, thirteen personal testimonies or memoirs, eleven spiritual or reflective works, seventeen histories (mostly of a partisan and popular nature), as well as the fictional titles mentioned above. Of these, twenty have been written in languages other than French, five in Italian and Spanish, four in German and English and two in Dutch. In addition, a number of prominent French works have been translated into several languages. Henri Perrin's *Itinéraire* has Italian, German and English editions, and his diary *Journal d'un prêtre ouvrier en Allemagne* has been translated into English, German, Italian and Czech. Another book, *Les Prêtres-Ouvriers,* a set of documents collected by priests who remained at the factories, sold not only twelve thousand copies; also it was translated into German and English. And all of this does not take into account the thousands of both religious and secular mass-media articles which appeared in France and abroad. Even a few documentary films have been shown on the subject.[29]

A brief sampling of the press found in the English-speaking west provides a flavor of the variety and breadth of interest shown toward the worker-priests. Quite naturally a number of British Catholic publications addressed the issue. Most thorough of these was the Dominican monthly *Blackfriars*. It defended the necessity of ecclesiastical action but had this to say in favor of the French radical clergy at issue: "The priest-workmen are witnesses searching out, for the future, the touchstones of grace in this atheistic milieu." Anglican publications gave attention to the controversy as well. *France, pays de mission?* was received with favor as was the Mission de Paris which grew out of its critical observations. Writing in *Spectator* the Anglican worker-priest Michael Gedge stated that it was "impossible not to sympathize with the French priests against the Vatican in this case."

So important was this avant-garde ministry to the Anglicans that a working panel was set up in 1963 so that British and French experts could share their experiences. *Priests and Workers,* the book which grew out of this discussion, called the French worker-priest apostolate "the most courageous and extensive experiment undertaken by any Christian church anywhere to bridge the gulf fixed since the nineteenth century between organized religion and the working class." The dialogue closed with this final appraisal by the Anglican suffragan bishop Edward Wickham: "Whenever the question of the church and the poor or the church and the workers is raised, the worker-priests of France will trouble the conscience of a comfortable church just as the poor man of Nazareth does himself."[30]

Some Canadian publications addressed worker-priest concerns as well. Since the French condemnation the Jesuit monthly *Relations* published articles concerning proletarian mission work in France and was an avid advocate of worker-priest ministries. In one article, the mission of René Giroux, a Windsor, Ontario worker-priest, was described. The more popular *Saturday Night,* published out of Toronto, described the worker-priest issue using the cold war rhetoric so prevalent in the North American mass media of the day.[31]

In the United States vast interest was displayed toward the worker-priests at a number of different levels. The great breadth of Catholic attention given to these clergy was not surprising. At the more academic level, a number of reviews addressed the issue. *Cross Currents,* voice of the avant-garde Catholic intelligentsia, published two articles on the subject, and Bertha Mugraver, who had spent some time in French industrial ghettos, wrote an article defending the worker-priests in the *American Catholic Sociological Review*. The Catholic mass media picked up on the issue as well. Surprisingly enough, the anti-Marxist tabloid of the Brooklyn diocese *The Tablet* dealt with the worker-priests in a nonpartisan more descriptive way. The popular

Catholic *The Commonweal* was not so reticent. Its 1949 article spoke of "the heroism of the worker-priest" which it likened to "the spirit of the early church." Even when the hierarchy condemned the experiment, *Commonweal* maintained its earlier respect. Although it upheld the church's decision, one of its articles hastened to add, "most of us would not be worthy of loosing the latchet of the shoes of these wholly dedicated men, some of whom are genuine saints." Articles by Sally Whelan Cassidy and Michael de la Bedoyere in the monthly *The Catholic World* echoed the stance of *Commonweal*, and the Jesuit weekly *America* was captivated equally by the French apostolate.[32]

American radical Catholicism was more inclined to side with the worker-priests in the controversy. Peter Maurin's and Dorothy Day's Catholic Worker movement, with its own lifestyle of radical poverty, was a case in point. Day herself was convinced that attacks on the avantgarde ministry were coming from "the rich and powerful" and that the priests had been doing precisely "what Jesus Christ Himself had told them to do." She concluded: "We still do not see why there should be such a furor in the church while the great mass of priests . . . go along wholeheartedly with Capitalism."[33]

Non-Catholics were interested as well. Among Protestant publications, the liberal and ecumenical *Christian Century* defended the worker-priests in glowing terms even in the midst of the Cold War. In over ten articles on the subject the well-known Protestant periodical critiqued the hierarchy and endorsed the condemned clergy. America's popular secular magazines picked up on the controversy also. Articles appeared in *Time, The New Yorker, Nation,* the social democratic *New Republic* and others. An especially thorough and balanced overview of the worker-priest movement appeared in *The New York Times Magazine* on December 26, 1965.[34]

Certainly the mass publicity given to the worker-priests, whether in France or abroad, was a mixed blessing. There were the inevitable distortions and romanticizings, and the men themselves were often the victims of publicity-seeking journalists. They were used by the press and often abused. Nevertheless, in spite of much misinformation, the worker-priests had impacted profoundly upon the western public during the years of the cause célèbre. The mountain of information disseminated about them is incontrovertible testimony to that.

Meanwhile that impact turned full circle coming to rest perhaps most heavily upon the protagonists themselves—the bishops and the worker-priests. The issues of 1954 would not go away, and *recherche* surrounding the question of how one could be totally priest and totally worker continued. The *soumis* became the French hierarchy's guide in this delicate issue while the episcopate's leadership sought to restore a worker priesthood without disobeying the will of Rome. Shortly after March 1, 1954 a number of bishops, including Cardinal Feltin, met at Bagneux to hear their obedient worker-priests present an apologetic for the necessity of missionary clergy doing manual labor. These views were presented a few days later in the presence of both Cardinals Feltin and Liénart. The road back to the factories had begun.[35]

In Paris soon thereafter Feltin sought to organize an entire proletarian mission throughout his archdiocese. He appointed Father Robert Frossard to coordinate this ambitious program. Archbishop Feltin called it the "Boucle de la Seine," and it was structured to include "the laity of the Action Catholique Ouvrière, the parish clergy and the priests who will again take up work." In the Nord, Cardinal Liénart concentrated his attention upon reorganizing the newly legal Mission de France and supporting the continuing work of the Mission de la Mer. Cardinal Gerlier of Lyon sought to save a worker-priest ministry by permitting his auxiliary bishop Alfred Ancel to set up a Prado *équipe* with priestly part-time laborers and lay brothers who toiled full-time at the factory.[36]

All of these efforts accomplished little. It was not the French hierarchy which needed convincing; it was Rome. Catholic radicalism continued to grow within the working class apostolates, and the Vatican's suspicions of these programs increased as well. Nevertheless, by 1959 Cardinal Feltin was convinced that enough time had elapsed for him to press a successful case at the Vatican for a return to full-time labor for his *prêtres au travail* ("priests at work"). He was wrong. Even a personal visit to the new pope John XXIII did not help. Within a month of his audience Feltin received a negative response to his request from Cardinal Pizzardo at the Holy Office. "Factory work is incompatible with the priestly life," declared the Vatican missive, and a series of arguments followed which were simply a repeat of the Holy See's logic in 1953 and 1954. The Pizzardo letter was a severe blow to those Catholics committed to a fully incarnational proletarian mission. Not only had Feltin's request been denied; also even those priests working part-time had to abandon their manual toil.[37]

However, the battle was not yet over. Cardinal Liénart took it to the halls of the Second Vatican Council. Bringing documentation prepared by the *soumis* worker-priests the aging prelate from Lille worked quietly and effectively to overturn the earlier papal decisions. With the help of bishops and worker-priests in attendance with him, he submitted a report to Pope Paul VI calling for a legitimization of the *prêtres au travail*. He won the support of the Pontiff, and even more important the Vatican Council itself endorsed this form of ministry in its document on the priesthood by a vote of 2,243 to 11. The worker-priests had been vindicated by church authority at the highest level.[38]

Meanwhile, the worker-priests, who in 1954 had become the *restés au travail*, took another road. For them the *recherche* continued as well, and this choice had its lasting impact also. In their case communication with the bishops was much more difficult. Often letters were exchanged, but these were filled habitually with misunderstanding and acrimony. The correspondence between Cardinal Gerlier and Joseph Gouttebarge and between Cardinal Feltin and Henri Barreau are two cases in point. Over the years attempts were made to break this impasse, but although hostilities had softened, a modus vivendi could not be reached. In spite of these communication difficulties the *restés au travail* sought to preserve their *équipes* and continue a collective *recherche*. Initially Jean-Marie Marzio maintained his national role as secretary, but with time, strategic divisions began to emerge. The more moderate group hoped to continue a dialogue with the institutional church, while the more radical priests felt that faith must be sought solely in the midst of proletarian life. As the years passed these men became immersed more and more in working class life. The demands of labor and struggle drew them further away from ecclesiastical life, but its mark upon them was there to stay. Some continued to write letters to their bishops; others met collectively to study social theology; and even those who became atheists retained an interest in the church's proletarian apostolates.[39]

In spite of their divergent paths both the *soumis* and *restés au travail* remained in fundamental accord. They were unanimous in their conviction that an effective sacerdotal *présence* in the proletariat demanded priests who worked full-time and were active in the organizations of the working class movement.

What about today? Have the worker-priests faded into history, or have they left an indelible mark which still impacts upon the present? There is the nearly unanimous conviction that they were a leading impetus to the birth and success of the Second Vatican Council and the spirit which emerged in its wake. Since Vatican II the Catholic Church has become increasingly militant in its espousal of the poor and oppressed, and there are those who feel that the worker-priests were vitally important in pioneering this trend. So many of the values and practices of current liberation theology in the third world found their precursors in the experience of these French and Belgian trailblazers. Their identification with the poor and oppressed, their methodology of *recherche,* their openness to Marxist analysis and activists, their increasing militancy in the cause of social justice, their more grass-roots notions of the church and their assessments of spirituality—all these were adopted to a striking degree by subsequent liberation theologians. In many instances, even the vocabulary of both groups has been the same. Although to a large extent the ties between the two are indirect, some French Catholic activists—Jean-Marie Domenach and Jacques Loew in particular—point to identifiable links between the pioneer worker-priests and their avant-garde distant cousins in Latin America.[40]

More specifically, the model of worker-priest ministries has been adopted throughout the industrialized west. Examples have been cited in Windsor, Ontario, and the Anglican Church in Britain has pushed forward with its own forms both in urban missions and on the high seas. A Canadian Anglican Daniel Heap worked in a factory as part of his religious vocation, and since 1976 the group PRROQ (prêtres, religieux et religieuses ouvrier(e)s du Québec) has practiced this unique form of ministry to manifest its and the church's solidarity with the proletariat. In all these instances, the French pioneers had served as role models.[41]

By the 1970s a growing number of American denominations began to pay increasing attention to this type of pastoral vocation. Almost ten per cent of the Episcopal Church's clergy was employed outside of the institutional church, and a number of these were involved in creative apostolates to the poor. The Methodists have had a Worker-Priest Task Force in their national Board of Missions, and the Metropolitan New York Synod of the Lutheran Church in America has a "Worker-Priest" ministry not unlike the French model almost four decades ago. These types of apostolates may be found in other industrial nations as well. Scotland, Japan, Italy, Spain and North Africa have them, and they have been in Germany for years.[42]

These experiences have inspired practical and pastoral studies which have led to further expansion of this sacerdotal form. Gregor Siefer of Germany expanded his thesis on the subject into a book called *The Church and Industrial Society: A Survey of the Worker-Priest Movement and Its Implications for the Christian Mission* (1960). Not only did he find this model of priesthood valid, but also he insisted that it was necessary for a church in a "state of mission" within the industrialized nations. Karl Reko, a Missouri Synod Lutheran pastor from the United States, conducted a study on worker-priest ministries in order to assess their feasibility for the seminary students which he taught. A Canadian Lutheran seminarian Fred Ludolph undertook a similar project to shed light on his own vocational pilgrimage. Finally the Vatican Council's "Decree on the Ministry and Life of Priests," which had validated the worker-priest apostolate once more, and a study by the World Council of Churches, which grew out of a 1971 Worker-Priests' conference, are further testimony to the impact these French pioneers made upon the entire Christian Church in the West.[43]

Last of all, in France itself the worker-priests have returned with full force. Since 1965, when only an initial twenty-five were allowed, the movement has expanded to over nine hundred, a full three per cent of the nation's Catholic clergy. All the initial obstacles placed before them by the hierarchy have been removed. They work full-time, they are active in the trade unions, and they have a Secrétariat National at Paris. This nationwide organization publishes a mimeographed periodical called *Courrier p.o.* which contains reports of its *équipes*. It describes national meetings, analyzes public events within the church and evaluates the continued experiences of its priests in proletarian life. Catholic Church publications, whether missionary or popular, still print articles about and interviews with worker-priests, and these pieces are uniformly positive.[44] Whether in France or elsewhere the worker-priests have left their mark, and they continue to do so. They have captured the hearts and visions of a wider public, and their living *recherche* has spawned a multitude of parallel missionary forms within the working class and among the poor.

Behind the specifics of worker-priest ministries, these pioneer clergy represent a paradigm of liberation thought and praxis for the industrial west. Few will deny the oppressive reality faced by the peasant and worker masses of the third world, but similar injustices are more easily hidden behind the productivity, technology and glitter of the western capitalistic democracies. Yet a closer examination of these nations reveals pockets of poverty and oppression not unlike those found in Latin America, Africa and southern Asia. Blacks, Hispanics and indigenous peoples come to mind immediately, but often forgotten are the men and women who make up the industrial work force. The western proletariat's occasional prosperity and trade union gains have obscured, on occasion, the grim and often unjust side of wage labor. Nonetheless, job insecurity, frequent lay-offs, unsafe working conditions, society's prejudice in favor of the business and professional classes, the vulnerability of one-industry towns and the massive shutdown of labor intensive sectors of the economy in the name of "high tech" capital investments all point to the life of oppression and injustice endured by the working class on a daily basis. These realities, from the hidden underside of our society, establish the relevance of a worker-priest ministry.

Such a model is only one paradigm among many that have taken root as a Christian response to the ravages of the Industrial Revolution. The North American social gospel, the pro-labor Catholic priests, the Catholic Worker movement, Cesar Chavez' farm laborers' union and the grass-roots labor-church alliance in Pittsburgh are other efforts in this direction, other examples of radical Christianity addressing itself to injustices experienced by the toiling classes. The Detroit Conference (1975) reissued the call: Christians of the white west must hear the cries of the poor and marginalized and struggle with them against their oppressors and for a world of peace and justice. A sacred memory of Christians fighting for human liberation must be recovered so that current believers might find historical roots which will inspire them to live out a gospel of emancipation. The Belgian and French worker-priests are one clear and significant example of that heritage. Their concrete impact has been assured. They have left a treasure of ideas and practices which have affected profoundly both the Christian church and sectors of the working class. As such, they were and are a paradigm of liberation for the industrial west.

This is the on-going legacy of those one hundred pioneers who were the first worker-priests. This has been the story of their pilgrimage. Those who are still alive prefer to remain anonymous. They seek and have sought a daily witness of *présence* and not the flashy notoriety of stars. As this book comes to a close a few of them continue to live their priestly vocation trudging to and from work, the rhythm of almost four decades, a working class lifetime. But whether they have remained practicing priests or have married and raised families, whether they work for the union after retirement or simply live on their small pensions, these men will be forever linked in a *communauté de destin* with that decade in which they were the church's pioneers within the proletariat. They have become immortal by that *recherche* which made them worker-priests forever "after the order of Melchizedek." To those who would follow in their steps, let them hear the words of Dorothy Day as one who knew their path: "The depth of the suffering of the world is measureless, a bottomless abyss, and our only approach to it is through the dark night of the soul, a taste of which the priest workmen of France are now having. God bless them all."[45]

BIBLIOGRAPHY

A. INTERVIEWS (WORKER-PRIESTS AND THEIR TEAMS)

Ancel, Monsignor Alfred, first worker-bishop. Private interview in Lyon, France, June 14, 1979.

Bardini, Aldo, worker-seminarian. Private interview in Bagnolet, France, May 10, 1980.

Barreau, Henri, worker-priest. Private interview in Gagny, France, May 16, 1979.

Bordet, Michel, worker-priest. Private interview in Simian-la-Rotonde, May 27, 1983.

Bouche, Albert, associated with the worker-priests. Private interview in Paris, May 13, 1983.

Bouyer, Louis, worker-priest in Fils de la Charité order. Private interview in Colombes, France, May 21, 1979.

Bureillier, Jean, worker-priest after 1954. Private interview in Lyon, France, June 14, 1979.

Cagne, Bernard, worker-priest. Private interview in Paris, France, June 21, 1979.

Chavanneau, André, worker-priest. Private interview in Limoges, France, May 31, 1983.

Chauveau, Bernard, worker-priest. Private interview in Boulogne-Billancourt, France, May 11, 1979.

Combe, Maurice, worker-priest. Private interview in Lyon, France, June 14, 1979.

Cottin, Jean, worker-priest. Private interview in Paris, France, June 17, 1980.

Courtoy, Albert, Belgian worker-priest. Private interview in Liège, Belgium, June 8, 1983.

Daniel, Yvan, co-author of *France, pays de mission?* and member of the Mission de Paris. Private conversation in Paris, France, May 14, 1979.

Depierre, André, worker-priest. Private interview in Montreuil, France, June 20, 1979.

Dillaye, R.P. Césaire, director of the Nanterre Capuchin worker-priest team. Private interview in Paris, France, May 14, 1979.

Flagothier, Louis, Belgian worker-priest. Private interview in Liège, Belgium, June 8, 1983.

Garnier, Yves, worker-priest. Private interview in Limoges, France, May 31, 1983.

Genthial, Gabriel, worker-priest. Private interview in Courbevoie, France, June 11, 1979.

Gray, Jean, worker-priest. Private interview in Auxerre, France, June 11, 1983.

Guichard, Albert, worker-priest. Private interview in Paris, France, June 21, 1983.

Guilbert, Paul, Prado worker-priest. Private interview in Venissieux, France, May 16, 1983.

Hollande, Jacques, superior and director of the Mission de Paris. Private interview in Paris, France, May 28, 1979.

Jaudon, Jacques, worker-priest. Private interview in Grenoble, France, June 15, 1983.

Jourjon, Antoine, worker-priest after 1954. Private interview in Lyon, France, June 14, 1979.

Lacroix, Bernard, Fils de la Charité worker-priest. Private interview in Grenoble, France, June 15, 1983.

Lafond, Michel, worker-priest after 1954. Private interview in Lyon, France, June 14, 1979.

Laval, Francis, worker-priest. Private interview in St. Etienne, France, May 19, 1983.

Legendre, Jean, Dominican worker-priest. Private interview in Plateau d'Assy, France, June 6, 1983.

Loew, Jacques, worker-priest. Private interview in Fribourg, Switzerland, May 14, 1980.

Olhagaray, Jean, worker-priest. Private interview in Paris, France, June 13, 1979.

Pacalet, Robert, worker-priest. Private interview in Lyon, France, July 5, 1979.

Pfaff, Robert, worker-priest. Private interview in Paris, France, June 10, 1983.

Piet, André, Dominican worker-priest. Private interview in Marseille, France, June 2, 1983.

Poulat, Emile, worker-priest. Private interview in Paris, France, May 20, 1983.

Riousse, Jacques, worker-priest. Private interview in Escarenne, France, June 3, 1983.

Robert, Joseph, Dominican worker-priest. Private interviews in Paris, France, June 27, 1979 and Hellemes, France, July 12, 1979.

Screppel, Jacques, Dominican worker-priest. Private interview in Hellemes, France, June 9, 1983.

Talé, Philbert, worker-priest. Private interview in Antony, France, June 1, 1983.

Tarby, Jean, Prado worker-priest. Private interview in Chartres, France, June 13, 1983.

Tiberghien, Bernard, worker-priest. Private interview in Dunkerque, France, June 12, 1980.

Vico, Francis, worker-priest. Private interview in Montluçon, France, May 24, 1980.

Vidal, François, worker-priest. Private interview in Marseille, France, June 2, 1983.

Volot, Jean, worker-priest. Mission de la Mer. Private interview in Paris, France, May 19, 1980.

B. OTHER INTERVIEWS

Augros, Louis, superior and director of the Mission de France seminary. Private interview in St. Symphorien-de-Lay, July 4, 1979.

Bédarida, Renée and François, Catholics in the Resistance. Private interview in Guelph, Ontario, Oct., 3, 1977.

Bidault, Georges, Catholic Resistance and M.R.P. leader. Private interviews in Paris, France, May 31, 1977 and May 18, 1979.

Blanquart, Louisette, J.O.C.F. and Communist militant. Private interview in Paris, France, June 22, 1979.

Body, Jean, A.C.O. leader. Private interview in Paris, France, June 8, 1977.

Boudot, René, J.O.C. and A.C.O. militant and friend of Robert Pfaff. Private interview near Longuyon, France, June 4, 1980.

Bratteau, Jean, C.G.T. militant. Private interview in Paris, France, June 19, 1980.

Cartayrade, Roger, J.O.C. leader. Private interview in Paris, France, July 6, 1979.

Chenu, Marie-Dominique, Dominican theologian. Private interview in Paris, France, May 15, 1979.

Congar, Yves, Dominican theologian. Private interview in Paris, France, May 15, 1979.

Couvreur, Gilles, Mission de France priest. Conversation in Paris, France, May 31, 1979.

Domenach, Jean-Marie, editor of *Esprit*. Private interviews in Paris, France, July 6, 1977 and May 17, 1979.

Duclos, Jacques, Communist Party leader. Private interview in Paris, France, May 7, 1973.

Frossard, Monsignor Robert, diocesan coordinator of missionary apostolates and auxiliary bishop of Paris. Private interview in Paris, France, July 2, 1979.

Hourdin, Georges, Catholic press leader. Private interview in Paris, France, June 21, 1979.

Hua, Maxime, A.C.O. chaplain. Private interview in Paris, France, May 9, 1979.

Jacquet, Joseph, J.O.C. and C.G.T. militant. Private interview in Lyon, France, June 14, 1979.

Laudrain, Maurice, Catholic Marxist of Popular Front period. Private interview in Paris, France, May 22, 1973.

Ludolph, Fred, Canadian Lutheran seminary student. Conversation in Waterloo, Ontario, Oct., 17, 1983.

LeSourd, Père Henri, secretary of Cardinal Suhard and Sulpician. Conversation in Paris, France, May 17, 1979.

Maire, Paul, A.C.O. chaplain. Private interview in Paris, France, June 8, 1977.

Moine, André, Communist Party leader. Private interview in Paris, France, June 13, 1977.

Mollard, Georges, missionary parish pastor. Private interview in Paris, France, June 5, 1980.

Montuclard, Maurice, leader of the movement Jeunesse de l'Eglise. Private interview in Lyon, France, June 14, 1983.

Nautin, Pierre, friend of worker-priests and historian of the early church. Private interview in Paris, France, June 19, 1980.

Perrot, Daniel, Mission de France professor and missionary parish priest. Private interview in Paris, France, May 10, 1979.

Pézeril, Monsignor Daniel, priest friend of the worker-priests and auxiliary bishop of Paris. Private interview in Paris, France, June 12, 1979.

Rémond, René, Catholic Action figure and historian. Private interview in Paris, France, May 22, 1979.

Trilles, Lucien, C.G.T. militant. Private interview in Avignon, France, May 26, 1980.

Vilette, André, J.O.C. leader. Private interview in Paris, France, June 15, 1980.

Villain, Jean, director of Jesuit Action Populaire. Private interview in Paris, France, June 6, 1979.

Vinatier, Jean, Mission de France priest. Private interview in Fontenay-sous-Bois, France, June 7, 1980.

C. UNPUBLISHED DOCUMENTS

Jeunesse Ouvrière Chrétienne, unpublished papers called "Prêtres-Ouvriers," n.d.
Mission de France: "Documents divers," 1949–1959. Fontenay-sous-Bois, France.
Mission de Paris: Private papers, 1943–1955. St. Denis, France.
Mission de Paris: Cahiers, 1955. St. Denis, France.
Private Papers:
> Bardini, Aldo, worker-seminarian, Bagnolet, France.
> Barreau, Henri, worker-priest, Gagny, France.
> Bouche, Albert, priest, Paris, France.
> Boudot, René, J.O.C. militant, Cons-la-Grandville, France.
> Combe, Maurice, worker-priest, St. Etienne, France.
> Flagothier, Louis, worker-priest, Liège, Belgium.
> Guilbert, Paul, worker-priest, Venissieux, France.
> Jaudon, Jacques, worker-priest, Grenoble, France.
> Laval, Francis, worker-priest, St. Etienne, France.
> Olhagaray, Jean, worker-priest, St. Jean de Luz, France.
> Pacalet, Robert, worker-priest, Lyon, France.
> Piet, André, worker-priest, Marseille, France.
> Screppel, Jacques, worker-priest, Hellemes, France.
> Vidal, François, worker-priest, Marseille, France.

D. PERIODICAL SOURCE MATERIAL

Action Catholique Etudiante (1952–1954).
Action Populaire (1908–1914, 1919–1939, 1945–1954), Jesuit social Catholic publications. Includes *Dossiers de, Revue de* and *Travaux de* . . .
America (1953–1954), Jesuit publication.
Association Catholique (1876–1908), Social Catholic periodical associated with Albert de Mun and René de la Tour du Pin.
L'Aube (1932–1940, 1944–1946), Christian Democratic and M.R.P. daily.
Avant-Garde (1944–1946), newspaper of the Jeunesses Communistes.
Blackfriars (1945–1954), Dominican publication, England.

Cahiers du Communisme (1946–1954), P.C.F. review.

Catholic Worker (1945–1954), U.S. Catholic radical newspaper.

Catholic World (1950–1954), U.S. Catholic publication.

Christian Century (1945–1954), liberal Protestant publication, U.S.

Chronique Sociale de France (1902–1914, 1919–1954), progressive social Catholic publication. Includes *Chronique du Sud-Est*.

Commonweal (1946–1954), liberal Catholic publication, U.S.

Conseil National (1942–1954), documents of national congresses of the Jeunesse Ouvrière Chrétienne (J.O.C.).

La Croix (1945–1954), most well-known French Catholic daily.

Documentation Catholique (1919–1939, 1945–1954), periodical collection of relevant materials on French and Vatican Catholicism.

Economie et Humanisme (1942–1954), publication of Father Lebret's research *équipe*.

Equipe Ouvrière (1940–1954), publication for J.O.C. militants.

Esprit (1932–1940, 1945–1954), progressive Catholic review founded by Emmanuel Mounier.

Etudes (1945–1954), French Jesuit publication.

Eveil Démocratique (1905–1910), newspaper of Marc Sangnier's Sillon.

Force Ouvrière (1945–1954), newspaper of the faction, then the union C.G.T.-F.O.

Forces Nouvelles (1952–1954), M.R.P. publication.

France Catholique (1944–1954), conservative Catholic newspaper.

France Nouvelle (1945–1954), newspaper of the P.C.F.

France-Soir (1946–1954), sensationalist press, Parisian daily.

L'Humanité (1940–1954), major daily of the P.C.F.

Jeunes Forces Rurales (1952–1954), newspaper of the Jeunesse Agricole Chrétienne.

Jeunesse de l'Eglise (1943–1953), cahiers and bulletins of Maurice Montuclard's *équipe*.

Jeunesse Ouvrière (1930–1954), popular newspaper of the J.O.C.

Lettre aux Aumôniers (1938–1952), publication for Catholic Action chaplains.

Lettre aux fédéraux (1941–1954), publication for heads of J.O.C. federations.

Lettres aux communautés (1945–1954), publication of the Mission de France. Includes *Unis pour . . .*

Masses Ouvrières (1943–1954), review for Catholic Action chaplains, Action Catholique Ouvrière.

Paris-Presse-Intransigéant (1946–1954), sensationalist press, Parisian daily.

Le Peuple (1945–1954), publication of the C.G.T.

La Quinzaine (1952–1954), leftist Catholic newspaper.

Relations (1950–1970), Jesuit publication, Canada.

Le Sillon (1899–1910), review of Sangnier's Sillon.

Spectator (1945–1954), British publication.

Le Syndicalisme (1933–1940, 1944–1954), newspaper of the C.F.T.C. Includes *Syndicalisme Chrétien*.

Tablet (1952–1954), New York Catholic newspaper.

Témoignage (1945–1954), newspaper of the Action Catholique Ouvrière (A.C.O.). Includes *Pages Sprirituelles*.

Témoignage Chrétien (1945–1954), progressive Catholic Resistance newspaper.

Terre Humaine (1952–1954), publication of the M.R.P.

Time (1945–1954), Canadian edition.

Vie Catholique (1924–1938), pluralistic newspaper for progressive Catholics.

Vie Intellectuelle (1945–1954), Dominican theological review.

Vie Ouvrière (1940–1954), newspaper of the C.G.T.

Vie Spirituelle (1945–1954), progressive Dominican review.

E. BOOKS AND ARTICLES

Abell, Aaron I. *American Catholicism and Social Action.* Garden City, N.Y.: Hanover House, 1960.

Allen, Lewis. "Resistance and the Catholic Church in France" in Hawes, Stephen and White, Ralph, eds. *Resistance in Europe: 1933–1945.* Baltimore: Penguin Books, 1976.

Allen, Richard. *The Social Passion.* Toronto: University Press, 1973.

Alzin, Josse. *Jésus Incognito.* Paris: Téqui, 1953.

Ancel, Alfred. *Cinq ans avec les ouvriers.* Paris: Centurion, 1963.

Andreu, Pierre. *Grandeurs et erreurs des prêtres-ouvriers.* Paris: Amiot-Dumont, 1955.

———. *Histoire des prêtres-ouvriers.* Paris: Nouvelles Editions Latines, 1960.

Anglade, Jean. *Le Chien du Seigneur.* Paris: Plon, 1952.

———. *Les Greffeurs d'orties.* Paris-Genève: La Palatine, 1958.

"Après la mort de Michel Favreau." *Semaine Religieuse de Bordeaux* (Apr., 1951), 1.

Arnal, Oscar L. *Ambivalent Alliance: The Catholic Church and the Action Française, 1899–1939.* Pittsburgh: University Press, 1985.

———. "Beyond the Walls of Christendom." *Contemporary French Civilization* VII, 1 (Fall, 1982), 41–62.

————. "Catholic Roots of Collaboration and Resistance in France in the 1930s." *Canadian Journal of History/Annales Canadiennes d'Histoire* XVII, (Apr., 1982), 87–110.

————. "A Missionary 'Main Tendue' toward French Communists: The 'Témoignages' of the Worker-Priests, 1943–1954." *French Historical Studies* XIII, 4 (Fall, 1984), 529–56.

————. "The Nature and Success of Breton Christian Democracy." *Catholic Historical Review* LXVIII, 2 (Apr., 1982), 226–48.

————. "Stillborn Alliance: Catholic Divisions and the Main Tendue." On-Demand Supplement of the *Journal of Modern History.* Chicago, Mar., 1979, D1001–27.

————. "Why the French Christian Democrats Were Condemned." *Church History* 49, 2 (June, 1980), 188–202.

Augros, Louis. *De l'église d'hier à l'église de demain.* Paris: Cerf, 1980.

Aumont, Michèle. *Les Dialogues de la vie ouvrière.* Paris: Spes, 1953.

Barbieri, Frane. *Organizzazione cattolica.* Florence: Parenti, 1957.

Barnes, Samuel H. "The Politics of French Christian Labor." *Journal of Politics* 21 (Feb., 1959), 105–22.

Barthélemy-Madaule, Madeleine. *Marc Sangnier (1873–1950).* Paris: Seuil, 1973.

Bastié, Jean. *La Croissance de la banlieue Parisienne.* Paris: Presses Universitaires de France, 1964.

Baum, Gregory. *Catholics and Canadian Socialism.* Toronto: Lorimer, 1980.

————. *The Priority of Labor.* New York: Paulist Press, 1982.

————. *The Social Imperative.* New York: Paulist Press, 1979.

———— and Cameron, Duncan. *Ethics and Economics.* Toronto: Lorimer, 1984.

Bédarida, Renée. *Les Armes de l'esprit. "Témoignage Chrétien" (1941–1944).* Paris: Editions Ouvrières, 1977.

Benda, Julien. *The Treason of the Intellectuals.* New York: W.W. Norton & Co., 1956 (1928).

Bergeron, André. *Confédération Force Ouvrière.* Paris: EPI, 1971.

Bergounioux, Alain. *Force Ouvrière.* Paris: Seuil, 1975.

Berthe, Léon-Noël. *JOC, je te dois tout.* Paris: Editions Ouvrières, 1980.

Beschet, Paul. *Mission en Thuringe.* Paris: Editions Ouvrières, 1947.

Bleitrach, Danielle, et al. *Classe ouvrière et social-démocratie: Lille et Marseille.* Paris: Editions sociales, 1981.

Bloch, Marc. *Strange Defeat.* New York: Oxford University Press, 1949.

Boland, Charles. *Dure Percée.* Brussels: Foyer Notre Dame, 1968.

————. "Prêtres en milieu de travail." *Evangéliser* (Mar., 1947), 438–52.

Bosworth, William. *Catholicism and Crisis in Modern France*. Princeton, N.J.: University Press, 1962.

Boulard, Fernand. *Essor ou déclin du clergé français*. Paris: Cerf, 1950.

————. *An Introduction to Religious Sociology*. Translated by M.J. Jackson. London: Darton, Longman and Todd, 1960.

————. *Problèmes missionnaires de la France rurale*. Paris: Cerf, 1945.

Bouscaren, Anthony T. "Origins of French Christian Democracy." *Thought* XXI, (Win., 1956–1957), 542–66.

Bousquet, Hadrien. *Hors des barbelés*. 2nd edition. Paris: Spes, 1945.

Bouvier, Pierre. *Travail et expression ouvrière*. Paris: Galilée, 1980.

Breunig, Charles. "The Condemnation of the Sillon." *Church History* 26 (Sept., 1957), 227–44.

Bron, Jean. *Histoire du mouvement ouvrier français*. 3 vol. Paris: Editions Ouvrières, 1968.

Brown, Robert McAfee. *Theology in a New Key*. Philadelphia: Westminster Press, 1978.

Brugerette, J. *Le Prêtre français et la société contemporaine*. 3 vol. Paris: P. Lethielleux, 1935–1938.

Bruhat, Jean. *Histoire du mouvement ouvrier français*. Vol. 1. Paris: Editions Ouvrières, 1968.

Byrnes, Robert F. "The French Christian Democrats in the 1890s." *Catholic Historical Review* 36, 4 (Oct., 1950), 286–306.

"Cahiers mensuels des futurs prêtres." *Servir* (July, 1943), 588–91.

Caillot, Robert. *L'Usine: la terre et la cité*. Paris: Editions ouvrières, 1958.

Caire, Guy. *Les Syndicats ouvriers*. Paris: Presses Universitaires de France, 1971.

Callot, Emile-François. *Le Mouvement républicain populaire*. Paris: M. Rivière, 1978.

Camp, Richard L. *The Papal Ideology of Social Reform: A Study in Historical Development, 1878–1967*. Leiden: E.J. Brill, 1969.

Cantril, Hadley. *The Politics of Despair*. New York: Collier Books, 1962.

Caron, Jeanne. *Le Sillon et la Démocratie chrétienne, 1894–1910*. Paris: Plon, 1967.

Cesbron, Gilbert. *Les Saints vont en enfer*. Paris: R. Laffont, 1952.

Chansou, Joseph. *Sous l'épiscopat du cardinal Saliège, 1929–1956*. Toulouse: J. Chansou, 1978.

Une Charité inventive. Paris: Centurion, 1975.

Chenu, M.-D. *La "Doctrine Sociale" de l'église comme idéologie*. Paris: Cerf, 1979.

————. *Pour une théologie du travail*. Paris: Seuil, 1954.

Chombart de Lauwe, P. *La Vie quotidienne des familles ouvrières*. Paris: Centre National de la Recherche Scientifique, 1956.

Christophe, Paul. *Les Catholiques et le Front Populaire*. Paris: Desclée, 1979.

Chronique des prêtres-ouvriers. Paris: Editions universitaires, 1963.

Coady, M.M. *Masters of Their Own Destiny*. New York: Harper and Row, 1967.

Cogley, John. "They Are Priests and Workers Both." *New York Times Magazine*. Dec. 26, 1965, 6–7, 33–36.

Collinet, Michel. *Essai sur la condition ouvrière*, 1951.

Collonge, André. *Le Scandale du XXe siècle et le drame des prêtres-ouvriers*. Paris: Oliver Perrin, 1957.

Combe, Maurice. *L'Alibi*. Paris: Gallimard, 1969.

Congar, Yves. *Vrai et fausse réforme dans l'Eglise*. Paris: Cerf, 1950.

Coninick, Léon de. "Les Conversations de Dachau." *Nouvelle Revue Théologique* (Nov., 1945), 1169–83.

Costa du Rels, Adolfo. *Les Etendards du Roi*. Paris: Plon, 1956.

Courrier p.o., May, 1980.

Coutrot, Aline and Dreyfus, François. *Les Forces religieuses dans la société française*. Paris: Armand Colin, 1965.

Cronin, John F. *Catholic Social Principles*. Milwaukee: Bruce, 1950.

Daniel, Yvan. *Aux frontières de l'église*. Paris: Cerf, 1978.

———. *Témoignages sur l'abbé Godin*. (Liège: Pensée Catholique, 1946) in *Etudes Religieuses*, no's. 575–576.

Daniel, Yvan and Le Mouel, Gilbert. *Paroisses d'hier, paroisses d'aujourd'hui*. Paris: Grasset, 1957.

Daniélou, Jean. "Mission chrétienne et mouvement ouvrier." *Bulletin du cercle St. Jean Baptise* (Feb., 1950), 1–4.

Dansette, Adrien. *Destin du Catholicisme français (1926–1956)*. Paris: Flammarion, 1957.

Darbon, Michel. *Le Conflit entre la droite et la gauche dans le Catholicisme français 1830–1953*. Toulouse: Privat, 1953.

Dariel, Jean-Loup. *Chez les prêtres-ouvriers*. Paris: Frédéric Chambriand, 1950.

Day, Dorothy. *Loaves and Fishes*. New York: Harper and Row, 1983 (1963).

Debès, Joseph. *Naissance de l'Action Catholique Ouvrière*. Paris: Editions Ouvrières, 1982.

Delbrêl, Madeleine. *Nous autres, gens des rues*. Paris: Seuil, 1966.

———. *Ville marxiste, terre de mission*. Paris: Cerf, 1957.

Deliat, Roger. *Vingt ans chez Renault*. Paris: Editions ouvrières, 1973.

Denniston, Robin, ed. *Part Time Priests? A Discussion*. London: Skeffington, 1960.

Deroo, André. *L'Episcopat français, 1930–1954*. Paris: Bonne Presse, 1955.

Deygas, Gérard. *La C.F.T.C., cinquante ans d'histoire*. Paris: Gérard Deygas, 1969.

Dillard, Contre-Amiral. *La Vie et la mort du R.P. Dillard*. Paris: Oeuvres Françaises, 1947.

Dillard, Victor. *Suprême Témoignage*. Paris: Spes, 1946.

Di Nola, Alfonso M. *Cristo in tuta*. Parme: U. Guanda, 1955.

Dolléans, Edouard and Dehove, Gérard. *Histoire du travail en France*. Paris: Editions Domat Montchréstien, 1955.

Domenach, Jean-Marie and Montvalon, Robert de. *The Catholic Avant-Garde: French Catholicism since World War II*. New York: Holt, Rinehart and Winston, 1967.

Doncoeur, R.P. Paul. *La Crise du sacerdoce*. Paris: Flammarion, 1932.

Dorr, Donal. *Option for the Poor: A Hundred Years of Vatican Social Teaching*. Maryknoll, N.Y.: Orbis Books, 1983.

Droulers, Paul. *Politique sociale et christianisme: le Père Desbuquois et l'Action Populaire*, I–II. Paris: Editions Ouvrières, 1969–1981.

Dumortier, Francis and Biteau, Roger. "Depuis 1944, les prêtres-ouvriers." *Masses Ouvrières* (June, 1979), 29–41.

Duquesne, Jacques. *Les Catholiques français sous l'occupation*. Paris: Grasset, 1966.

———. *Les Prêtres*. Paris: Grasset, 1965.

Duroselle, Jean-Baptiste. *Les Débuts du Catholicisme social en France (1822–1871)*. Paris: Presses Universitaires de France, 1951.

Duthoit, Eugène. *Le Catholicisme, lien social*. Paris: Spes, 1929.

———. *L'Economie au service de l'homme*. Paris: Flammarion, 1932.

———. *Vers une économie ordonnée*. Lyon: Chronique Sociale de France, 1932.

Economic Justice. New York: Division for Mission in North America, Lutheran Church in America, 1980.

Edwards, David L., ed. *Priests and Workers*. London: SCM Press, 1961.

Ehrmann, Henry W. *French Labor from Popular Front to Liberation*. New York: Oxford University Press, 1947.

Einaudi, Mario and Goguel, François. *Christian Democracy in Italy and France*. Notre Dame, Ind.: University of Notre Dame Press, 1952.

Elbow, Matthew H. *French Corporative Theory*. New York: Columbia University Press, 1953.

Evensen, Norma. *Paris: A Century of Change, 1878–1978*. New Haven: Yale University Press, 1979.

Fabrègues, Jean de. *Le Sillon de Marc Sangnier*. Paris: Perrin, 1964.

Faupin, Jacques. *La Mission de France.* Paris: Casterman, 1960.

Fauvet, Jacques. *Histoire du Parti Communiste Français.* Paris: Fayard, 1977.

Fauvet, Jacques. *La IVe république.* Paris: Fayard, 1959.

Flory, Albert. *Albert de Mun.* Paris: Bonne Presse, 1941.

Fogarty, Michael P. *Christian Democracy in Western Europe, 1820–1953.* Notre Dame, Ind.: University Press, 1957.

Fremantle, Anne, ed. *The Papal Encyclicals in Their Historical Context.* New York: New American Library, 1956.

Freire, Paulo. *Pedagogy of the Oppressed.* Trans. by Myra Ramos. New York: Seabury, 1968.

Frémontier, Jacques. *La Forteresse ouvrière Renault.* Paris: Fayard, 1971.

Fridenson, Patrick. *Histoire des usines Renault.* 2 vol. Paris: Seuil, 1972.

Galenson, Walter. *Trade Union Democracy in Western Europe.* Berkeley: University of California Press, 1961.

Gelin, Joseph. *Nüremberg, 1943–1945. L'Expérience d'un prêtre-ouvrier.* Seine: Petit-Clamart, 1946.

George, Pierre. *Géographie économique: La Métallurgie du fer.* Paris: Centre de Documentation Universitaire, n.d.

———. *La Ville.* Paris: Presses Universitaires de France, 1952.

Gerrell, Frank. "Paris Dispatch." *New Republic.* Apr. 5, 1954, 6.

Glorieux, Palémon. *Un Homme providentiel.* Paris: Bonne Presse, 1946.

Godin, Henri. *L'Aumônier et la mystique préjociste,* 1936.
> *Le Christ dans la construction du foyer,* 1943.
> *Jeunesse qui reconstruit,* 1942.
> *Missel jociste,* 1937.

Godin, Henri and Daniel, Yvan. *La France pagan? The Mission of Abbé Godin.* Translated by Maisie Ward. London: Sheed and Ward, 1950.

Godin, Henri and Daniel, Yvan. *France, pays de mission?* Paris: Abeille, 1943.

Goguel, François. *France under the Fourth Republic.* Ithaca, N.Y.: Cornell University Press, 1952.

Graham, B.D. *The French Socialists and Tripartisme, 1944–1947.* Toronto: University Press, 1965.

Grandmesnil, Georges. *Action Catholique et S.T.O.* I–II. Paris: Editions Ouvrières, 1947.

Groussard, Serge. *L'Homme de la nuit.* Paris: Palatine, 1957.

Guéry, Louis. *Vendredi Saint tous les jours.* Fontenay-le-Comte: Lussaud, 1947.

———. *Volontaire pour le Christ.* Angers: H. Siraudeau, 1948.

Gugliellmi, J.-L. and Perrot, M. *Salaires et revendications sociales en France, 1944–1952*. Paris: Armand Colin, 1952.

Guitton, Georges. *Léon Harmel*. 2 vol. Paris: Spes, 1927.

Hamilton, Richard F. *Affluence and the French Worker in the Fourth Republic*. Princeton, N.J.: University Press, 1967.

Handy, Robert T., ed. *The Social Gospel in America, 1870–1920*. New York: Oxford University Press, 1966.

Harmel, Léon. *A Key to Labor Problems*. London: Catholic Truth Society, 1896.

———. *Manual d'une corporation chrétienne*. Tours: Alfred Mame et fils, 1876.

Heer, Friedrich. "The Priest-Workers in France." *Cross Currents* IV, 3 (Spr.-Sum., 1954), 262–74.

Hellman, John. *Emmanuel Mounier and the New Catholic Left, 1930–1950*. Toronto: University Press, 1981.

———. "French 'Left Catholics' and Communists in the 1930s." *Church History* XLV (Dec., 1976), 507–23.

———. *Simone Weil*. Waterloo, Ont.: Wilfrid Laurier University Press, 1982.

———. "Vichy Background." On-Demand Supplement of *Journal of Modern History*. Chicago: University Press, 1977.

Hennion, Jean-Robert, ed. *Problèmes du catholicisme français*. Paris: Julliard, 1954.

Hochwälder, Fritz. *Sur la terre comme au ciel*. Paris: Table ronde, 1952.

Hodiak, Bohdan. "Prophets in Steeltown." *The Christian Century*. May 8, 1985, pp. 460–462.

Hoffman, Stanley, et al. *In Search of France*. New York: Harper and Row, 1963.

Hoog, Georges. *Histoire du Catholicisme social en France, 1871–1931*. Paris: Doumat, 1946.

Hourdin, Georges. *La Presse Catholique*. Paris: Arthème Fayard, 1957.

Hoyt, Michael. "How to Make Steel: Agitate and Organize." *Christianity and Crisis* March 4, 1985, pp. 62–65.

———. "In Pennsylvania's Steel Valley, Churches Assail Bank about Vanishing Jobs." *National Catholic Reporter*. September 23, 1983.

"Il y a dix ans mourait le cardinal Suhard." *Informations Catholiques Internationales* (May 1, 1959), 13–24.

Irving, R.E.M. *Christian Democracy in France*. London: Allen and Unwin, 1973.

Isambert, F.-A. *Christianisme et classe ouvrière*. Paris: Casterman, 1960.

Jansen, Alain. *Il n'y aura qu'un visage*. Paris: Julliard, 1954.

Jarlot, Georges. *Doctrine pontificale et histoire*. Rome: Presses de l'Universitaire grégorienne, 1964.

Jeanneney, Jean-Noël. *François de Wendel en République*. 3 vol. Paris: Champion, 1976.

Just, Bela. *En la Mission de Paris*. Saint-Sébastien: Dinor, 1954.

Kedward, H.R. *Resistance in Vichy France*. Oxford: University Press, 1978.

Kee, Alistair, ed. *A Reader in Political Theology*. Philadelphia: Westminster, 1974.

Kothen, Robert. *The Priest and the Proletariat*. Translated by Frank Maher. New York: Sheed and Ward, 1950.

Larkin, Maurice. *Church and State after the Dreyfus Affair*. London: Macmillan, 1974.

Latreille, André. *De Gaulle, la Libération et l'église*. Paris: Cerf, 1978.

———. *Histoire de Lyon et du lyonnais*. Toulouse: Privat, 1975.

Launay, Michel. "La Crise du Sillon dans l'été 1905." *Revue Historique* 498 (Apr.–June, 1971), 393–426.

Le Bas, Maurice. *Pierre de Porcaro, prêtre-ouvrier, mort à Dachau (1904–1945)*. Paris: Lethielleux, 1948.

Le Bras, Gabriel. *Etudes de sociologie religieuse*. 2 vol. Paris: Presses Universitaires de France, 1955–1956.

Le Bras, Gabriel. *Introduction à l'histoire de la pratique religieuse en France*. 2 vol. Paris: Presses Universitaires de France, 1942–1945.

Lebret, Louis-Joseph. *Guide pratique de l'enquête sociale*. Paris: Presses Universitaires de France, 1952.

———. *Les Professions maritimes à la recherche du bien commun*. Paris: Dunod, 1939.

Leclerq, Jacques. "Holiness and the Temporal." *Cross Currents* IV, 4 (Win., 1954), 92–108.

Lemire, Jules. *Le Travail de nuit des enfants dans les usines à feu continu*. Paris: Alcan, 1911.

Lepp, Ignace. *Le Monde chrétien et ses malfaçons*. Paris: Aubier, 1956.

"Letter from Paris". *New Yorker*. Oct. 24, 1953, 78–79.

Levard, Georges. *Chances et périls du syndicalisme chrétien*. Paris: Arthème Fayard, 1955.

Lhande, Pierre. *Le Christ dans la banlieue*. Paris: Plon, 1927.

Loew, M.-R. *Les Dockers de Marseille*. L'Arbresle: Economie et Humanisme, 1945.

———. *Journal d'une mission ouvrière*. Paris: Cerf, 1959.

———. *Mission to the Poorest*. Translated by Pamela Carswell. London: Sheed and Ward, 1950.

Lorwin, Val. R. *The French Labor Movement*. Cambridge: Harvard University Press, 1954.

Lubac, Henri de. *Catholicisme*. Paris: Cerf, 1952.

McManners, John. *Church and State in France, 1870–1914*. New York: Harper and Row, 1972.

Maitre, Jacques. "Les Sociologies du Catholicisme français." *Cahiers International de Sociologie* XXIV (Jan.–June, 1958), 104–24.

Maritain, Jacques. *Integral Humanism*. Translated by Joseph Evans. New York: Scribner's, 1936.

Marteaux, Jacques. *L'Eglise de France devant la révolution marxiste*. 2 vol. Paris: Table Ronde, 1958–1959.

Martin, Benjamin F. Jr. *Count Albert de Mun*. Chapel Hill: University of North Carolina Press, 1978.

Mayeur, Jean-Marie. *Un Prêtre démocrate: l'abbé Lemire (1853–1928)*. Tournai: Casterman, 1968.

Merrien, Jean. *Missionnaire de la mer*. Paris: Table Ronde, 1953.

Michel, René, ed. *Zwischen Abfall und Bekehrung. Abbé Godin und eine Pariser Mission*. Offenburg: Dokumente Verlag, 1950.

Michonneau, Georges. *The Missionary Spirit in Parish Life*. Westminster, Md.: Newman Press, 1952.

———. *Revolution in a City Parish*. Translation of *Paroisse, communauté missionnaire*. London: Blackfriars, 1949.

——— and Meurice, R. *Catholic Action and the Parish*. Translated by Edmond Bonin. Westminster, Md.: Newman Press, 1955.

Minces, Juliette. *Le Nord*. Paris: François Maspero, 1967.

Minguet, René. *Géographie industrielle de Paris*. Paris: Hachette, 1957.

Montuclard, Maurice. *Conscience religieuse et démocratie*. Paris: Seuil, 1963.

———. *Les Evenements et la foi*. Paris: Seuil, 1951.

———. "Aux origines de la démocratie chrétienne." *Archives de Sociologie des Religions* 6 (July-Dec., 1958), 47–89.

Moody, Joseph N., ed. *Church and Society: Catholic Social and Political Thought and Movements, 1789–1950*. New York: Arts, Inc., 1953.

Moody, Joseph N. "The Dechristianization of the French Working Class." *Review of Politics* 20 (Jan., 1958), 46–69.

Moon, Parker Thomas. *The Labor Problem and the Social Catholic Movement in France*. New York: Macmillan, 1921.

Moore, Robert Samuel. *Pit-men, Preachers and Politics*. London: Cambridge University Press, 1974.

Morelli, A.G. *Terre de détresse*. Paris: Bloud et Gay, 1947.

Mounier, Emmanuel. *Oeuvres*. 4 vol. Paris: Seuil, 1961.

Mouriaux, René. *La C.G.T.* Paris: Seuil, 1982.

Mugraver, Bertha. "Variations in Pastoral Role in France." *American Catholic Sociological Review* 11 (Mar., 1950), 15–24.

Mun, Albert de. *La Conquête du peuple.* Paris: P. Lethielleux, 1908.

———. *Ma vocation sociale.* Paris: P. Lethielleux, 1908.

———. *La Question sociale, sa solution corporative.* Reims: n.d.

Murphy, Francis J. "La Main Tendue." *Catholic Historical Review* 60,2 (July, 1974), 255–70.

Noguères, Henri, et al. *Histoire de la Résistance en France.* 4 vol. Paris: Laffont, 1967–1976.

O'Brien, David J. *American Catholics and Social Reform.* New York: Oxford University Press, 1959.

Osgood, Samuel. *The Fall of France.* Boston: Heath, 1965.

Ott, Barthelemy. *Georges Bidault, l'indomptable.* Paris: Editions du Vivarais, 1978.

Paxton, Robert. *Vichy France.* New York: Knopf, 1972.

Paxton, Robert and Marrus, Michael. *Vichy France and the Jews.* New York: Basic Books, 1981.

Peek, Tim and Davis, Dave. "The Preacher Who Wouldn't Quit." *Philadelphia Inquirer,* February 24, 1985.

Pélissier, Jean. *Si la Gestapo avait su.* Paris: Bonne Presse, 1945.

Perconte, Jean-Pierre. "La J.O.C. et la J.O.C.F. dans le diocèse de Grenoble." Unpublished Masters' thesis, Grenoble, 1977.

Le Père Guérin. Paris: Editions Ouvrières, 1972.

Perrin, Henri. *Itinéraire d'Henri Perrin.* Paris: Seuil, 1958.

———. *Journal d'un prêtre-ouvrier en Allemagne.* Paris: Seuil, 1945.

Petrie, John, ed. *The Worker-Priests.* London: Routledge and Kegan Paul, 1956.

Peyrefitte, Christel. "Le Clergé français est-il en crise?" *Commentaire* 1,2 (Sum. 1978), 163–72.

Pézeril, Daniel. *Rue Notre Dame.* London: Burns Oates, 1953.

Pezet, Ernest. *Chrétiens au service de la cité, de Léon XIII, au Sillon et au M.R.P. (1891–1965).* Paris: Nouvelles Editions Latines, 1965.

Piet, André. *A travers le reél.* Paris: Pensée universelle, 1978.

Poël, Ivar H. *Arbetarprästerna. Ett socialetiskt experiment.* Stockholm: Verbum, 1968.

Pohoyles, Egon. "Vatican Boomerang." *The Nation,* Oct. 24, 1953, 332.

Politi, Sirio. *Una Zolla di terra.* Vincence: La Locusta, 1961.

Ponson, Christian. *Les Catholiques lyonnais et la Chronique Sociale.* Lyon: Presses Universitaires de Lyon, 1979.

Potel, Julien. *Le Clergé français.* Paris: Centurion, 1967.

Poujol, Geneviève. *L'Education populaire*. Paris: Editions ouvrières. 1981.

Poulain, Jean-Claude. *CFDT, le rêve et la vie*. Paris: Editions sociales, 1981.

Poulat, Emile. *Une Eglise ébranlée*. Paris: Casterman, 1980.

———. "Une enquête anticléricale de pratique religieuse en Seine-et-Marne 1903." *Archives de la Sociologie des Religions* 6 (July–Dec., 1958), 127–48.

———. Le *"Journal d'un prêtre d'après-demain" (1902–1903) de l'abbé Calippe*. Paris: Casterman, 1961.

———. *Naissance des prêtres-ouvriers*. Paris: Casterman, 1965.

Le Prêtre dans la J.O.C. Paris: Editions Ouvrières, 1952.

Les Prêtres-Ouvriers. Paris: Minuit, 1954.

"Les Prêtres-ouvriers en 1979." *Lettre-Temps Présent* (Apr., 1979), 10–13.

"Les Prêtres-ouvriers liégois." *La Wallonie*, Mar. 30, 1983, 1, 10.

Priest-Workman in England. London: S.P.C.K., 1951.

PRROQ. *Le Groupe PRROQ, le monde ouvrier et l'église*. Montréal: PRROQ, 1982.

Pucheu, Abbé. *Le Prêtre-Ouvrier, homme de dieu, source et resources spirituelles*. Paris: no address, 1952.

Quéffelec, Henri. *Le Jour se lève sur la banlieue*. Paris: Grasset, 1954.

Rauch, R. William, Jr. *Politics and Belief in Contemporary France*. The Hague: Nijhoff, 1972.

Reko, H. Karl. "Determinative Factors in the Ability of Christ Seminary—Seminex Graduates to Conduct Worker-Priest Ministries in the United States." Unpublished thesis, c. 1980.

Remi, Fernand. *Mission publique: Mouvement précurseur des prêtres-ouvriers*. Paris: Editions de l'Oeuvre de tous, 1951.

Rémond, René. *Les Catholiques, le communisme et les crises 1929–1939*. Paris: Armand Colin, 1960.

———. "Droite et gauche dans le catholicisme français contemporain." *Revue française de science politique* VIII (1958), 529–44, 803–20.

Rémond, René ed. *Forces religieuses et attitudes politiques dans la France contemporaine* in *Cahiers de la Fondation Nationale des Sciences Politiques*. Paris: Armand Colin, 1965.

Rétif, Louis. *J'ai vu naître l'église de demain*. Paris: Editions Ouvrières, 1971.

Reynaud, Jean-Daniel. *Les Syndicats en France*. Paris: Armand Colin, 1966.

Rice-Maximin, Edward. "The Main Tendue." *Contemporary French Civilization* (Win., 1980), 193–210.

Rollet, Henri. *L'Action sociale des catholiques en France*. Paris: Boivin, 1958.

———. *Albert de Mun et le parti catholique*. Paris: Boivin, 1949.

Ross, Eva J. "The Sociology of Religion in France Today." *American Catholic Sociological Review* 11 (Mar., 1950), 3–14.

Ross, George. *Workers and Communists in France*. Berkeley: University of California Press, 1982.

Rougier, Louis. "French Worker-Priest Idea Backfires." *Saturday Night* (Mar. 27, 1954), 7–8.

Rowe, John. *Priests and Workers: A Rejoinder*. London: Darton, Longman and Todd, 1965.

Saint-Pierre, Michel de. *Les Nouveaux Prêtres*. Paris: Table Ronde, 1964.

Sangnier, Marc. *L'Education sociale du peuple*. Paris: Au Sillon, 1904.

———. *Les Syndicats et la démocratie*. Paris: Au Sillon, 1906.

Schalk, David L. *The Spectrum of Political Engagement*. Princeton, N.J.: University Press, 1979.

Scholl, S.H. *Cent cinquante ans de mouvement ouvrier chrétien en Europe de l'Ouest (1789–1939)*. Louvain-Paris, 1966.

Shorter, Edward and Tilly, Charles. *Strikes in France*. Cambridge: University Press, 1974.

Siefer, Gregor. *The Church and Industrial Society*. Translated by Isabel and Florence McHugh. London: Darton, Longman and Todd, 1964.

Six, Jean-François. *Charles de Foucauld aujourd'hui*. Paris: Seuil, 1966.

———. *Cheminements de la Mission de France*. Paris: Seuil, 1967.

———. *Vie de Charles de Foucauld*. Paris: Seuil, 1962.

Sutcliffe, Anthony. *The Autumn of Central Paris*. Montreal: McGill-Queens Press, 1971.

Symanowski, Horst. *Die Welt des Arbeiters*. Frankfurt-am-Main: Stimme Verlag, 1964.

Talmy, Robert. *Albert de Mun*. Paris: Bloud et Gay, 1965.

———. *Aux sources du Catholicisme social: l'école de la Tour du Pin*. Tournai: Desclée, 1963.

———. *René de la Tour du Pin*. Paris: Bloud et Gay, 1964.

———. *Le Syndicalisme chrétien en France, 1871–1930*. Paris: Bloud et Gay, 1966.

Tessier, Gaston. *Un Progrès social: la Journée du huit heures*. Paris: Spes, 1923.

———. *Le Syndicalisme chrétien en 1945*. Paris: C.F.T.C., 1945.

Un Théologien en liberté: Jacques Duquesne interroge le Père Chenu. Paris: Centurion, 1975.

Thompson, E.P. *The Making of the English Working Class.* New York: Random, 1963.

Thompson, Ian B. *The Lower Rhône and Marseille.* Oxford: University Press, 1975.

———. *The Paris Basin.* Oxford: University Press, 1973.

Thormann, G.C. "Christian Trade Unionism in France." Dissertation, Columbia University, 1951.

Tiersky, Ronald. *French Communism, 1920–1972.* New York: Columbia University Press, 1974.

La Tour du Pin, René. *Vers un ordre social: Jalons la route, 1882–1907.* Paris: Nouvelle Librairie Nationale, 1907.

Touraine, Alaine. *L'Evolution du travail ouvrier aux usines Renault.* Paris: Centre National de la Recherche Scientifique, 1955.

Trimouille, Pierre. *Léon Harmel et l'usine chrétienne du Val des Bois.* Lyon: Centre d'Histoire du Catholicisme, 1974.

Truman, Tom. *Catholic Action and Politics.* London: Marlin Press, 1960.

Véret, Charles. *J'ai vu grandir la J.O.C.* Paris: Editions Ouvrières, 1977.

Vidler, Alec R. *A Variety of Catholic Modernists.* Cambridge: University Press, 1970.

Vignaux, Paul. *De la CFTC à la CFDT.* Paris: Editions Ouvrières, 1980.

Villain, Jean. *La Charte du travail et l'organisation économique et sociale de la profession.* Paris: Spes, 1942.

———. *L'Enseignement social de l'église.* Paris: Spes, 1954.

———. *Le Myth du communisme.* Paris: Spes, 1936.

———. *Le Problème de la nationalisation au regard de la pensée sociale chrétienne.* Paris: Spes, 1944.

Vinatier, Jean. *Le Cardinal Liénart et la Mission de France.* Paris: Centurion, 1978.

———. *Le cardinal Suhard.* Paris: Centurion, 1983.

Voillaume, René. *Au coeur des masses.* I–II. Paris: Cerf, 1969.

Wearmouth, Robert P. *Methodanism and the Working-Class Movements of England, 1800–1850.* London: Epworth, 1947.

Weil, Simone. *La Condition Ouvrière.* Paris: Gallimard, 1951.

———. *Waiting for God.* Translated by Emma Craufurd. New York: Harper and Row, 1951.

Werth, Alexander. *France, 1940–1955.* London: Robert Hale, 1956.

Wickham, E.R. *Church and People in an Industrial City.* London: Lutterworth, 1967.

Williams, John R., ed. *Canadian Churches and Social Justice.* Toronto: Lorimer, 1984.

Williams, Philip M. *Crisis and Compromise: Politics in the Fourth Republic.* London: Longmans, 1964.

Wolff, Philippe. *Histoire de Toulouse*. Toulouse: Privat, 1974.

The Worker Pastor. New York: Metropolitan New York Synod, LCA, c.1980.

Wright, Gordon. *France in Modern Times*. Chicago: Rand McNally, 1974.

———. *The Reshaping of French Democracy*. Boston: Beacon Press, 1970 (1948).

Wright, John, ed. *The Church Today: The Collected Writings of Emmanuel Cardinal Suhard*. Chicago: Fides, 1953.

Yates, Willard Ross. "Power, Principles and Doctrine of the Mouvement Républicain Populaire." *American Political Science Review* LII, 2 (June, 1958), 419–36.

Zirnheld, Jules. *Cinquante années du syndicalisme chrétien*. Paris: Spes, 1937.

Zudaire, Christano. *Quijotes a lo divino*. Barcelona: Editorial franciscana, 1950.

Zuurdeeg, J. *De Franse priester-arbeiders in conflick met hun Kerk*. Delft: W. Gaade, 1954.

NOTES

I. THE PARADIGM OF THE WORKER-PRIESTS

1. Jean-Pierre Dubois-Dumée, "Les Prêtres-Ouvriers, présence du Christ dans un monde païen." *Témoignage Chrétien,* July 11, 1952, pp.1, 4.

2. One excellent example of this theological dialogue is Alistair Kee's *A Reader in Political Theology* (Philadelphia: Westminster, 1974).

3. For a thorough analysis of the Detroit conference, read Gregory Baum, "The Christian Left at Detroit, 1976" in *The Social Imperative* (New York: Paulist Press, 1979).

4. Ibid., p.36; Robert McAfee Brown, *Theology in a New Key* (Philadelphia: Westminster Press, 1978), p.11.

5. Brown, *Theology,* pp.60–74, 138–141.

6. E.P. Thompson, *The Making of the English Working Class* (New York: Random, 1963); E.R. Wickham, *Church and People in an Industrial City* (London: Lutterworth, 1957); Robert P. Wearmouth, *Methodism and the Working-Class Movements of England, 1800–1850* (London: Epworth, 1947); and Robert Samuel Moore, *Pit-men, Preachers and Politics* (London: Cambridge University Press, 1974) illustrate British Christian involvement in the midst of urban and industrial squalor.

7. Works to consult on the U.S. and Canadian social gospel are Robert T. Handy, ed., *The Social Gospel in America, 1870–1920* (New York: Oxford University Press, 1966) and Richard Allen, *The Social Passion* (Toronto: University Press, 1973).

8. For a glimpse of Catholic social consciousness during this period, see David J. O'Brien, *American Catholics and Social Reform* (New York: University Press, 1959) and Aaron I. Abell, *American Catholicism and Social Action* (Garden City, N.Y.: Hanover House, 1960). Dorothy Day's *Loaves and Fishes* (New York: Harper and Row, 1983 [1963]) and M.M. Coady's *Masters of Their Own Destiny* (New York: Harper and Row, 1967) are descriptions of these two movements by the founders themselves. Gregory Baum analyzes the Antigonish movement skillfully in his *Catholics and Canadian Socialism* (Toronto: Lorimer, 1980). Donal Dorr's *Option for the Poor: A Hundred Years of Vatican Social Teaching* (Maryknoll, N.Y.: Orbis Books, 1983) is a superb analysis of the ambiguities and development of papal teaching in these areas from *Rerum Novarum* to the present.

9. Gregory Baum provides excellent analyses on the recent social encyclicals and the Canadian bishops' statements since 1975 in his works *The Priority of Labor* (New York: Paulist Press, 1982) and *Ethics and Economics* (with Duncan Cameron) (Toronto: Lorimer, 1984). Also see John R. Williams, ed., *Canadian Churches and Social Justice* (Toronto: Lorimer, 1984) and *Economic Justice* (New York: Division for Mission in North America, Lutheran Church in America, 1980). For brief analyses of the D.M.S. and Network coalition, consult Tim Peek and Dave Davis, "The Preacher Who Wouldn't Quit," *Philadelphia Inquirer*, Feb. 24, 1985; Michael Hoyt, "In Pennsylvania's 'Steel Valley,' churches assail bank about vanishing jobs," *National Catholic Reporter*, Sept. 23, 1983; Bohdan Hodiak, "Prophets in Steeltown," *The Christian Century*, May 8, 1985, pp.460–462; and Michael Hoyt, "How to make steel: Agitate and organize," *Christianity and Crisis*, Mar. 4, 1985), pp.62–65.

10. Brown, *Theology*, p.179.

II. THE FRANCE OF THE WORKER-PRIESTS (1943–1954)

1. One intriguing study which portrays this vividly is Stanley Hoffmann, et al., *In Search of France* (New York: Harper and Row, 1963). Another is a more detailed, descriptive account by Alexander Werth called *France, 1940–1955* (London: Robert Hale, Ltd. 1956).

2. For a brief description of the 1930s era, one may consult Gordon Wright, *France in Modern Times* (Chicago: Rand McNally, 1974), pp.363–395.

3. This state of affairs is analyzed with great passion by the historian Marc Bloch in his *Strange Defeat* (New York: Oxford University Press, 1949). A good study on the varying opinions as to why France fell in 1940 is found in the Problems in European Civilization series: Samuel Osgood, *The Fall of France, 1940* (Boston: Heath, 1965).

4. Julian Benda's, *The Treason of the Intellectuals* (New York: W.W. Norton & Co., 1956 [1928]) is a contemporary account of this phenomenon for one point of view.

5. Two fine works dealing with this intellectual engagement are David L. Schalk's *The Spectrum of Political Engagement* (Princeton, N.J.: University Press, 1979) and John Hellman's *Emmanuel Mounier and the New Catholic Left* (Toronto: University Press, 1981). In fact, this latter book provides a good picture of the intellectual stirrings within Catholicism of which the worker-priests were a vital part.

6. There are a large number of books and articles on this exciting transition in French Catholic life. I cite a few examples: Hellman, *Emmanuel Mounier;* René Rémond, *Les Catholiques, le communisme et les crises, 1929–1939* (Paris: Armand Colin, 1960); Oscar L. Arnal, *Ambivalent Alliance: the Catholic Church and the Action Française* (Pittsburgh: University Press, 1985); John Hellman, "French 'Left Catholics' and Communism in the Nineteen-Thirties," *Church History* 45, 4 (December, 1976), pp.507–523; Francis J. Murphy, "La Main

Tendue," *Catholic Historical Review* 60, 2 (July, 1974), pp.255–270; Edward Rice-Maximin, "The Main Tendue," *Contemporary French Civilization* (Winter, 1980), pp.193–210; John Hellman, "Vichy Background," On-Demand Supplement of the *Journal of Modern History* (Chicago, 1977), pp.D1111–D1144; Oscar L. Arnal, "Stillborn Alliance: Catholic Divisions and the Main Tendue," On-Demand Supplement of the *Journal of Modern History* (Chicago, March, 1979), pp.D1001–1027; Oscar L. Arnal, "Catholic Roots of Collaboration and Resistance in France in the 1930s," *Canadian Journal of History/Annales Canadiennes d'Histoire* XVII, 1 (April, 1982), pp.87–110.

7. To date, the definitive study of the Vichy regime in English is Robert O. Paxton's, *Vichy France* (New York: Alfred A. Knopf, 1972).

8. Some excellent studies on these matters, which may be consulted, are Ronald Tiersky, *French Communism, 1920–1972* (New York: Columbia University Press, 1974); Jacques Fauvet, *Histoire du Parti Communiste Français* (Paris: Fayard, 1977); Jacques Duquesne, *Les Catholiques français sous l'occupation* (Paris: Bernard Grasset, 1966); Renée Bédarida, *Les Armes de l'Esprit: Témoignage Chrétien* (Paris: Editions Ouvrières, 1977); Renée Bédarida, personal interview, Guelph, Ontario (October, 1977). H.R. Kedward's *Resistance in Vichy France* (Oxford: University Press, 1978) is a superior work of research on France's resistance movement. The interviews within the book bring the period to life. The most thorough work on the French resistance is Henri Noguères, et al., *Histoire de Résistance*, 4 Vol. (Paris: Robert Laffont, 1967–1976).

9. Duquesne's work provides some information on these matters. For more details, see Emile Poulat, *Naissance des prêtres-ouvriers* (Paris: Casterman, 1965); Andrien Dansette, *Destin du catholicisme français, 1926–1956* (Paris: Flammarion, 1957) and especially Chapters III and IV of this book.

10. Georges Bidault, personal interview, Paris (May, 1977). A thorough and fine study of the *tripartiste* phase of the Fourth Republic is Gordon Wright's *The Reshaping of French Democracy* (Boston: Beacon Press, 1970 [1948]).

11. For histories and analyses of the Fourth Republic, consult Philip M. Williams, *Crisis and Compromise: Politics in the Fourth Republic* (London: Longmans, 1964). Jacques Fauvet, *La IVᵉ république* (Paris: Fayard, 1959) and François Goguel, *France under the Fourth Republic* (Ithaca, N.Y.: Cornell University Press, 1952). For a study of the Socialist Party, see B.D. Graham, *The French Socialists and Tripartisme, 1944–1947* (Toronto: University Press, 1965). The most thorough study in English on the Mouvement Républicain Populaire is R.E.M. Irving's *Christian Democracy in France* (London: George Allan & Unwin Ltd., 1973).

12. For details, see Tiersky, *French Communism*, pp.112–225; George Ross, *Workers and Communists in France: From Popular Front to Eurocommunism* (Berkeley: University of California Press, 1982); and Richard F. Hamilton, *Affluence and the French Worker in the Fourth Republic* (Princeton: University Press, 1967).

13. The following works present a rather comprehensive picture of the postwar church in France, its structures, its activities and the fate of its avant-

garde efforts: William Bosworth, *Catholicism and Crisis in Modern France* (Princeton: University Press, 1962); Aline Coutrot and François Dreyfus, *Les Forces religieuses dans la société française* (Paris: Armand Colin, 1965); and Dansette, *Destin*. Irving's *Christian Democracy in France* gives a thorough picture of the vicissitudes of the M.R.P.

III. THE WORLD FROM WHICH THEY CAME: MISSIONARY APOSTOLATES TO THE PROLETARIAT

1. Maurice Montuclard, *Conscience religieuse et démocratie* (Paris: Seuil, 1963), p.66; H. Danzas, "Les Devoirs de la classe dirigéante," *Association Catholique* II, 4 (1876), pp.505–519. For some studies on the birth of French social Catholicism, consult Parker T. Moon, *The Labor Problem and the Social Catholic Movement in France* (New York: Macmillan, 1921); Matthew H. Elbow, *French Corporative Theory* (New York: Columbia University Press, 1953); Georges Hoog, *Histoire du Catholicisme social en France, 1871–1931* (Paris: Doumat, 1946); Joseph N. Moody, *Catholic Social and Political Thought and Movements* (New York: Arts, Inc., 1953) and Benjamin F. Martin Jr., *Count Albert de Mun* (Chapel Hill, N.C.: University of North Carolina Press, 1978), pp.8–20. For a study of precursors to De Mun and La Tour du Pin, see Jean-Baptise Dursoselle, *Les Débuts du catholicisme social en France (1822–1871)* (Paris: Presses Universitaires de France, 1951).

2. "Chronique de l'Oeuvre . . . ," *Association Catholique* II (1876), p.273; Marc Sangnier in John McManners, *Church and State in France, 1870–1914* (New York: Harper and Row, 1972), p.82.

3. La Tour du Pin Chambly, "Du régime corporatif," *Association Catholique* XVI, 2 (Aug. 15, 1883), pp.145–172; La Tour du Pin Chambly, "Un programme qui vient à son heure," *Association Catholique* XXXVIII, 1 (1894), pp.15–31; "La Loi sur les syndicats professionnels," *Association Catholique* XVI, (July 15, 1883), pp.5–9; A. de Mun, "Le Repos du dimanche," *Action Libérale Populaire*, Apr. 4, 1907, p.1; J. Brugerette, *Le Prêtre français et la société contemporaine*, Vol. III (Paris: P. Lethielleux, 1935), p.36.

4. For some good studies on this phase of Christian Democracy, see Maurice Montuclard, "Aux origines de la démocratie chrétienne," *Archives de Sociologie des Religions* 6 (July–Dec., 1958), pp.47–89; Robert F. Byrnes, "The French Christian Democrats in the 1890s," *Catholic Historical Review* 36, 4 (Oct., 1950), pp.286–306; Anthony T. Bouscaren, "Origins of French Christian Democracy," *Thought* XXI, 123 (Winter, 1956–1957), pp.542–566; R.E.M. Irving, *Christian Democracy in France* (London: Allen and Unwin, 1973), pp.19–51; Pierre Trimouille, *Léon Harmel et l'usine chrétienne du Val des-Bois, 1840–1914* (Lyon: Presses Universitaires, 1974) and Oscar L. Arnal, "The Nature and Success of Breton Christian Democracy," *Catholic Historical Review* LXVIII, 2 (April, 1982), pp.226–248.

5. Maurice Larkin, *Church and State after the Dreyfus Affair* (London: Mac-

millan, 1974), pp.161, 163–164. For the definitive look at Father Calippe's testimony, see Emile Poulat, *Le "Journal d'un prêtre d'après-demain" (1902–1903) de l'abbé Calippe* (Paris: Casterman, 1961).

6. Marc Sangnier, quoted in Hoog, *Histoire*, p.134; APP B 2/1540: "Société . . . ," Dec. 9, 1900, #24; Nov. 1, 1901, #34; "Meeting . . . ," July 24, 1902, #68–#71; Marc Sangnier, "Un congrès syndical au Sillon," *Eveil Démocratique*, Oct. 21, 1906, p.1; L. Antoine, "De Intervention . . . ," *Le Sillon* (Mar. 10, 1901), pp.134–139; APP B 2/1540; "Rapport," Jan. 11, 1907, #676; Marc Sangnier, "La Guerre de classes," *Eveil Démocratique*, Sept. 8, 1907, p.1; Marc Sangnier, "Les Patrons," *Eveil Démocratique*, Nov. 1, 1908, p.1; Marc Sangnier, "Hier et demain," *Eveil Démocratique*, Apr. 7, 1907, p.1. For further material on Sangnier, Sillon and the church's condemnation of both, see Jeanne Caron, *Le Sillon et la démocratie chrétienne* (Paris: Plon, 1967); Alec R. Vidler, *A Variety of Catholic Modernists* (Cambridge: University Press, 1970); Charles Breunig, "The Condemnation of the Sillon," *Church History* 26, (Sept., 1957), pp.227–244; and Oscar L. Arnal, "Why the French Christian Democrats Were Condemned," *Church History* 49, 2 (June, 1980), pp.188–202.

7. Christian Ponson, *Les Catholiques Lyonnais et la Chronique Sociale* (Lyon: Presses Universitaires, 1979), pp.53–151, 217–260; "Les Semaines Sociales se présentent," *Chronique Sociale de France* 62 (May–June, 1964), pp.223–240; Louis Coirard, "Le Catholicisme social en face du Socialisme," *Chronique Sociale de France* (Feb., 1912), pp.41–48; "Regards sur les classes . . . Semaine Sociale de Bordeaux," *Documentation Catholique* (Aug. 5, 1939), pp.931–980; Eugène Duthoit, "Economie dirigée économie humaine," *Chronique Sociale de France* (Feb., 1932), pp.69–79; M. Gonin, "Où en est le syndicalisme révolutionnaire," *Chronique Sociale de France* (Apr. 25, 1913), pp.121–126; "Libération de la classe ouvrière," *Chronique Sociale de France* LIV, no.3 (special number) (June–July, 1945), pp.283–396.

8. R.P. Jean Villain, "L'Action Populaire," *Chronique Sociale de France* 60 (Apr. 1952), pp.215–219; "Cinquante années d'apostolat social," *Revue de l'Action Populaire* 69 (June, 1953), pp.481–498; "La Conquête des ames," *Dossiers de l'Action Populaire* (June 10, 1929), pp.699–706; J.C., "L'Attrait du communisme," *Dossiers de l'Action Populaire* (July 10, 1933), pp.1393–1414; "Syndicalisme et salariat," *Année Sociale Internationale* (1910–1914), pp.521–552; M.N., "La Vie à l'usine," *Dossiers de l'Action Populaire* (Feb. 25, 1926), pp.145–160; A. de Soras, "La Mission pastorale de l'Eglise . . . ," *Travaux de l'Action Populaire* 30 (May, 1949), pp.321–337; M.A.D., "Richesses du quartier ouvrier," *Revue de l'Action Populaire* 70 (July–Aug., 1953), pp.652–661; "Prêtres-ouvriers travaillant à Paris" (Dec. 8, 1949), 1p. in Mission de Paris papers (1949) (hereafter referred to as MDP); Henri Perrin, *Itinéraire. d'Henri Perrin* (Paris: Seuil, 1958), pp.66, 88–90, 117–118, 157–161; Père Jean Villain of Action Populaire, interview, Paris (June 6, 1979). A thorough study of the team is Paul Drouler's, *Le Père Desbuquois et l'Action Populaire*, I–II (Paris: Editions Ouvrières, 1981).

9. Three such studies which include some significant social analysis and data are J. Brugerette, *Le Prêtre français et la Société contemporaine*, I–III (Paris:

P. Lethielleaux, 1935–1938); R.P. Doncoeur, *La Crise du sacerdoce* (Paris: Flammarion, 1932); Pierre Lhande, *Le Christ dans la banlieue* (Paris: Plon, 1927).

10. Le Bras, *Introduction* . . . , I–III (Paris: Presses Universitaires de France, 1942–1945) and Le Bras, *Etudes* . . . , I–III (Paris: Presses Universitaires de France, 1955–1956). See also his "Connaissance des Villes," *Masses Ouvrières* (July, 1945), pp.41–46. Emile Poulat, letter, Jan. 11, 1986, p.4.

11. Fernard Boulard, *Problèmes* . . . (Paris: Cerf, 1945); Eva J. Ross, "The Sociology of Religion in France Today," *American Catholic Sociological Review* 11 (Mar., 1950), p.11. Boulard's later *An Introduction to Religious Sociology* (trans. by M.J. Jackson, London: Darton, Longman and Todd, 1960) is a useful update of his earlier work. Poulat, letter.

12. Simone Weil, *La Condition ouvrière* (Paris: Gallimard, 1951); Simone Weil, *Waiting for God*, trans. by Emma Craufurd (New York: Harper and Row, 1951), p.ix; Jacques Loew, interview, Fribourg, Swit. (May 14, 1980); John Hellman, *Simone Weil* (Waterloo, Ontario: Wilfrid Laurier University Press, 1982); Jean-François Six, *Cheminements de la Mission de France* (Paris: Seuil, 1967), pp.40–41; Madeleine Delbrêl, *Ville marxiste, terre de mission* (Paris: Cerf, 1957); Madeleine Delbrêl, *Nous autres, gens des rues* (Paris: Seuil, 1966).

13. Ross, "The Sociology of Religion," pp.7–8; Louisette Blanquart, interview, Paris (June 22, 1979). Two of Lebret's significant works in this field are *Les Professions maritimes à la recherche du bien commun* (Paris: Dunod, 1939) and *Guide pratique de l'enquête sociale* (Paris: Presses Universitaires de France, 1952). "Manifeste d'Economie et Humanisme," *Economie et Humanisme* (Feb.–Mar., 1952), pp.3–52; L.-J. Lebret and Henri-Charles Desroches, "La Méthode d'Economie et Humanisme," *Economie et Humanisme* (Mar.–July, 1944), pp.121–134, 225–249; M.-R. Loew, *Les Dockers de Marseille* (L'Arbresle: Economie et Humanisme, 1946). Father Daniel Perrot recalls that Father Lebret was one of the theologians most favored by his Mission de France students (interview, Paris, May 10, 1979).

14. Maurice Montuclard, interview, Lyon (June 14, 1983); "Le Centre de recherche," *Jeunesse de l'Eglise*, III (1944), pp.22–33; *La Crise de la civilisation chrétienne*, V (1945); *L'Evangile Captif*, X (1949); *Le Temps du pauvre* IX (1948); *Délivérance de l'homme*, VII (1947); Maurice Montuclard, *Les Evénements et la foi* (Paris: Seuil, 1951).

15. Adrien Dansette, *Destin du catholicisme français* (Paris: Flammarion, 1957), pp.121–123, 131; Jacques Maritain, *Integral Humanisme*, trans. by Joseph Evans (New York: Scribner's, 1936); *Un Théologien en liberté: Jacque Duquesne interroge le Père Chenu* (Paris: Centurion, 1975) pp.5–107; F. Gay, "Ce que nous voulons être," *Vie Catholique*, Sept. 20, 1924, p.1.

16. Emmanuel Mounier, "Débat à haute voix," *Esprit* (Feb., 1946), pp.166–167; Jean Daniélou, "Mission chrétienne et mouvement ouvrier," *Bulletin du cercle St. Jean Baptise* (Feb., 1950), pp.1–4; M.-D. Chenu, *Pour une théologie du travail* (Paris: Seuil, 1954), pp.58–59; Perrin, *Itinéraire*, pp.126–127. Some examples of influential works published by some of these theologians during this period are: Henri de Lubac, *Catholicisme* (Paris: Cerf, 1952) and

Yves Congar, *Vrai et fausse réforme dans l'Eglise* (Paris: Cerf, 1950). Poulat, letter, Jan. 11, 1986, p.4.

17. Francis J. Murphy, "La Main Tendue," *Catholic Historical Review* 60, 2 (July, 1974), pp.255–270; John Hellman, *Emmanuel Mounier and the New Catholic Left* (Toronto: University Press, 1981), p.297; Oscar L. Arnal, "Stillborn Alliance," on demand supplement of *Journal of Modern History* (1979), p.D1003; Jean Vinatier, *Le Cardinal Liénart et la Mission de France* (Paris: Centurion, 1978), pp.68–74; Joseph Chansou, *Sous l'épiscopat du cardinal Saliège* (Toulouse: J. Chansou, 1978). "Lettre de S.G. Monseigneur l'évêque de Lille . . . ," *Semaine Religieuse de Lille* (Sept. 1, 1929), pp.439–450; Mgr. Liénart, "Deuxième lettre," *Semaine Religieuse de Lille* (Sept. 15, 1929), pp.467–470.

18. "Déclaration de l'épiscopat français sur la personne humaine, la famille, la société," *Documentation Catholique* (Mar. 18, 1945), pp.228–229.

19. Arnal, "Stillborn Alliance," pp.D1015–1016; "Lettre de S.G. Monseigneur l'évêque de Lille . . . ," pp.441, 446–447, 450; Jacques Duquesne, *Les Catholiques français sous l'occupation* (Paris: Grasset, 1966), pp.35–56; "Déclaration de l'Assemblée . . . ," *Documentation Catholique* (Mar. 28, 1948), p.388; "Une Note de S. Em. le cardinal Liénart . . . ," *Documentation Catholique* (Apr. 10, 1949), pp.471–472; "Un Décret de la Suprême Congrégation du Saint-Office . . ." *Documentation Catholique* (July 31, 1949), pp.961–962; "Lettre des cardinaux français sur le décret . . . ," *Documentation Catholique* (Sept. 25, 1949), pp.1217–1224; Perrin, Itinéraire, pp.187–194.

20. Emmanuel Cardinal Suhard, *The Church Today* (Chicago: Fides, 1953), pp.153–154, 282–284.

21. For descriptions of the Mission de France and its ideas, consult Vinatier, *Cardinal Liénart;* Jacques Faupin, *La Mission de France* (Paris: Casterman, 1960); Jean-François Six, *Cheminements de la Mission de France* (Paris: Seuil, 1967); Louis Augros, *De l'église d'hier à l'église de demain* (Paris: Cerf, 1980); "Regard sur notre histoire," *Lettre aux communautés* (Nov., 1954), pp.4–16; and Oscar L. Arnal, "Beyond the Walls of Christendom," *Contemporary French Civilization* VII (Fall, 1982), pp.41–62. I received valuable personal testimonies on this history from Louis Augros, St. Symphorien-de-Lay (July, 1979); Daniel Perrot, and Jean Vinatier, Fontenay-sous-Bois (June, 1980).

22. Perrot, Augros, Vinatier interviews; Francis Vico, interview, Montluçon (May, 1980); Augros, *De l'église,* pp.56, 58–66; Claude Wiener, "Le Séminaire de la Mission," *Lettre aux Amis de la Mission de France* (May, 1953), pp.6–7; Vinatier, *Cardinal Liénart,* p.85; *Mission de France* in unpublished papers, Mission de France (1945–1954), pp.12–14; Bernard Striffling, interview, Courbevoie (June, 1979); Joseph Robert, interview, Hellemes (July, 1979); "Quelques réflexions sur l'évangelisation de notre secteur," *Lettre aux Communautés* (Feb. 10, 1951), pp.1–8; Jean Vinatier, "Au coeur du malaise rural," *Lettre aux Communautés* (Apr. 15, 1951), pp.1–8; Jean Volot, interview, Paris (May, 1980); "Les Stages," *Unis pour . . . aux communautés et aux stagiaires* (Apr., 1949), pp.4–5.

23. Père Lévèsque, "Thérèse missionnaire," *Lettre aux Communautés* (June

30, 1952), pp.4–5, 9; Vinatier, "Au coeur . . . ," pp.6–8; Daniel Perrot, "Perspectives missionnaires," *Lettre aux Amis de la Mission de France* (May, 1953), p.3.

24. Suhard, *Church Today*, pp.26–27, 153–154; Aline Coutrot and François Dreyfus, *Les Forces Religieuses dans la société française* (Paris: Colin, 1965), pp.120–121; Henri Godin and Yvan Daniel, *France pays de mission?* (Paris: Abeille, 1943), pp.40, 44–47; Gustave Bardy, "Sur l'origine des paroisses," *Masses Ouvrières* (Mar., 1947), pp.42–58 and (Apr., 1947), pp.42–66; "Masses déchristianisées," *Masses Ouvrières* (July, 1945), pp.59–84.

25. Louis Rétif, *J'ai vu naître l'église de demain* (Paris: Editions Ouvrières, 1971), pp.31–40. Emile Poulat has an interesting analysis of the Colombes parish in his *Une Eglise ébranlée* (Paris: Casterman, 1980), pp.201–213.

26. Georges Michonneau, *Revolution in a City Parish*, trans. of *Paroisse, Communauté Missionnaire* (London: Blackfriars, 1949), pp.25–40, 54–59, 80–97, 115–130; Rétif, *J'ai vu*, pp.56–57, 72; Louis Rétif, "Soubassements sociologiques d'une paroisse," *Masses Ouvrières* (Feb., 1951), p.77; Césaire Dillaye, interview, Paris (May, 1979); Louis Bouyer, interview, Colombes (May, 1979); Bernard Cagne, interview, Paris (June, 1979).

27. Perrot, Robert, Striffling interviews; "Paroisse St.X.," *Lettre aux Communautés* (Apr. 15, 1951), pp.10–14; Abbé Guinard, "Monographie d'une paroisse ouvrière *Masses Ouvrières* (Feb., 1946), pp.77–86; "Orientation communautaire et vie materielle des paroisses du bassin mineur de l'Herault," *Masses Ouvrières* (May, 1947), pp.31–60; "Point de vue d'un curé . . . (1950–1951), 1p. in MDP (1950).

28. Jean-Pierre Perconte, *La J.O.C. et la J.O.C.F. dans le diocèse de Grenoble*, unpublished Master's thesis (Grenoble, 1977), pp.16, 23, 25–29, 31, 69–73, 88–89, 123–128; William Bosworth, *Catholicism and Crisis in Modern France* (Princeton: University Press, 1962), pp.116–117; Charles Veret, *J'ai vu grandir la J.O.C.* (Paris: Editions Ouvrières, 1977), pp.168–197; Léon-Noël Berthe, *JOC je te dois tout* (Paris: Editions Ouvrières, 1980); *Lettre aux fédéraux*, Oct., 1941, pp.1–2; *Equipe Ouvrière*, June, 1941, p.217; "Les Réquis," *Conseil National* 76 (1943), pp.1–10; "Les Aspirations des travailleurs et l'ordre social," *Nouvelle série*, no.10, pp.1–4.

29. Joseph Cardijn, "Formation spirituelle des chrétiens pour la masse," *Masses Ouvrières* (Nov., 1945), pp.1–2; Roger Cartayrade, interview, Paris (July 6, 1979); André Villette, interview, Paris (June 25, 1980); Joseph Cardijn, "L'Eglise devant la révolution mondiale," *Masses Ouvrières* (Apr., 1947), p.10; *Jeunesse Ouvrière*, Aug. 4, 1946; p.1; André Millard, "Notre témoignage chrétien," *Masses Ouvrières Supplement*, 1947, p.4; Blanquart interview.

30. *Lettre aux fédéraux*, May, 1952, p.5.

31. Perconte, *La J.O.C.*, pp.34–36; Bosworth, *Catholicism*, pp.98, 109, 113, 155; Pius XI, July 8, 1937 in *Documentation Catholique* (Sept. 25, 1937), p.387; "Lettre de Son Eminence le Cardinal Suhard . . . ," *Document J.O.C.* #7, July–Aug., 1946, p.3; *Lettre aux féderaux*, May, 1949, pp.7–8; *Le Prêtre dans la J.O.C.* (Paris: Editions Ouvrières, 1952), pp.105–110; *Le Père Guérin*, (Paris: Editions Ouvrières, 1972), p.21; Henri Godin, *France Pagan?*, trans. by Maisie Ward (London: Sheed and Ward, 1950), pp.20–29.

32. *Lettre aux fédéraux*, Dec., 1952, pp.3–4; "Action au travail," *Conseil National* 142A, 1953, pp.19–23; Perconte, *La J.O.C.*, pp.69–73; *Jeunesse Ouvrière*, June 15, 1936, p.1; *Equipe Ouvrière*, Nov.–Dec., 1944, p.3; *Lettre aux fèdèraux*, Sept., 1953, p.9; Joseph Jaquet, interview, Lyon (June 14, 1979); Blanquart interview; René Boudot, interview, Longuyon (June 4, 1980); "Marseille report," 1948, pp.25–27 in MDP (1948); "J.O.C. et mouvement ouvrier," *Conseil National* 137, 1952, p.57; *Lettre aux fèdèraux*, Dec., 1944, pp.10–11; "Positions," *Conseil National* 107A, 1949, 29042.

33. Bosworth, *Catholicism,* pp.109–111; Joseph Debès, *Naissance de l'Action Catholique Ouvrière* (Paris: Editions Ouvrières, 1982), pp.34–48, 69–77, 157–256; "A nos lecteurs," *Pages spirituelles, témoignage,* Oct.–Nov., 1946, p.1; André Millard, "Alerte!" *Témoignage,* July–Aug., 1949, pp.1–3; Maxime Hua, "Condamnations," *Témoignage,* Sept.–Oct., 1949, pp.1–7; "Nos prêtres," *Témoignage,* Feb. 1947, p.16.

34. Bosworth, *Catholicism,*· pp.110–116, Debès, *Naissance,* pp.157–256; A.D., "Ensemble prêtres-laïques," *Témoignage,* Mar., 1953, p.1; A.D., "Devenons ce que nous voulons être," *Témoignage,* Feb., 1953, p.1; Maxime Hua, "Vers une grande A.C.O.," *Témoignage,* Jan., 1950, pp.1–2; "Textes fondamentaux sur l'A.C.O.," *Témoignage,* May, 1950, pp.1–6; Maxime Hua, interview, Paris (May, 1979); Jean Body, interview, Paris (June, 1977).

35. Bernard Lacroix, interview, Grenoble (June 15, 1983).

36. Alfred Ancel, *Cinq ans avec les ouvriers* (Paris: Centurion, 1963), pp.16, 23, 28–43; Gregor Siefer, *The Church and Industrial Society,* trans. by Isabel and Florence McHugh (London: Darton, Longman and Todd, 1964), p.87; Paul Guilbert, interview, Venissieux (May 16, 1983); Jean Tarby, interview, Chartres (June 13, 1983); *Prêtres du Prado* 21 (Sept., 1954), pp.1–21 in MDP (1954).

37. Siefer, *The Church,* pp.88–89, 130; Jean-François Six, *Charles Foucauld aujourd'hui* (Paris: Seuil, 1966), p.12; "Note sur la congrégation des Petits Frères de Jésus . . . ," Rome (Jan. 23, 1949), pp.1–2 in MDP (1949); "Les Prêtres-Ouvriers." *Le Dossier de la Semaine,* no.170 (Apr. 21, 1952), pp.3, 6 in MDP (1952); Mgr. de Provendres and P. Voillaume, "Prêtres-ouvriers" (Jan. 27, 1949), pp.1–4 in MDP (1949); A Wankenne, S.J., "Prêtres-ouvriers," *Revue Quital Belge* (Jan., 1953), pp.411–421 in MDP (1953). Jean-François Six has written a biography called *Vie de Charles de Foucauld* (Paris: Seuil, 1962), and René Voillaume's *Au Coeur des masses,* I–II (Paris: Cerf, 1969) is a thorough summary of De Foucauld's vision and that of the order inspired by his witness.

38. The papal social encyclicals for this period can be found in any number of source books. For example, see Anne Fremantle, ed., *The Papal Encyclicals in Their Historical Context* (New York: New American Library, 1956). For more comprehensive analyses of papal social teaching, see M.-D. Chenu, *La "Doctrine sociale" de l'église comme idéologie* (Paris: Cerf, 1979); Emile Poulat, *Une Eglise ébranlée;* and Richard L. Camp, *The Papal Ideology of Social Reform* (Leiden: E.J. Brill, 1969).

IV. THE WORLD TO WHICH THEY CAME: THE FRENCH WORKING CLASS

1. André Deléage, "Réflexions sur mon stage," pp.1–6 in Mission de Paris papers (hereafter referred to as MDP) (1954); Marseille report to Mgr. Delay (1948), pp.22–23 in MDP (1948).

2. Simone Weil, *La Condition Ouvrière* (Paris: Gallimard, 1951), pp.23–24, 250–251.

3. "Contre-témoignage de l'église dans la classe ouvrière," pp.6–7 in "Les Témoignages des laïcs" Cahiers de la Mission de Paris (hereafter referred to as Cahiers MDP) (1955); Emile Rideau, "A nous chrétiens," *Travaux de l'Action Populaire* 16 (Jan., 1948), p.5; "Abrégé du rapport," pp.3–4, 6 in Cahiers MDP (1955), "Le Régime économique et la vie des travailleurs," pp.17–18, 20, 22 in Cahiers MDP (1955); Alaine Touraine, *L'Evolution du travail ouvrier aux usines Renault* (Paris: Centre National de la Recherche Scientifique, 1955), pp.11, 22, 26, 37–43, 53–57; Michel Collinet, *Essai sur la condition ouvrière* (Paris: Editions Ouvrières, 1951), pp.71–72; P. Chombart de Lauwe, *la Vie Quotidienne des familles ouvrières* (Paris: Centre National de la Recherche Scientifique, 1956), pp.21, 24–25; "Quinze jours dans le Jura" (July 13, 1945), p.17 in MDP (1945).

4. "Le Régime économique," p.19; "Abrégé du rapport," pp.3–4.

5. "Problème missionnaire" (1950), p.4 in MDP (1950).

6. Jacques Frémontier, *La Forteresse ouvrière Renault* (Paris: Fayard, 1971), p.14; Patrick Fridenson, *Histoire des usines Renault*, I (Paris: Seuil, 1972), pp.1–4, 297; René Minguet, *Géographie industrielle de Paris* (Paris: Hachette, 1957), pp.187–188; Touraine, *L'Evolution*, pp.11, 13, 27, 37, 54–55, 58, 100, 102, 118, 131, 137, 143–144; Pierre George, *Géographie économique: La Métallurgie du fer* (Paris: Centre de Documentation Universitaire, n.d.), pp.136–137.

7. George, *Géographie économique*, pp.70–73, 135–140. The history of capital concentration in the steel industry can be noted in the history of its most prominent family: Jean-Noël Jeanneney, *François de Wendel en République*, 3 vol. (Paris: Champion, 1976). "Travail et repos d'un haut-fourniste au cours de 1950," 6pp. in René Boudot, private papers (1951).

8. Danielle Bleitrach, et al. *Classe ouvrière et social-démocratie: Lille et Marseille* (Paris: Editions sociales, 1981), pp.26–27, 29, 56, 59–61, 100; M.-R. Loew, *Les Dockers de Marseille* (L'Arbresle: Economie et Humanisme, 1945), pp.6–15, 21, 27–51; Ian B. Thompson, *The Lower Rhône and Marseille* (Oxford: University Press, 1975), pp.11, 17; "J.O.C. Fédération Marseille-Nord," *Conseil National* (1954), pp.1–4; Juliette Minces, *Le Nord* (Paris: François Maspero, 1967), pp.10–11, 14, 18–19, 31–32; André Latreille, *Histoire de Lyon et du Lyonnais* (Toulouse: Privat, 1975), pp.473, 475–477; "Problème missionnaire," p.41 in MDP (1950); Philippe Wolff, *Histoire de Toulouse* (Toulouse: Privat, 1974), pp.507, 509, 517, 522.

9. "Le Régime économique," pp.35–37; Chombart de Lauwe, *Vie quotidienne*, p.29; Richard F. Hamilton, *Affluence and the French Worker in the Fourth*

Republic (Princeton: N.J.: University Press, 1967), pp.186–187, 191–192, 195.

10. Rideau, "A nous chrétiens," pp.3–5; "Travail et repos," 3rd pg.; Hamilton, *Affluence*, pp.68, 71–73, 76; Val R. Lorwin, *The French Labor Movement* (Cambridge: Harvard University Press, 1954), p.113; Chombart de Lauwe, *Vie Quotidienne*, pp.140, 149–152; Collinet, *Essai*, pp.143–145; J.-L. Guglielmi and M. Perrot, *Salaires et revendications sociales en France, 1944–1952* (Paris: Colin, 1952), pp.166–167, 172, 175.

11. Guy Caire, *Les Syndicats Ouvriers* (Paris: Presses Universitaires de France, 1971), pp.55–70, 76; René Mouriaux, *La CGT* (Paris: Seuil, 1982), p.17, 34–49; Lorwin, *French Labor*, pp.21–43.

12. Caire, *Les Syndicats*, pp.80–88; Mouriaux, *La CGT*, pp.56–84; Lorwin, *French Labor*, pp.54–88; George Ross, *Workers and Communists in France*. (Berkeley: University of California Press, 1982), pp.8–13; Henry W. Ehrmann, *French Labor from Popular Front to Liberation* (New York: Oxford University Press, 1947), pp.31–165.

13. Caire, *Les Syndicats*, pp.96–99, 334; Ross, *Workers and Communists*, pp.x–xii, 19–43; Mouriaux, *La CGT*, pp.89–91; Lorwin, *French Labor*, pp.91–116.

14. Léon Jouhaux, *Force Ouvrière*, Dec. 20, 1945, p.1; "Rendons à César," *Force Ouvrière*, July 4, 1946, p.1; F.O., "En toute clarté," *Force Ouvrière*, Oct. 23, 1947, p.1; "La Conférence Nationale . . . ," *Force Ouvrière*, Dec. 25, 1947, p.11; Caire, *Les Syndicats*, pp.101–103; Alain Bergounioux, *Force Ouvrière* (Paris: Seuil, 1975), pp.32, 58–88, 92–96, 105–110, 127–128; André Bergeron, *Confédération Force Ouvrière* (Paris: EPI, 1971), pp.19–31; Benoît Frachon, *Le Peuple*, July 19, 1950; R. Arrachard, "Notre vielle maison," *Vie Ouvrière*, Dec. 24–30, 1947, pp.1, 3; Benoît Frachon, "Une seule section syndicale . . . ," *Vie Ouvrière*, Mar. 27–Apr. 2, 1947, pp.1, 3; Benoît Frachon, "La Grande conspiration contre la C.G.T.," *Vie Ouvrière*, Jan. 7–13, 1948, p.5.

15. Gérard Deygas, *La C.F.T.C., cinquante ans d'histoire* (Paris: Gérard Deygas, 1969), pp.13–14, 29–61; Guy Caire, *Les Syndicats*, p.91; Lorwin, *French Labor*, p.64; G.C. Thormann, *Christian Trade Unionism in France*, dissertation (New York: Columbia University, 1951), pp.36–56; Jean-Claude Poulain, *CFDT, le rêve et la vie* (Paris: Editions sociales, 1981), pp.17–21. Poulain, the author, was one of the worker-priests who had much difficulty with the Catholic trade union leadership. For some observations about the leadership's personal trade union life, see Gaston Tessier, *Le Syndicalisme chrétien en 1945* (Paris: C.F.T.C., 1945) and Jules Zirnheld, *Cinquante années du syndicalisme chrétien* (Paris: Spes, 1937).

16. Deygas, *La C.F.T.C.*, pp.57–117; Caire, *Les Syndicats*, pp.92–95; Gérard Adam, *La C.F.T.C., (1940–1958)* (Paris: Colin, 1964), pp.10–11; Thormann, *Christian Trade Unionism*, pp.59–97; Gaston Tessier, "Pour la paix sociale," *Vie Catholique*, Apr. 21, 1934, p.1; Charles Flory, "L'Importance et les difficultés de la propagande syndicale chrétienne," *Vie Catholique*, Aug. 1, 1925, p.1; "Méthodes de la C.F.T.C.," *Vie Catholique*, Nov. 21, 1931, p.9; Gaston Tessier, "Syndicalisme des fonctionnaires," *Syndicalisme chrétien* (Nov.,

1933), p.876; "Syndicalisme chrétien et corporatisme fasciste," *Syndicalisme chrétien* (Nov., 1934), pp.887–889 and (Feb., 1934), pp.895–897; J. Zirnheld, "Un Bilan," *Syndicalisme,* July, 1936, p.1; "La Grève générale," *Syndicalisme,* Apr., 1937, p.1; William Bosworth, *Catholicism and Crisis in Modern France* (Princeton, N.J.: University Press, 1962f), pp.266–267.

17. Gaston Tessier, "Novembre, 1919–Novembre 1944," *Syndicalisme,* Nov. 4, 1944, p.1.

18. Maurice Bouladoux, "A propos de l'unité," *Syndicalisme,* Mar. 10, 1945, p.1.

19. Benoît Frachon, "A tous les travailleurs de France," *Vie Ouvrière,* Dec. 11–16, 1947, p.6; "Où sont les adhérents de la C.F.T.C.?" *Vie Ouvrière,* Aug. 7–13, 1947, p.11; "L'U.G.F.F. condamne les dirigeants nationaux F.O. et C.F.T.C.," *Vie Ouvrière,* July 29–Aug. 4, 1948, p.5; Bureau de la C.G.T., "Vive l'unité de la classe ouvrière," *Le Peuple,* Mar. 28–Apr. 4, 1951, p.1; Paul Vignaux, *De la CFTC à la CFDT* (Paris: Editions Ouvrières, 1980), pp.31–32, 40–46; Poulain, *CFDT,* pp.44–45; Adam, *La C.F.T.C.,* pp.99–100, 104, 107–109; Thormann, *Christian Trade Unionism,* pp.155–157.

20. Deygas, *La C.F.T.C.,* pp.136–142, 150–153, 159; Caire, *Les Syndicats,* p.100; Vignaux, *De la CFTC,* pp.30–31; Adam, *La C.F.T.C.,* pp.57–71, 76–78, 111–119; 129–135, 152–157, 168–181, 189–215; Thormann, *Christian Trade Unionism,* pp.111–122, 136–139, 165–224; Bosworth, *Catholicism,* pp.267–276, 278.

21. Deygas, *La C.F.T.C.,* pp.143–144, 148–149, 155–156, 162–166; Caire, *Les Syndicats,* p.100; Vignaux *De la C.F.T.C.,* pp.30, 83, 122; Adam, *La C.F.T.C.,* pp.71–75, 79–80, 219–273; Thormann, *Christian Trade Unionism,* pp.123–135.

22. Edward Shorter and Charles Tilly, *Strikes in France* (Cambridge: University Press, 1974), pp.127–128; Frémontier, *La Forteresse ouvrière,* p.60; Weil, *Condition ouvrière,* pp.158–159.

23. H.R. Kedward, *Resistance in Vichy France* (Oxford: University Press, 1978), pp.256, 261–263, 270–271; Ehrmann, *French Labor,* pp.238–279; "Peuple de France," *L'Humanité,* Aug. 15, 1940, p.1; "Contre les déportations en Bochie," *L'Humanité,* Jan., 1943, p.1; "Intensifions la préparation à l'insurrection nationale," *L'Humanité,* July 20, 1943, p.1; "L'Action des vaillants F.T.P.F.," *L'Humanité,* Jan. 18, 1944, p.4; "Après le discours de Laval," *Vie Ouvrière,* June 27, 1942, p.1; "Pendant 12 jours, à Montceau-les-Mines, 5.000 mineurs font grève," *Vie Ouvrière,* Feb., 1942, p.1; Jacques Duclos, interview, Paris (May 7, 1973); André Moine, interview, Paris (June 13, 1977).

24. Ross, *Workers and Communists,* pp.45–46, Caire, *Les Syndicats,* pp.103–105; Shorter and Tilly, *Strikes,* pp.137–139; F.O., "En toute clarté;" F.O., "Etat d'alerte," *Force Ouvrière,* Sept. 3, 1953, p.1; Benoît Frachon, "A tous les travailleurs de France," *Vie Ouvrière,* Dec. 11–16, 1947, pp.6–7; "Dans les mines de fer . . . ," *Vie Ouvrière,* Jan. 6–12, 1949, p.9.

25. Ross, *Workers and Communists,* pp.59–63; Vignaux, *De la CFTC,* p.46; Marcel Dufriche, "Paix au Vietnam," *Vie Ouvrière,* Mar. 17–23, 1949, p.5; Eugène Henaff, "Contre le pacte de mort," *Vie Ouvrière,* July 14–20, 1949, pp.1,

7; Benoît Frachon, La Paix est un combat," *Le Peuple*, May 26–June 2, 1949, p.1; Jules Duchat, "Vers le congrès des peuples pour la paix," *La Peuple*, Aug, 1, 1952, p.1.

26. Lorwin, *French Labor*, pp.149–151, 153–158; Walter Galenson, *Trade Union Democracy in Western Europe* (Berkeley: University of California Press, 1961), p.12; Jean Bratteau, interview, Paris (June 19, 1980); Lucien Trilles, interview, Avignon (May 26, 1980); Benoît Frachon, "Qui avait raison?" *Vie Ouvrière*, Feb. 5–11, 1948, pp.1, 3; "Le Patronat s'oppose à la baisse des prix," *Le Peuple*, Feb. 27–Mar. 4, 1948, pp.1, 3; "Résolution sur les salaires et les prix," *Le Peuple*, Feb. 27–Mar. 4, 1948, p.6.

27. Trilles interview; Lorwin, *French Labor*, pp.171–173; Caire, *Les Syndicats*, pp.373–374, 408–415; Meeting announcement, C.G.T.-Syndicat des Metaux de Venissieux, Lyon (Feb. 1, 1954), 1p. in MDP (1954).

28. Lorwin, *French Labor*, pp.256–265; Calenson, *Trade Union Democracy*, pp.8–9; "Document . . . Les Comités d'Entreprises," *Lettre aux fédéraux* (July–Aug., 1945), pp.11–12; Pierre Bouvier, *Travail et expression ouvrière* (Paris: Galilée, 1980), pp.11–22, 28–29; Maurice Combe, *L'Alibi* (Paris: Gallimard, 1969), pp.20–34, 36–39. M. Combe was a St. Etienne worker-priest until the papal condemnation of 1954. Maurice Montuclard wrote a thesis on these *comités* which was published by the Centre National de la Recherche Scientifique.

29. "Ma vie chez Citroën" (1947) in MDP (1947); Combe, *L'Alibi*, pp.37–40, 80–81, 96–103, 109–116, 232–237, 252–273; Bouvier, *Travail*, pp.22–24; Lorwin, *French Labor*, pp.234–248; Jean-Daniel Reynaud, *Les Syndicats en France* (Paris: Colin, 1966), pp.142–149.

30. G.B., "Simples Réflexions" (Oct., 1948), pp.1–6 in MDP (1954); Bleitrach, *Classe ouvrière*, pp.27–28, 30, 56, 59, 100; Minces, *Le Nord*, pp.13–14, 31–33; Loew, *Les Dockers*, pp.48–51; Pierre Lhande, *Le Christ dans la Banlieue* (Paris: Plon, 1927), pp.3, 5, 10–12, 159–163; Charles Pautet, "Mission de Paris" (June 11, 1945), p.1 in MDP (1945); "18 mois à Belleville" (1949), p.1 in MDP (1949); Ross, *Workers and Communists*, p.7; Norma Evenson, *Paris: A Century of Change, 1878–1978* (New Haven: Yale University Press, 1979), pp.204–231; Anthony Sutcliffe, *The Autumn of Central Paris* (Montreal: McGill-Queens Press, 1971), pp.222–247; Ian B. Thompson, *The Paris Basin* (Oxford: University Press, 1973), pp.11–13, 15–16, 23; Jean Bastié, *La Croissance de la Banlieue Parisienne* (Paris: Presses Universitaires de France, 1964), pp.343–423.

31. Bastié, *La Croissance*, pp.346–347; Bleitrach, *Classe ouvrière*, p.100; Minces, *Le Nord*, pp.32, 43–44; André Depierre, report, Montreuil (1949), p.2 in MDP (1949); "18 mois," p.1; "Problème missionnaire," p.11; "Le Régime économique," pp.29–32; Jean Dubernet, "Dans un quartier comme tien," *Equipe Ouvrière*, Nov., 1950, p.2; Hamilton, *Affluence*, p.83; Evenson, *Paris*, pp.232, 235; Chombart de Lauwe, *Vie quotidienne*, pp.70, 81–90.

32. Rideau, "A nous chrétiens," p.4; "Le Régime économique," pp.29, 35; Hamilton, *Affluence*, p.149; Lorwin, *French Labor*, pp.112, 129; Chombart de Lauwe, *Vie quotidienne*, pp.118, 122–123, 190–195, 203.

33. "Quinze jours," pp.15–31; "18 mois," pp.2–3; André Deléage, "Ré-

flexions sur mon stage," p.5 in MDP (1954); Hamilton, *Affluence,* pp.52, 78, 99; Chombart de Lauwe, *Vie quotidienne,* pp.60–62, 91–93; Jean-Claude Poulain, Les Halles (Oct., 1949), p.3 in MDP (1949); "Problème missionnaire," p.11; "Travail et repos," pp.2–3; Hadley Cantril, *The Politics of Despair* (New York: Collier Books, 1962), p.69; Frémontier, *Forteresse,* p.58; Geneviève Poujol, *L'Éducation populaire* (Paris: Editions ouvrières, 1981), pp.26–27, 96–98.

34. Rideau, "A nous chrétiens," pp.6–8; "18 mois," pp.3–4; "Problème missionnaire," pp.5–7; "Essai de compréhension des aspirations ouvrières" (1950?), pp.3–10 in MDP (1950); "Abrégé," p.7; "Le Régime économique," pp.52–55; Cantril, *Politics,* pp.50–53.

35. Hamilton, *Affluence,* p.37.

36. Père André Capuchin, "Sacerdos et . . . Opifex" (1949), p.1 in MDP (1949); "Introduction historique," p.15 in Cahiers MDP (1955); Hamilton, *Affluence,* pp.24–33, 103–106, 137–145, 249, 259; Cantril, *Politics,* pp.100, 102, 105–106, 111–112.

37. "Rapport sur un project de mission," Paris (Dec. 14, 1946), pp.12–13 in MDP (1947); Marseille report (1948), pp.9–17; "Quatrième partie-Les Témoignages Sacerdotaux," p.6 in Cahiers MDP (1955); Gilbert Ponchaut and Lomme-Lez-Lille," (Oct. 3, 1964), pp.1–3 in Jacques Screppel papers; Cantril, *Politics,* p.53; "Quelques points acquis" (Sept. 1, 1948), pp.2, 4 in René Boudot papers (1948); Lhande, *Le Christ,* pp.64, 80; Hamilton, *Affluence,* pp.93–94.

38. Marseille report, pp.3–4, 8; Jean-Marie Lepetit, report, Paris 20ᵉ (Oct., 1949), p.2 in MDP (1949); "Problème missionnaire," pp.15–16; "Introduction historique," p.15; "Ma vie chez Citroën," p.2.

39. "Problème missionnaire," pp.6–7, 12.

40. "Ma vie chez Citroën," p.4; Deléage, "Réflexions," p.5; "Les Témoignages des laïcs," pp.2, 4–6, 9, 16, 19, 22–24, 46. The study *France, pays de mission?* by Fathers Henri Godin and Yvan Daniel, which was so influential in the birth of the worker-priest movement, illustrated this alienation graphically.

41. Marseille report, pp.7–8, 20; P. Besnard, Paris 18ᵉ (1949), p.1 in MDP (1949); "Problème missionnaire," pp.15–17; "Les Témoignages des laïcs," pp.8, 20, 22, 29bis–29ter.

V. THE WORLD OF WORKER-PRIEST ORIGINS

1. Emile Poulat's *Naissance des Prêtres-Ouvriers* (Paris: Casterman, 1965) is undoubtedly the most thorough and definitive study on worker-priest origins in both the narrow and broader contexts.

2. Yvan Daniel was also a member of the Mission de Paris (although not as a worker-priest) as well as a *curé* in an Ivry missionary parish. For more data on his life, consult Yvan Daniel, ed., *Témoignages sur l'abbé Godin* (Liège: Pensée Catholique, 1946) in *Etudes Religieuses,* no's.575–576 and Yvan Daniel, *Aux frontières de l'église* (Paris: Cerf, 1978).

3. Henri Godin and Yvan Daniel, *France Pagan? The Mission of Abbé*

Godin, introduction and trans. by Maisie Ward (London: Sheed and Ward, 1950), pp.3–4, 8; Poulat, *Naissance*, p.52. For a rather hagiographic study on Godin, read P. Glorieux, *Un homme providentiel* (Paris: Bonne Presse, 1946).

4. Godin and Daniel, *France*, pp.12–14, 22–23, 29; Poulat, *Naissance*, pp.57–62. During his Jociste period Godin was a prolific author. He wrote a number of very practical manuals for the Jocistes under his charge. These include: *L'Aumônier et la mystique préjociste* (1936) *Missel jociste* (1937), *Jeunesse qui reconstruit* (1942) and *Le Christ dans la construction du foyer* (1943).

5. Godin and Daniel, *France*, pp.19–20, 27, 31, 39.

6. Henri Godin and Yvan Daniel, *France, pays de mission?* (Paris, 1943), pp.9, 23–25, 39, 41, 46.

7. Ibid., pp.38, 57–58, 90, 99, 140, 145.

8. Ibid., pp.49, 71, 91.

9. "Il y a dix ans mourait le Cardinal Suhard," *Informations Catholiques Internationales* (May 1, 1959), pp.13–24; *The Church Today: The Collected Writings of Emmanuel Cardinal Suhard*, intro. by John Wright (Chicago: Fides, 1953), pp.vii–viii. A cameo of Suhard's personality is sensitively developed in Jean Vinatier's, *Le Cardinal Liénart et la Mission de France* (Paris: Centurion, 1978), pp.29–30. For a critical appraisal of his war-time activities, see appropriate sections in Robert Paxton, *Vichy France* (New York: Knopf, 1972) and Robert Paxton and Michael Marrus, *Vichy France and the Jews* (New York: Basic Books, 1981). The most thorough work on Cardinal Suhard is the definitive biography by Jean Vinatier, *Le cardinal Suhard* (Paris: Centurion, 1983).

10. Poulat, *Naissance*, pp.36–37. For further details on this history from a personal witness, consult Daniel, *Aux frontières*.

11. Such was the testimony given to me by a large number of former worker-priests. Some examples are: Henri Barreau, interview, Gagny (May 16, 1979); Francis Laval, interview, St. Etienne (May 19, 1983); Jacques Jaudon, interview, Grenoble (June 15, 1983); Louis Flagothier and Albert Courtoy, interviews, Liège, Belgium (June 8, 1983).

12. Text of retreat by Louis Augros, "Sacerdoce dans l'église," pp.1–21 in Mission de Paris papers (hereafter cited as MDP) (1943–1944); "Mois d'études et de conversations pour la mise au point de la Mission de Paris" (Dec. 19, 1943–Jan. 16, 1944), pp.1–5 in MDP (1943–1944). For full details of the retreat, see Poulat, *Naissance*, pp.94–108.

13. Poulat, *Naissance*, pp.95–96, 103–110; "Mois d'études," pp.1–5.

14. "Consignes de S.E. le Cardinal" (Jan. 13–14, 1944), p.1 in MDP (1943–1944).

15. Poulat, *Naissance*, p.112; Godin and Daniel, *France pagan?* p.60; "Autour d'un père de la classe ouvrière," funeral mass, p.1 in MDP (1943–1944); André Retif, "La Mission de Paris," *Etudes* (Mar., 1949), p.3.

16. Introduction historique," pp.8–9 in MDP (1955); "Prêtres-ouvriers français," pp.2–7 in MDP (1954); Poulat, *Naissance*, pp.209, 211–212, 246, 252, 258, 270.

17. Poulat, *Naissance*, pp.259–270. The personal reminiscences of Rodhain can be found in *Une charité inventive* (Paris: Centurion, 1975), pp.46–100.

18. For some examples, consult Joseph Gelin, *Nüremberg, 1943–1945*. *L'expérience d'un prêtre-ouvrier* (Seine: Petit-Clamart, 1946); A.G. Morelli, *Terre de détresse* (Paris: Bloud et Gay, 1947); Paul Beschet, *Mission en Thuringe* (Paris: Editions Ouvrières, 1947); Ulrich, "La Vie religieuse en captivité," *Etudes* (Apr., 1945), pp.24–39; Léon de Coninck, "Les Conversations de Dachau," *Nouvelle Revue Théologique* (Nov., 1945), pp.1169–1183; "Cahiers mensuels des futurs prêtres." *Servir* (July, 1943), pp.588–591.

19. Poulat, *Naissance*, pp.196–197, 200–201.

20. Hadrien Bousquet, *Hors des Barbelés*, 2nd edition (Paris: Spes, 1945), pp.20, 27, 48, 60, 63–64, 70, 73–75, 80–81, 111–116.

21. Victor Dillard, *Suprême Témoignage* (Paris: Spes, 1946), pp.5–6, 17, 32, 34, 36–39, 41–42, 46. For further details on Dillard's life and testimony, see Contre-Amiral Dillard, *La Vie et la mort du R.P. Dillard* (Paris: Oeuvres Françaises, 1947) and A. de Soras, "Le Père Victor Dillard," *Etudes* (Oct., 1945), pp.84–105.

22. Emile Poulat's *Naissance des prêtres-ouvriers* is a brilliant and thorough account of this constellation of persons and events.

23. "Clergé de la Mission de Paris" (Mar., 1944), p.1 in MDP (1943–1944); "Mission Ouvrière de Toulouse," June, 1951, 1p. in MDP (1951); untitled biographical list, 10pp. (1951) in MDP (1951); Joseph Sanguedolce, et al, *Joseph Gouttebarge* in Robert Pacalet, private papers; Jacques Hollande, interview, Paris (May 28, 1979).

24. Albert Bouche, interview, Paris (May 13, 1983); André Depierre, interview, Montreuil (June 20, 1979); Sanguedolce, *Joseph Gouttebarge*, pp.3, 17; Maurice Combe, interview, Lyon (June 14, 1979); Henri Perrin, *Itinéraire d'Henri Perrin* (Paris: Seuil, 1958), p.9.

25. Jean Volot, interview, Paris (May 19, 1980); Bernard Cagne, interview, Paris (June 21, 1979); Barreau interview; Charles Pautet, "Le Père Charles Pautet . . . à Monsieur," Aug. 7, 1947, p.1 in MDP (1947); Père Robert, "Rapport sur mon engagement," Paris (Jan. 22, 1949), p.1 in MDP (1949); Joseph Robert, interview, Paris (June 27, 1979).

26. Jacques Loew, interview, Fribourg, Swit. (May 14, 1980); Bernard Tiberghien, interview, Dunkerque (June 12, 1980); Jacques Screppel, interview, Hellemes (June 9, 1983).

27. Volot, Cagne, Barreau interviews; Pautet, "Le Père Charles . . . ," p.1; P. Jean-Marie Petit, report, Paris 20ᵉ (Oct., 1949), p.1 in MDP (1949) Père Roger Deliat, report Boulogne-Billancourt (1949), p.1 in MDP (1949); Roger Deliat, *Vingt ans chez Renault* (Paris: Editions ouvrières, 1973), pp.15, 17; Sanguedolce, *Joseph Gouttebarge*, pp.5–6.

28. Perrin, *Itinéraire*, pp.11–23; Depierre, Tiberghien, Laval, Jaudon interviews; Jean Gray, interview, Auxerre (June 11, 1983).

29. Laval, Combe, Jaudon, Flagothier, Courtoy, Gray interviews; "Addenda" (Oct. 13, 1949), 1p. in MDP (1949); Jacques Hollande, letter to Msgr. Touvet (May 12, 1953), 1p. in MDP (1953); Striffling, Vivez, Genthial interviews, Courbevoie (June 11, 1979); Garnier and Chavanneau interviews, Limoges (May 31, 1983); Jacques Riousse, interview, Escarenne (June 3, 1983);

Philbert Talé, interview, Antony (June 1, 1983); Albert Guichard, interview, Paris (June 21, 1983).

30. Gray, Guichard interviews; Emile Poulat, interview, Paris (May 20, 1983).

31. Deliat, *Vingt ans*, pp.18–19; Robert, "rapport," p.1.

32. Gray, Riousse, Striffling interviews; Paul Guilbert, interview, Venissieux (May 16, 1983); Bernard Chauveau, interview, Boulogne-Billancourt (May 11, 1979); Georges-Pierre Puységur, "Mission de la gare," Paris 13ᵉ (Dec. 26, 1948), pp.1–3 in MDP (1948).

33. Albert Gauche, "Aux ouvrièrs chrétiens," 1954, p.1 in MDP (1954); Barreau interview; Robert, "rapport," p.1.

34. Henri Perrin, *Journal d'un prêtre-ouvrier en Allemagne* (Paris: Seuil, 1945), pp.18, 27–28, 72, 105–106, 144–145, 149–168, 239–240, 277–278, 314, 316–317.

35. Depierre, Robert interviews; Robert Pacalet, interview, Lyon (July 5, 1979); Francis Vico, interview, Montluçon (May 24, 1980).

36. Michel Bordet, interview, Simian-la-Rotunde (May 27, 1983); "Témoignages des prêtres," p.102 in Cahiers de la Mission de Paris (1955); Jean Cottin, interview, Paris (June 17, 1980); Sanguedolce, *Joseph Gouttebarge*, p.7; Jean-Pierre Perconte, *La J.O.C. et la J.O.C.F. dans le diocèse de Grenoble*, unpublished research paper (Grenoble, 1977); Pierre Riche, report, Paris 20ᵉ (Oct., 1949), p.1 in MDP (1949); Robert, "rapport," pp.1–2.

37. "Témoignages des prêtres," p.99; Gauche, "Aux ouvriers," p.1; Sanguedolce, *Joseph Gouttebarge*, p.14; Deliat, report, p.1; Robert Pfaff, interview, Paris (June 10, 1983); François Vidal, interview, Marseille (June 2, 1983).

38. Poulat, *Naissance*, pp.411–412, 414, 444; *Témoignage Chrétien*, July 1962, pp.1, 4.

39. "De quelques problèmes autour de la Mission de Paris" (Mar. 27, 1945), pp.1–4 in MDP (1945); "Quelques notes sur la Mission de Paris" (Feb., 1946), p.1 in MDP (1943–1944).

40. Robert Kothen, *The Priest and the Proletariat*, trans. by Frank Maher (New York: Sheed and Ward, 1950), pp.32–37; André Retif, "La Mission de Paris," *Etudes* (Mar., 1949), p.11; Bernard Tiberghien, "Réflexions sur la Mission de Paris," June 16, 1945, p.3 in MDP (1945); P. Lucien Lacour, "La Mission de Paris," Oct., 1949, p.4 in MDP (1949); "Quelques notes," p.2; "L'Eglise en marche," c. 1946, p.2 in MDP (1943–1944).

41. Depierre interview; Andre Depierre, "Monde moderne, monde chrétien," *Esprit* (Aug.–Sept., 1946), pp.321–344; André Depierre, "De la mission à la communauté de quartier, foyer de vie humaine," *Economie et Humanisme* (Nov.–Dec., 1946), pp.570–577; André Depierre, report July, 1945, pp.8–9 in MDP (1945).

42. Poulat, *Naissance*, pp.239–243; André Depierre, "Adieu à un ami," *Témoignage Chrétien*, May 18, 1945, pp.1–2.

43. Poulat, *Naissance*, pp.188–196; Charles Boland, *Dure Percée* (Brussels: Foyer Notre Dame, 1968), pp.27–28, 30–34, 44, 48–52.

44. Boland, *Dure Percée*, pp.61, 63; Poulat, *Naissance*, pp.470–474, 477;

"Fraternité des O.V.P." (June 15, 1947), pp.4–6, 18 in MDP (1947); Père Damien Reumont, "Fraternité des Ouvriers de la Vièrge des Pauvres" (1947), pp.2–3 in MDP (1947).

45. Poulat, *Naissance,* pp.446–451; "Journée des religieux missionnaires" (Feb. 6, 1949), pp.1–2, 4; "Rapport sur un projet de mission," p.12 in "Fraternité des O.V.P."; R.P. Césaire Dillaye, interview, Paris (May, 1979).

46. Poulat, *Naissance,* pp.451–452, 454–457; "Journée des religieux," p.4; Perrin, *Itinéraire,* pp.93–103, 108, 117, 120–126, 128–129, 132–140; "Fraternité des O.V.P.," p.3; Père Villain, Action Populaire, interview, Paris (June 6, 1979).

47. Poulat, *Naissance,* pp.415–431; Loew interview.

48. "La Mission de Paris" (Oct., 1949), p.1 in MDP (1949); Perrin, *Itinéraire,* pp.162, 178, 183; Daniel Perrot, Mission de France, interview, Paris (May 10, 1979); Robert interview.

49. Alfred Ancel, interview, Lyon (June 14, 1979); Alfred Ancel, *5 ans avec les ouvriers* (Paris: Centurion, 1963), pp.31, 34; "Fraternité des O.V.P.," pp.3–4.

50. Poulat, *Naissance,* pp.525–536; John Petrie, ed., *The Worker-Priests* (London: Routledge and Kegan Paul, 1956), p.15.

VI. THE WORLD OF WORKER-PRIEST NATURALIZATION

1. Jacques Jaudon, worker-priest, interview, Grenoble (June 15, 1983); André Piet, worker-priest, interview, Marseille (June 2, 1983); Joseph Robert, worker-priest, interview, Paris (June 17, 1979); and Bernard Chauveau, worker-priest, interview, Boulogne-Billancourt (May 11, 1979).

2. Père du Mont, report, Ivry (Feb. 2, 1945), pp.1–3 in Mission de Paris papers (1945), hereafter referred to as MDP.

3. "Des prêtres, en milieu de travail," p.2 in MDP (1946).

4. "Le Responsable du groupe," note (1946), 1p. in MDP (1946).

5. François Vidal, worker-priest, interview, Marseille (June 2, 1983); Louis Flagothier, worker-priest, interview, Liège (June 8, 1983); "Les Prêtres-Ouvriers liégois," *La Wallonie,* March 30, 1983, pp.1, 10 in Louis Flagothier papers.

6. Henri Perrin, *Itinéraire d'Henri Perrin* (Paris: Seuil, 1958), pp.143–144.

7. Jacques Loew, worker-priest, interview, Fribourg, Swit. (May 14, 1980); M.-R. Loew, *Mission to the Poorest,* trans. by Pamela Carswell (London: Sheed and Ward, 1950), pp.21–22, 28.

8. Charles Boland, *Dure Percée* (Brussels: Foyer Notre Dame, 1968), pp.27–52.

9. Robert Pacalet, worker-priest, interview, Lyon (July 5, 1979).

10. Mgr. Alfred Ancel, worker-bishop, interview, Lyon (June 14, 1979); Alfred Ancel, *5 ans avec les ouvriers* (Paris: Centurion, 1963), pp.33–35.

11. Perrin, *Itinéraire*, pp.157, 159.

12. Père Charles Pautet, "A Monsieur le Chef du Personnel . . . Renault." (Aug. 7, 1947), p.1 in MDP (1947).

13. Pacalet interview.

14. André Deléage, "Réflexions sur mon stage," pp.1–2 in MDP (1954).

15. Gabriel Genthial, Bernard Striffling and Jacques Vivez, worker-priests, interview, Courbevoie (June 11, 1979); Henri Barreau, worker-priest, interview, Gagny (May 16, 1979); Louis Bouyer, worker-priest, interview, Colombes (May 21, 1979).

16. "Problème missionnaire," Limoges report (1950), p.21 in MDP (1950).

17. Jean Olhagaray, worker-priest, interview, Paris (June 13, 1979); Barreau interview.

18. "Quelques points acquis" (Sept. 1, 1948) in René Boudot, private papers (1948); Jean Legendre, worker-priest, interview, Plateau d'Assy (June 6, 1983); Jean Cottin, worker-priest, interview, Paris (June 17, 1980).

19. Perrin, *Itinéraire*, p.159.

20. Roger Deliat, *Vingt ans O.S. chez Renault* (Paris: Editions Ouvrières, 1973), p.22.

21. Marseille report to Mgr. Delay (1948), pp.21–22 in MDP (1948).

22. Ibid. pp.21–23; Michel Bordet, worker-priest, interview, Simian-la-Rotonde (May 27, 1983).

23. "Déclaration des travailleurs chrétiens," p.3 in MDP (1953); Deliat, *Vingt ans*, p.25; René Boudot, friend of worker-priest, interview, Cons-la-Grandville (June 4, 1980); Maurice Combe, worker-priest, interview, Lyon (June 14, 1979); Perrin, *Itinéraire*, p.159; Bernard Tiberghien, worker-priest, interview, Dunkerque (June 12, 1980); Césaire Dillaye, Capuchin, interview, Paris (May 14, 1979); Yves Garnier and André Chavanneau, worker-priest, interviews, Limoges (May 31, 1983); Jean Tarby, worker-priest, interview, Chartres (June 13, 1983); Philbert Talé, worker-priest, interview, Antony (June 1, 1983); Paul Guilbert, worker-priest, interview, Venissieux (May 16, 1983); Jean Gray, worker-priest, interview, Auxerre (June 11, 1983); Bernard Cagne, worker-priest, interview, Paris (June 21, 1979); André Piet, worker-priest, interview, Marseille (June 2, 1983); Robert Pfaff, worker-priest, interview, Paris (June 10, 1983); Albert Courtoy, worker-priest, interview, Liège (June 8, 1983); Robert, Flagothier, Bordet, Vidal, Legendre, Jaudon, Barreau and Chauveau interviews; Joseph Sanguedolce, et. al., *Joseph Gouttebarge*, p.26 in Robert Pacalet, private papers; Ch. Monier, "Formation d'une section syndicale" (Sept.–Oct., 1953), p.1 in MDP (1953).

24. Loew, *Mission*, pp.23–24; Loew and Tiberghien interviews; "Mission de Paris" (c. 1950), p.3 in MDP (1943–1944); Perrin, *Itinéraire*, p.257; Genthial, Striffling, Vivez interviews; Francis Vico, worker-priest, interview, Montluçon (May 24, 1980); untitled biographical list, 10pp. (1951), p.3 in MDP (1951); list to Père Hollande, Lyon (July 9, 1951), 1p. in MDP (1951); Francis Laval, worker-priest, St. Etienne, interview (May 19, 1983); "Relevé des services," Jan. 11, 1983, 1p. in Francis Laval papers; "La Mission de Paris" (Oct.,

1949), p.1 in MDP (1949); P. Rosi, report, Paris 18ᵉ (Oct., 1949), p.1 in MDP (1949); Jean Volot, sailor-priest, interview, Paris (May 19, 1980); Jacques Riousse, worker-priest, interview (June 3, 1983); Père Damien, "Fraternité des O.V.P." (July 21, 1947), p.2 in MDP (1947); Ancel, *5 ans*, pp.42, 45; Ancel interview; P. Pierre Riche, reports, Paris 20ᵉ (Oct., 1949), p.1 in MDP (1949); Robert Kothen, *The Priest and the Proletariat*, trans. by Frank Maher (New York: Sheed and Ward, 1948), pp.35–37; P. Jean-Marie Marzio, report, Paris 12ᵉ (Oct., 1949), p.1 in MDP (1949). Jean Sulivan's novel *Car, je t'aime, ô éternité*, published by Gallimard in Paris, is a novel based upon Father Rosi's ministry.

25. Henri Barreau, "Project de Déclaration," p.2 in Henri Barreau, private papers.

26. Pacalet, Barreau, Robert, Jaudon interviews; André Depierre, worker-priest, interview, Montreuil (June 20, 1979); Père Joseph Robert, "Rapport sur mon engagement de prêtre-ouvrier," Paris (Jan. 22, 1949), p.4 in MDP (1949); Chauveau, Bouyer and Cottin interviews.

27. "Témoignages des prêtres ayant été au travail," p.115 in *Cahiers de la Mission de Paris* (1955).

28. G.B., "Simple Réflexions" (Oct., 1948–July, 1950), pp.1–2 in MDP (1954); André Deléage, "Réflexions sur mon stage," p.4 in MDP (1954); Pfaff, Bordet and Piet interviews; *Joseph Lafontaine*, p.3 in Jacques Jaudon private papers.

29. Vico, Pacalet interviews; Deliat, *Vingt ans*, pp.33–39; "Conclusions des journées de prêtres-ouvriers" (Feb. 16–17, 1952), p.2 in MDP (1952); "La Fin d'un apôtre moderne" (1951), 1p. in MDP (1951); Sanguedolce, *Joseph Gouttebarge; Joseph Lafontaine;* Père Jacques, "A la memoire de nos camarades," *Eveil Syndical* (June, 1950) in Jacques Screppel, private papers.

30. Depierre and Cagne interviews, Riche, Olhagaray, Lepetit, handwritten report (Dec., 1948–Jan., 1949), Ménilmontant in MDP (1949); "Ma Vie chez Citroën" (1947), pp.1–5 in MDP (1947).

31. Jean Leclère, letter, Bordeaux (June, 1953), p.1 in MDP (1953); Albert Gauche, "Àux ouvriers chrétiens" (1954), p.2 in MDP (1954); Henri Barreau, "Tu es pour eux un démon!" p.13 in Henri Barreau, private papers; "Douze grévistes," p.1 in MDP (1954); Talé interview; Sanguedolce, *Joseph Gouttebarge*, pp.27–29, 37.

32. Piet, Laval and Robert interviews.

33. Marseille report, pp.28, 30–31; G.B., "Simple Réflexions," pp.6–9.

34. Perrin, *Itinéraire*, pp.159–160, 166–167; Loew interview; Loew, *Mission*, pp.21, 23–25.

35. Cottin, Bordet, Depierre, Vico, Genthial, Striffling, Vivez, Combe, Bouyer, Barreau, Olhagaray, Chauveau, Cagne, Pacalet, Dillaye, Loew, Talé, Pfaff, Guilbert, Piet, Laval, Jaudon interviews; Albert Guichard, worker-priest, interview, Paris (June 21, 1983); Bernard Lacroix, worker-priest, interview, Grenoble (June 15, 1983).

36. "Déclation de travailleurs chrétiens," p.3 in MDP (1953); Robert, Gray, Tarby, Chauveau, Cagne, Pacalet, Vico interviews; Emile Poulat, worker-priest, interview, Paris (May 20, 1983). Rumor has it that the Lyon

worker-priest Father Paul Magand resolved such interunion tensions by taking out membership in all three union federations (Jaudon and Bordet interviews; Emile Poulat, letter, Jan. 11, 1986, p.5).

37. Perrin, *Itinéraire*, p.163; Sanguedolce, *Joseph Gouttebarge*, p.26; P. Jean Olhagaray, report, Paris 20ᵉ (Oct., 1949), pp.3–4 in MDP (1949); Tiberghien, "Ma Vie," pp.3–5.

38. H. Barreau (c. 1949), p.1 in MDP (1949). Also Deliat, *Vingt Ans*, p.108; Bouyer interview.

39. Boudot, Depierre, Striffling, Genthial interviews; Gauche, "Aux ouvriers," p.2; M.-R. Loew, *Journal d'une mission ouvriére* (Paris: 1959), pp.109–110; Loew interviews; P. Henri Barreau, report, Malakoff (Oct., 1949), p.2 in MDP (1949); Jean Desailly (March, 1954), p.1 in Henri Barreau, private papers.

40. Screppel, Legendre, Flagothier, Courtoy interviews.

41. Depierre, Tiberghien and Loew interviews.

42. Vidal and Tiberghien interviews; Ch. Monier, "Formation d'une section syndicale" (Sept.–Oct., 1953), p.2 in MDP (1953).

43. Combe, Pacalet, Talé, Gray, Garnier and Chavanneau interviews; "Un prêtre-ouvrier de Donzère-Mondragon," *Marseillaise* (Oct. 29, 1952), 1p. in MDP (1954); Deliat, *Vingt ans*, p.31. *L'Alibi* (Paris: Gallimard, 1969) is Maurice Combe's book about his work on a *comité d'entreprise* and is well worth consulting.

44. *Joseph Lafontaine*, p.13; Vico interview.

45. Sanguedolce, *Joseph Gouttebarge*, pp.24, 26, 28, 39, 44–45; Joseph Gouttebarge, letter to Cardinal Gerlier (Mar. 14, 1954), p.2 in MDP (1954). Francis Laval was also an editor of his trade-union newspaper for the miners (Laval interview).

46. Barreau interview; Secrétariat d'information, "Notes confidentielles du 1ᵉʳ et 8 juin 1951," 1p. in MDP (1954); "Conclusions des journées de prêtres-ouvriers" (Feb. 16–17, 1952), p.2 in MDP (1952); Père Jacques Hollande, interview, Paris (May 28, 1979).

47. Loew, Cottin, Chauveau, Flagothier, Courtoy, Legendre and Screppel interviews; "Des prêtres-ouvriers de Limoges," 1p. in MDP (1954); Jacques Screppel, handwritten notes, "Historique gréve Fives-Lille" (1950), pp.1–4 in Screppel papers; Bernard Tiberghien, "Ma Vie," pp.2–5.

48. Bordet interview; Sanguedolce, *Joseph Gouttebarge*, pp.37–38, 41–42.

49. Perrin, *Itinéraire*, pp.262, 265, 271, 273–76, 278–280, 283–286, 291, 295–298, 301.

50. Robert Pfaff, "Quelques réflexions . . . ," pp.6–8 in René Boudot, private papers.

51. Legendre, Screppel, Laval, Talé, Gray, Vidal, Pfaff, Guichard, Chauveau, Combe, Pacalet, Cottin, Robert, Loew and Barreau interviews; Jacques Screppel, "Premières intuitions," p.4 in Screppel papers; Deliat, *Vingt Ans*, p.31; "Un prêtre-ouvrier de Donzère-Mondragon," *Marseillaise*, Oct. 29, 1952, p.1 in MDP (1952); "Les Prêtres-Ouvriers du Rhône et de la Loire," Lyon (Mar. 4, 1953), pp.1–2 in MDP (1953); "Equipe de Marseille" (1953),

pp.1–4 in MDP (1953); Mgr. Raymond Touvet, letter to Jacques Hollande (May 11, 1953), 1p. in MDP (1953); Albert Gauche, "Aux ouvriers chrétiens" (1954), pp.1–4, in MDP (1954); H.-M. Féret, "Explication de vote" (1950), pp.1–8 in MDP (1950); G.B., "Simples Réflexions" (Oct., 1948–July, 1950), p.10 in MDP (1954).

52. Vico interview; Sanguedolce, *Joseph Gouttebarge,* pp.22–23, 80; Barreau interview; Henri Barreau, "Project de Déclaration," p.3 in Barreau papers. A number of the other worker-priests also marched for peace (Piet, Jaudon and Tarby interviews).

53. Bouyer and Cagne interviews; L. Bouyer and B. Cagne, "Pour ceux qui ne pourront jamais parler et qu'on ne voudra pas croire," Colombes (May 30, 1952), pp.1–4 in MDP (1952).

54. For a study on this issue, consult Oscar L. Arnal, "Missionary 'Main Tendue' Toward French Communists," *French Historical Studies* XIII, 4 (Fall, 1984), pp.529–556.

55. Poulat, Guichard, Talé interviews.

56. Abbé C.F. Boland, pp.554–555 in MDP (1947); "Découverte du travail et des travailleurs," *Masses Ouvrières* (Nov., 1945), pp.38–55; "Allemagne" (1948) in MDP (1948); Perrin, *Itinéraire,* pp.82–83, 85; Cagne, Pacalet, Vico, Depierre, Cottin and Loew interviews; Loew, *Mission,* pp.21–22; Sanguedolce, *Joseph Gouttebarge,* p.13; P. Charles Pautet, report, Boulogne-Billancourt (Oct., 1949), p.1 in MDP (1949).

57. Bordet interview; "Quelques points acquis" (Sept. 1, 1948), pp.5–7 in René Boudot, private papers; Père Legendre report, "Les Reformes de structure," p.8 in MDP (1945); "Problèmes de la mission à Arcueil" (Apr., 1945), p.2 in MDP (1945); "Les Reformes de structure," pp.8–9, 13.

58. Deliat, *Vingt ans,* p.22; Perrin, *Itinéraire,* p.171; Depierre, Barreau, Olhagaray interviews.

59. "Marseille reports," pp.25–27; Loew interview.

60. Vico, Combe, Talé interviews; P. Besnard, report, Paris 18ᵉ (1949), p.2 in MDP (1949); Perrin, *Itinéraire,* p.167; "Marseille report," p.25; "Sur le décret du Saint Office . . ." (Oct., 1949), p.5 in MDP (1949).

61. Pfaff, Gray, Laval, Legendre, Jaudon, Tarby, Talé, Combe, Barreau, Boudot interviews; "Note sur la situation religieuse créée par l'engagement des catholiques dans le mouvement ouvrier," pp.1–4 in MDP (1951); Roger Deliat, "Question à poser à l'équipe" (Mar. 19, 1953), p.1 in MDP (1953); letter, André Piet (?), Nov. 27, 1951 in François Vidal papers; Sanguedolce, *Joseph Gouttebarge,* pp.33–34.

62. Perrin, *Itinéraire,* p.194.

63. Hollande, Poulat, Barreau, Chauveau, Bouyer, Tiberghien, Cottin, Volot, Gray, Tarby, Talé, Guichard and Bordet interviews; Maxime Hua, A.C.O., interview, Paris (May 9, 1979); "Après la mort," p.1; Sanguedolce, *Joseph Gouttebarge,* pp.17–18, 22, 30.

64. Loew, *Mission,* pp.26, 29–32.

65. Ibid., pp.32–35.

66. Flagothier, Barreau and Depierre interviews; Louisette Blanquart, interview, Paris (June 22, 1979); Daniel Perrot, interview, Paris (May 10, 1979); Perrin, *Itinéraire*, pp.272–273, 275–276; Deliat, *Vingt ans*, p.24; "La Mission de Paris," p.2 in MDP (1943–1944); "L'Eglise en marche," p.2 in MDP (1943–1944); Robert Barrat, "Notre enquête sur les lectures spirituelles," *Témoignage Chrétien*, Oct. 1, 1948, p.4.

67. Pacalet interviews; Joseph Jacquet, interview, Lyon (June 14, 1979).

68. Vidal and Loew interviews; Loew, *Mission*, pp.169–170.

69. Perrin, *Itinéraire*, pp.158, 178; Ancel, Dillaye, Robert, Screppel and Legendre interviews; M.-D. Chenu, Dominican theologian, interview, Paris (May 15, 1979).

70. Poulat interviews; "La Mission de Paris" (Dec. 16, 1947), p.1 in MDP (1943–1944); "Marseille reports" p.31.

71. "Journée des religieux missionaires" (Feb. 6, 1949), pp.2–3 in MDP (1949); note, (Feb. 13, 1946), pp.1–3 in MDP (1947); Garnier interview; Loew, *Mission*, p.155.

72. Flagothier, Courtoy, Tiberghien, Pacalet, Depierre, Loew, Dillaye, Ancel, Garnier, Screppel and Laval interviews.

73. Talé, Tarby, Gray, Cagne, Chauveau, Hua, Bouyer, Poulat, Barreau, Robert, Depierre, Dillaye, Vico, Jaudon, Chavanneau, Guichard, Legendre, Screppel and Piet interviews; Henri Perrin, "Note sur les 2 articles . . ." (July 15, 1949), p.1 in MDP (1949); A.D., report, July 1945, p.13, in MDP (1945).

74. Flagothier, Chauveau, Laval, Combe, Tarby, Vico, Cottin, Cagne, Jaudon and Olhagaray interviews; "Quinze jours dans le Jura" (July 13, 1945), pp.1–17 in MDP (1945).

75. Laval, Loew and Depierre interviews; Perrin, *Itinéraire*, pp.117, 127–129, 133–138, 213–214, 225, 227, 231; Sanguedolce, *Joseph Gouttebarge*, pp.46–48; André Depierre, "Ce témoignage persévérant de Dieu," *Esprit* (Dec., 1950), p.906; J.-M. Domenach, of *Esprit*, interview, Paris (May 17, 1979).

76. Talé interview.

77. Cottin, Pacalet, Guichard, Chavanneau, Tiberghien, Chauveau, Flagothier, Gray, Dillaye, Olhagaray, Bordet, Legendre, Depierre and Pfaff interviews; Loew, *Mission*, pp.29–30, 37–40; "Quelques points acquis," pp.5–7.

78. Volot, Laval, Bouyer, Cagne and Screppel interviews; Jacques Screppel, "Association de la commune libre de la rue Jean Bart et adjacentes" (Sept. 22, 1950), pp.1–2 in Screppel papers; Perrin, *Itinéraire*, pp.182–183; Loew, *Mission*, pp.81–82, 86–90; M. Lespinasse, letter to Père Hollande, Boulogne (Feb. 8, 1954), pp.1–2 in MDP (1954); Sanguedolce, *Joseph Gouttebarge*, pp.30–31.

79. Volot, Loew, Tiberghien, Robert, Depierre, Piet and Vidal interviews; "Abrégé du rapport—III. Qui donc fera le pont?" p.11 in *Cahiers de la MDP* (1955).

80. Poulat, Talé, Garnier, Legendre, Laval, Barreau, Depierre, Vico, Loew, Dillaye and Olhagaray interviews; Perrin, *Itinéraire*, pp.104, 108, 115.

81. "Marseille report," pp.19–20; Charles Pautet, "Mission de Paris" (June 11, 1945), pp.2–3 in MDP (1945); Depierre report, pp.11–12; "La Mission de Paris" (Dec. 16, 1947), p.3 in MDP (1947).

82. Screppel interview; "Mission de Paris-Difficultés de la vie eucharistique" (1947), pp.1–2 in MDP (1947); Perrin, *Itinéraire*, pp.93, 99; note; (Feb. 9, 1946), 1p. in MDP (1943–1944).

83. Cagne and Dillaye interviews; Loew, *Journal*, p.24; Perrin, *Itinéraire*, p.162; André Retif, "La Mission de Paris," *Etudes* (March, 1949), pp.8–9; Loew, *Mission*, pp.65–66.

84. Courtoy, Guichard, Flagothier, Bordet, Tarby, Jaudon, Volot, Robert and Loew interviews; "Journée des religieux missionnaires" (Feb. 6, 1949), pp.5–6 in MDP (1949); Loew, *Mission*, pp.121–122; Loew, *Journal*, p.283.

85. Cagne, Depierre, Barreau, Chauveau, Guichard interviews; "La Mission de Paris" (1948), p.2 in MDP (1943–1944); "Ce que les jeunes pensent du prêtre," p.31 in MDP (1943–1944); "L'Eglise en marche," p.2 in MDP (1943–1944); letter, June 21, 1944, p.2 in MDP (1943–1944); "Retraits de la Mission de Paris" (1952), p.1 in MDP (1943–1944).

86. Perrot interview, Perrin, *Itinéraire*, pp.160, 162, 178; Père Damien, "Fraternité des O.V.P." (July 21, 1947), p.3 in MDP (1947); "La Mission de Paris" (Oct., 1949), p.2 in MDP (1949); "Journée des religieux," pp.1–7.

87. Deliat, *Vingt ans*, pp.29–30; Jacques Hollande, "Ordre du jour" (Nov. 26, 1952), p.1 in MDP (1952); "Notre solidarité ouvrière" (Sept. 28, 1952), p.1 in MDP (1952); "A l'ordre du jour 4 problèmes principaux" (1953), pp.1–3 in MDP (1953); Hollande to worker-priests, letter, Paris (June 1, 1950), 1p. in MDP (1950); secretariat report (1953), p.1 in MDP (1953); "Correspondants d'equipe," p.1 in MDP (1953); J.-M. Marzio, secretariat letter (June 27, 1953), p.1 in MDP (1953); J.-M. Marzio, secretariat letter (May 13, 1953), p.1 in MDP (1953).

88. Domenach, Hourdin, Villain, Ancel, Loew, Combe, Depierre, Blanquart, Montuclard, Cagne, Vico, Volot, Genthial, Vivez, Jaudon, Tarby, Guichard, Laval, Talé, Vidal, Poulat, Riousse, Garnier and Gray interviews.

89. Hua and Depierre interviews; four letters from the *curé* of St. Francis Xavier (1943) in MDP (1943–1944); Godin letter (1943), pp.1–9 in MDP (1943–1944); "La Mission de Paris" p.5 in MDP (1943–1944); "La Mission de Paris" (July, 1950), p.2 in MDP (1943–1944).

90. Bordet, Volot, Tiberghien, Cottin, Chauveau, Barreau, Robert, Striffling, Chavanneau, Guichard, Bouyer, Cagne and Loew interviews; Loew, *Mission*, pp.69–70, 74, 108; Loew, *Journal*, pp.159, 172, 274.

91. Gray, Piet, Jaudon, Laval, Tarby, Legendre, Vico, Screppel, Cagne, Bouyer and Perrot interviews; "Problème missionnaire," Limoges report (1950), pp.23–24.

92. Jaudon, Poulat, Talé and Combe interviews; Jean-Marie Marzio, "Project d'une équipe de P.O. dans la région de Caen," pp.1–3 in Vidal papers; "Pour un travail apostolique dans le milieu ouvrier de Lyon" (Nov., 1945), pp.1–8; A.D., report (July, 1945), p.3 in MDP (1945); Michel Lemonon, "Té-

moignages des prêtres ayant été au travail," p.102 in *Cahiers MDP* (1955); note (Feb. 13, 1946), p.2 in MDP (1947).

93. Boudot interview; Roger Cartayrade, J.O.C. leader, interview, Paris (July 6, 1979); "La Mission de Paris," pp.2–3 in MDP (1943–1944); Dewitte letter to Godin (Nov. 8, 1943), p.2 in MDP (1943–1944); Godin response, p.1 in MDP (1943–1944); "Note," pp.1–5 in MDP (1943–1944).

94. Albert Denis, "Paroisse et communautés humaines," *Masses Ouvrières* (July, 1948), p.38; "Soutien du prêtre aux foyers chrétiens," *Masses Ouvrières* (Aug.–Sept., 1947), pp.69–70; Joseph Cardijn, "Les Responsabilités des prêtres devant les problèmes actuels de la jeunesse ouvrière," *Masses Ouvrières* (Dec., 1947), p.22.

95. M.-D. Chenu, letters (Nov. 24, 1945), p.1 in MDP (1945) and (Nov. 25, 1949), pp.1–2 in MDP (1949); Chenu interview; Roger Beaunez, "Quelques réflections à la suite de notre soirée rue Cler," (July, 1946), pp.1–7 in MDP (1946).

96. Bouyer, Cottin, Cartayrade interviews; André Villette, J.O.C. leader, interview, Paris (June 25, 1980); Depierre report, pp.3–4; "Problème missionnaire," p.12.

97. "Témoignage," *Masses Ouvrières* (Apr., 1952), pp.66–72; J. Robert, "D'un prêtre-ouvrier," *Masses Ouvrières* (Mar.–Apr., 1948), pp.178–181; P. Depierre, "D'un prêtre de la Mission de Paris," *Masses Ouvrières* (Mar.–Apr., 1948), pp.182–192; M.-R. Loew, "Incroyance des masses," *Masses Ouvrières* (Feb., 1949), pp.17–36; Boudot, Blanquart, Hua and Jacquet interviews; "La Mission de Paris" (Oct., 1949), p.3 in MDP (1949); "Mission et Action Catholique," *Masses Ouvrières* (July, 1948), pp.1–5.

98. "Déclaration de l'Assemblée des cardinaux et archevêques de France" (Feb. 28, 1945) and (Mar. 4, 1948) in *Documentation Catholique* (Mar. 18, 1945), pp.228–229 and (Mar. 28, 1948), pp.385–386; Cardinal Suhard, note, "Apostolat auprès des masses déchristianisées" (1948), p.1 in MDP (1948).

99. Cottin, Loew and Jaudon interviews; Loew, *Journal,* pp.255, 328.

100. Flagothier, Courtoy, Piet, Pfaff, Bordet, Chauveau, Vico, Bouyer and Cagne interviews; "Rencontre de Longwy" (July 9, 1951), p.2 in Boudot papers; Cardinal Suhard, "La Mission de Paris" (1947), pp.1–2 in MDP (1947); "Esquisse d'une conception du monde et de l'eglise" (1948–1949), (Oct. 31, 1951), p.4 in MDP (1948).

101. "La Mission de Paris" (Dec. 16, 1947), p.4 in MDP (1943–1944); Depierre, Olhagaray, Tiberghien, Poulat, Talé, Ancel, Pacalet, Jacquet, Combe, Tarby, Volot, Screppel and Legendre interviews; "Mission de Paris," p.2 in MDP (1943–1944).

102. Loew interview; Loew, *Journal,* p.318; Perrin, *Itinéraire,* pp.246–248, 253–257.

VII. THE WORLD OF WORKER-PRIEST REFLECTION

1. "Mission et Action Catholique," Mar. 12, 1947, p.1 in Mission de Paris papers (hereafter referred to as MDP) (1947); Jacques Loew, interview, Fribourg, Swit. (May 14, 1980); Francis Vico, interview, Montluçon (May 24, 1980); "Retraite de Père Feret" (Oct. 12–16, 1948), pp.1–26 in MDP (1948); André Depierre, interview, Montreuil (June 20, 1979); Yves Congar, interview, Paris (May 15, 1979); "Rencontre des Prêtres-ouvriers de France" (Jan. 21–22, 1950), pp.1–3 in MDP (1950); Louisette Blanquart, interview, Paris (June 22, 1979); J.-M. Domenach, interview, Paris (May 17, 1979); Maurice Combe, interview, Lyon (June 14, 1979); Maurice Montuclard, interview, Lyon (June 14, 1983).

2. Vico, Depierre, Congar interviews; Bernard Tiberghien, interview, Dunkerque (June 12, 1980); Louis Bouyer, interview, Colombes (May 21, 1979); Jean Volot, interview, Paris (May 19, 1980); M.-D. Chenu, interview, Paris (May 15, 1979); P. Chenu, letter to Jacques Hollande (Nov. 25, 1949), pp.1–2 in MDP (1949); M.-D. Chenu, "Le Sacerdoce des prêtres-ouvriers," *Vie Intellectuelle* (Feb., 1954), pp.175–181.

3. Volot, Depierre, Domenach, interviews; Joseph Robert, interview, Paris (June 27, 1979); Msgr. Daniel Pézeriel, interview, Paris, (June 12, 1979); Henri Perrin, *Itinéraire d'Henri Perrin* (Paris: Seuil, 1958), p.225.

4. Chenu, Montuclard interviews. For details of this methodology, see Paulo Freire, *Pedagogy of the Oppressed*, trans. by Myra Ramos (New York: Seabury, 1968).

5. P. Jean-Marie Marzio, report, Paris 12ᵉ (Oct., 1949), p.2 in MDP (1949); P. Jean-Claude Poulain, "L'Eglise de la Mission de Paris à son nouvel archevêque Monseigneur Feltin," Les Halles (Oct., 1949), p.9 in MDP (1949); Volot interview; Albert Guichard (interview, Paris, June 21, 1983) echoed Volot's opinion.

6. "Notre mission d'église," (Oct.–Nov., 1951), p.1 in MDP (1951); "Rapport Jean Gray" (Mar., 1953), p.2 in MDP (1953); Philbert Talé, interview, Antony (June 1, 1983); André Piet, Marseille (June 2, 1983); Charles Pautet, "Mission de Paris," June 11, 1945, p.1 in MDP (1945); Henri Barreau, interview, Gagny (May 16, 1979).

7. "Projet des conversations" (1943), pp.1–2 in MDP (1943–1944); Abbé Dewitte, "La Direction des jeunes gens," p.33 in MDP (1943–1944); P. Hua, "Le Problème du laïcat," p.24 in MDP (1943–1944); Père Villain, "L'Action Catholique," pp.3–4 in MDP (1943–1944); "Consignes de S.E. le Cardinal" (Jan. 13, 1944), p.1 in MDP (1943–1944); "Note," p.1 in MDP (1943–1944).

8. Jean Legendre, interview, Plateau d'Assy (June 6, 1983); Césaire Dillaye, interview, Paris (May 14, 1979); François Vidal, interview, Marseille (June 1, 1983); Jean Gray, interview, Auxerre (June 11, 1983); Jacques Riousse, interview, Escarenne (June 3, 1983); André Depierre, report, Montreuil (1949), p.1 in MDP (1949).

9. Poulain, "L'Eglise," p.75; P. Jean-Marie Lepetit, report, Paris 20ᵉ

(Oct., 1949), p.2 in MDP (1949); "Des prêtres en milieu de travail," p.1 in MDP (1946); C.F. Boland, "Prêtres en milieu de travail," *Evangéliser* (Mar., 1947), p.448.

10. Robert, Dillaye interviews; "Problème missionnaire," Limoges report (1950), p.28 in MDP (1950).

11. Combe, Vidal interviews; André Chavanneau and Yves Garnier, interviews, Limoges (May 31, 1983); A.D., report (July, 1945), p.13 in MDP (1945).

12. P. Besnard, report, Paris 18ᵉ (1949), p.2 in MDP (1949); Robert Pacalet, letter to Père Hollande (Dec. 28, 1948), p.1 in MDP (1948).

13. Gray, Loew interviews; Jacques Loew, *Mission to the Poorest*, trans. by Pamela Carswell (London: Sheed and Ward, 1950), p.90; Jacques Screppel, interview, Hellemes (June 9, 1983); Besnard, report, p.1; P. Pierre Riche, report, Paris 20ᵉ (Oct., 1949), p.2 in MDP (1949).

14. Alfred Ancel, interview, Lyon (June 14, 1979); Barreau interview, Père Damien Reumont, "Fraternité des Ouvriers de la Vièrge des Pauvres" (1947), pp.2–3 in MDP (1947).

15. Letter, Saint-Brieuc (March 4, 1954) and "Raisons d'être des prêtres-ouvriers," p.5 in J.O.C. dossier on the worker-priests.

16. Roger Deliat, *Vingt ans O.S. chez Renault* (Paris: Editions Ouvrières, 1973), p.22.

17. Joseph Gouttebarge, "Cafard" (1950) in Joseph Sanguedolce, *Joseph Gouttebarge*, pp.18–21.

18. Henri Barreau, "Tu es pour eux un démon!" pp.13–14 in Henri Barreau (private papers); personal autograph in the hands of the author.

19. Emile Poulat, *Naissance des Prêtres-Ouvriers* (Paris: Centurion, 1965), p.395; A.D., report (July, 1945), p.14 in MDP (1945); Depierre interview.

20. "Des prêtres en milieu de travail—Raisons d'être de cette présence," pp.1–2 in MDP (1946).

21. "Fraternité des O.V.P." (June 15, 1947), p.2 in MDP (1947).

22. Ibid., pp.4–6, 8–10; Abbé C.F. Boland, "Prêtres en milieu de travail," pp.439–440; Reumont, "Fraternité," p.3. Not surprisingly the Belgian worker-priests Louis Flagothier and Albert Courtoy echoed the words of Father Reumont (interviews, Liège, Belgium, June 8, 1983).

23. Bernard Lacroix, interview, Grenoble (June 15, 1983); P. Lucien Lacour, "La Mission de Paris" (Oct., 1949), p.4 in MDP (1949); "Marseille report" (1948), pp.23–24, 29; Loew interview; Jacques Loew, *Journal d'une mission ouvrière* (Paris: Cerf, 1959), pp.437–438; "Quelques points acquis" (Sept. 1, 1948), p.3 in René Boudot, private papers; "Journée des religieux missionnaires" (Feb. 6, 1949), p.2 in MDP (1949).

24. Sanguedolce, *Joseph Gouttebarge*, p.9.

25. Bernard Chauveau, interview, Boulogne-Billancourt (May 11, 1979); A.D., report, pp.5, 7; "Equipe de Marseille" (1953), p.3 in MDP (1953); Henri Barreau, "Projet de Déclaration," p.2 in Henri Barreau, private papers.

26. "Notre solidarité ouvrière," report (Sept. 28, 1952), p.1 in MDP

(1952); This charity argument was employed also by Robert Pfaff of Longwy, interview, Paris (June 10, 1983).

27. Joseph Sanguedolce, *Joseph Gouttebarge*, p.33.

28. Bernard Striffling and Gabriel Genthial interviews, Courbevoie (June 11, 1979); Albert Gauche, "Aux ouvriers chrétiens," 1954, p.2 in MDP (1954).

29. P. Henri Barreau, report, Malakoff (Oct., 1949), p.4 in MDP (1949); Robert Pfaff, "Quelques réflexions sur et à propos du Directoire des prêtres-ouvriers de Mgr. Ancel," pp.2–3 in René Boudot, private papers.

30. Ibid., p.5.

31. "Problème missionnaire," pp.2–3, 8; Combe interview; Bernard Cagne, interview, Paris (June 21, 1979); Robert Pfaff, "Perspectives missionaires" (Oct. 14, 1953), p.1, René Boudot, private papers.

32. Perrin, *Itinéraire*, pp.187, 189, 193.

33. "Sur le décret du Saint Office et la Déclaration des 4 cardinaux français" (Oct., 1949), pp.2–10 in MDP (1949).

34. Loew interviews; Loew, *Journal*, pp.204, 206–209, 221–224, 226.

35. Sanguedolce, *Joseph Gouttebarge*, p.34; André Depierre, report, p.30.

36. "Le Problème missionnaire en France" (Nov. 29, 1946), pp.1–2 in MDP (1946); P. Besnard, report, Paris 18ᵉ (1949), p.2 in MDP (1949).

37. Andre Depierre, report, pp.3, 7; A.D., report, p.3; Flagothier, Gray interviews; P. Jean-Marie Lepetit, report, Paris 20ᵉ (Oct., 1949), p.1 in MDP (1949); Pfaff, "Quelques points acquis," p.7; Pfaff, "Quelques réflexions," p.4; Jacques Screppel, "Vocation Dominicaine et mission proletarienne," 1948, p.4 in Jacques Screppel, private papers.

38. P. Riche, P. Jean Olhagaray, P. Jean Lepetit, report (Dec., 1948–Jan., 1949), p.4 in MDP (1949); Pfaff, "Quelques points acquis," pp.11–12.

39. Loew, *Journal*, pp.357–358; A.D., report, pp.2, 6, 16–17.

40. "La Mission de Paris" (1948), pp.1–2 in MDP (1943–1944); "Quelques réflexions à amorce nos discussions" (April, 1948), p.6 in MDP (1948); A.D., report, p.13.

41. Père Robert, "Rapport sur mon engagement de prêtre-ouvrier," Paris (Jan. 22, 1949), p.2 in MDP (1949).

42. Père du Mont, report to Père Hollande, Ivry (Feb. 2, 1945), p.1 in MDP (1945); Père André, Capuchin, "Pourquoi je suis prêtre-ouvrier" (1949), p.2 in MDP (1949).

43. "Le Sacerdoce des prêtres-ouvriers," to Mgr. Ancel, pp.4–6 in MDP (1951).

44. Deliat, *Vingt ans*, pp.32–33.

45. "Fraternité des O.V.P.," pp.6, 12; Barreau, report, p.3.

46. "Problème missionnaire," pp.29–30; Sanguedolce, *Joseph Gouttebarge*, p.8.

47. Père André, pp.1–2; Screppel, "Vocation," pp.12–13; "Fraternité," p.14; Jean-Claude Poulain, Les Halles (Oct., 1949), p.2 in MDP (1949); "Questions," 1947, p.1 in MDP (1947).

48. "Fraternité," pp.7, 13; Robert, report, pp.3–4; "Note pour les sémi-

naristes qui feront un stage en usine" (July 15–Aug. 31, 1947), p.1 in MDP (1947).

49. C.F. Boland, "Travail d'usine et vie spirituelle," p.2 in MDP (1953); "Le Prêtre-Ouvrier," St. Alban-Leysse (Feb. 10, 1952), p.10 in MDP (1952); "Après la mort de Michel Favreau," *Semaine Religieuse de Bordeaux* (April, 1951), p.1; "Problème missionnaire," p.25.

50. Robert, "Rapport," p.3; Barreau, "Tu es pour eux," pp.13–14; H. Barreau, note (c. 1949), p.1 in MDP (1949); Boland, "Travail d'usine," p.4.

51. "Témoignages des prêtres ayant été au travail," p.104 in *Cahiers de la M.D.P.* (1955).

52. Ibid., p.111.

VIII. THE WORLD OF WORKER-PRIEST CONFLICT

1. S.-E. Monseigneur Montini, pp.8–9 in Mission de Paris papers (hereafter called MDP) (1946); Msgr. Tardini (Nov. 28, 1946), p.7 and Msgr. Ottaviani (Nov. 29, 1946), pp.10–11 both in MDP (1946).

2. "Audience de Sa Sainteté Pie XII" (Nov. 27, 1946), p.5 in MDP (1946).

3. Augros, Hollande, Laporte letter (Dec. 1, 1946), 1p. in MDP (1946).

4. For these articles, see *France-Soir* (July 15–18, 20–21, 23, 1949) and *Paris-Presse-Intransigeant* (July 16–20, 22–26, 1949). In *Chez les prêtres ouvriers* (Paris: Frédéric Chambriand, 1950) Jean-Loup Dariel, the author of the *France Soir* series defends and describes his stories about the worker-priests. Hollande, letter to Ancel (Aug. 6, 1949), pp.1–2 in MDP (1949); Hollande to Mgr. Chappoulie (Aug. 8, 1949) p.1 in MDP (1949); "Après le dechainement de la presse à sensation" (1949), pp.1–2 in MDP (1949).

5. Henri Perrin, "Note sur les 2 articles de Jean Balensi dans *Paris-Presse*" (July 15, 1949), pp.1–2 in MDP (1949).

6. "Sur le Décret du Saint Office et la Déclaration des 4 cardinaux français" (Oct., 1949), pp.1–11 in MDP (1949); "Résumé de la conversation entre Mgr. Chappoulie et les Pères Hollande, Laporte et Depierre de la Mission de Paris" (Oct. 17, 1949), pp.1–2 in MDP (1949).

7. Alfred Ancel, letter, Lyon (May 12, 1950), pp.1–3, 7–8 in MDP (1950).

8. "Project de Directoire pour les prêtres travaillant en usine" (May, 1951), p.1 in MDP (1951).

9. Ibid., pp.1, 3–6.

10. Alfred Ancel, ". . . aux prêtres-ouvriers du diocèse de Lyon," Lyon (Sept. 22, 1951), pp.2–13 in MDP (1951).

11. Jacques Hollande, letter (All Saints, 1951), pp.1–2 in MDP (1951); "Quelques réflexions sur et à propos du Directoire . . . ," p.1 in René Boudot, private papers; Robert Pfaff, "Quelques réflexions sur et à propos du Directoire . . . ," pp.1–2, 5–7 in Boudot papers; M.-R. Loew, *Journal d'une mission ouvrière* (Paris: Cerf, 1959), pp.247–249, 251–254.

12. L. Bouyer and B. Cagne, "Pour ceux qui ne pourront jamais parler et qu'on ne voudra pas croire," Colombes (May 30, 1952), pp.1–4 in MDP (1952); Louis Bouyer, interview, Colombes (May 21, 1979); Bernard Cagne, interview, Paris (June 21, 1979); Etienne Borne, "Polémiques et Dialogues," *Terre Humaine* (July–Aug., 1952), pp.123–128; "Deux prêtres passés à tabac," *Vie Intellectuelle* (July, 1952), pp.1–6; "Prêtres et 'Partisans'," *La Quinzaine* (?, 1952), p.13 in MDP (1954).

13. "Prêtres et 'Partisans' "; Louis Retif, "A.M. l'officier de police du Xe arrondissement," June 13, 1952, pp.1, 6.

14. Cagne, Bouyer interviews; Bernard Tiberghien, interview, Dunkerque (June 12, 1980); Jean Volot, interview, Paris (May 19, 1980); Robert Pacalet, interview, Lyon (July 5, 1979); Jacques Loew, interview, Fribourg, Swit. (May 14, 1980); Georges Mollard, interview, Paris (June 6, 1980); Jacques Jaudon, interview, Grenoble (June 15, 1983); Emile Poulat, interview, Paris (May 20, 1983); Philbert Talé, interview, Antony, (June 1, 1983); André Chauvaneau, interview, Limoges (May 31, 1983); Jacques Screppel, interview, Hellemes (June 9, 1983); Francis Laval, interview, St. Etienne (May 19, 1983); Michel Bordet, interview, Simian-la-Rotonde (May 27, 1983); Jean Gray, interview, Auxerre (June 11, 1983); Loew, *Journal*, pp.366–367.

15. Note on March 11 meeting (Mar. 19, 1952), pp.1–2 in MDP (1952).

16. Gregor Siefer, *The Church and Industrial Society* (London: Darton, Longman and Todd, 1964), pp.319–322, 327. For more details on this brief history of the Mission de France, see Jean-François Six, *Cheminements de la Mission de France* (Paris: Seuil, 1967); Jacques Faupin, *La Mission de France* (Paris: Casterman, 1960); Jean Vinatier, *Le Cardinal Liénart et la Mission de France* (Paris: Centurion, 1978) and "regard sur notre histoire," *Lettre aux Communautés* (Nov., 1954), pp.4–16. The author received a living testimony of these events from one of those nineteen seminarians (Aldo Bardini, interview, Bagnolet, May 10, 1980).

17. Siefer, *The Church*, p.320; Jacques Hollande, letter to Jean Desailly (Mar. 20, 1953), p.1 in MDP (1953); Jacques Hollande, letter to André Depierre (Mar. 20, 1953), p.1 in MDP (1953); Archevêché, letter to Hollande (May 11, 1953), p.1 in MDP (1953); Hollande, response to Archevêché (May 12, 1953), p.1 in MDP (1953); Screppel, Laval interviews; Albert Guichard, interview, Paris (June 21, 1983); Jean Legendre, interview, Plateau d'Assy (June 6, 1983).

18. Roger Deliat, *Vingt ans O.S. chez Renault* (Paris: Editions Ouvrières, 1973), p.125; Mgr. Delay, to Comité diocésain d'A.C.O. de Marseille (May 4, 1953), pp.1–3 in MDP (1953); Piet, Monnier, Gauche, letter to Mgr. Delay (May 5, 1953), p.1 in MDP (1953); Mgr. Delay, letter, May 27, 1953, pp.1–2 in MDP (1953) and in André Piet, private papers; "Equipe de Marseille" (1953), pp.2–4 in MDP (1953); Cardinal Feltin, letter, July 23, 1953, p.1 in MDP (1953); Siefer, *The Church*, pp.322–323. For further details on the Marseille incident, see "Equipe de Marseille," pp.1–4 in François Vidal, private papers.

19. Siefer, *The Church*, pp.321–323; Deliat, *Vingt ans*, pp.126–127; René

Desgrand, letter (Dec. 8, 1953), pp.1–2 and "Reunion de nonce avec les évêques," pp.1–3 both in François Vidal, private papers.

20. "The Green Paper," found in John Petrie, *The Worker-Priests* (London: Routledge & Kegan Paul, 1956), pp.158, 161; Gray interview. For the original French in all citations from the Petrie work, see *Les Prêtres-Ouvriers* (Paris: Minuit, 1954).

21. Ibid., pp.162, 164–168, 170.

22. Siefer, *The Church*, pp.323–324; J.-M. Marzio, letter (Oct. 23, 1953), p.1 in MDP (1953).

23. "Vous êtes des ouvriers, vous n'êtes plus des prêtres" (Dec., 1952), pp.2–4, 7 in MDP (1952).

24. "Document vert," *Les Prêtres-Ouvriers* (Paris: Minuit), pp.225–242. "Rapport Jean Gray," pp.1–3 in François Vidal, private papers; also see "Rapport Jean Gray," pp.1–3 in MDP (1953).

25. Emile Poulat, letter, Jan., 1953, pp.1–3 in MDP (1953); Michel Galais, Mar., 1953, pp.1–2 in MDP (1953); Bernard Chauveau, *La Quinzaine* (Sept. 15, 1953) in *Documentation Catholique* (Oct. 18, 1953), pp.1300–1301; René Besnard, Mar. 7, 1953, p.1 in MDP (1953); Poulat, Talé interviews; Yves Garnier, interview, Limoges (May 31, 1983); Jean Tarby, interview, Chartres (June 13, 1983); Louis Flagothier, interview, Liège, Belgium (June 8, 1953).

26. Yvan Daniel, "Il s'agit de notre conscience religieuse" (Jan., 1953), pp.1–3 in MDP (1953); Yvan Daniel, letter to Marzio (Mar. 7, 1953), pp.1–2 in MDP (1953); Loew, *Journal*, pp.327–329, 332.

27. "Notre action—le cas Desgrand," Section syndicale, C.F.T.C. (1953), pp.1–2 in MDP (1953); "Les Prêtres-Ouvriers du Rhône et de la Loire à l'U.D.-C.F.T.C. du Rhône," Lyon (Mar. 4, 1953), pp.1–2 in MDP (1953).

28. "La Trahison des dirigeants de F.O. et de la C.F.T.C.," *France Nouvelle*, Sept. 5, 1953, p.5; "Déclaration de Travailleurs Chrétiens sur les grèves d'Août 1953," pp.1–4 in MDP (1953).

29. "Cause Tessier-Barreau," April 24, 1953, pp.1–4; "Procès verbal d'audience," pp.7–8, 10, 12–13; Jean-Claude Poulain, brief to Monsieur l'Official, pp.1–22; "Parisien-Observations de l'avocat sur la Memoire remis par Monsieur l'abbé Poulain," pp.1–5, all in Henri Barreau, private papers.

30. Jaudon, Bordet interviews; Jacques Screppel, "Premières intuitions," private papers, p.5.

31. "Déclaration" (Nov., 1953), p.1 in MDP (1953).

32. Deliat, *Vingt ans*, pp.130, 133–135; Césaire Dillaye, interview, Paris (May 14, 1979); Jean Olhagaray, interview, Paris (June 13, 1979); Henri Barreau, interview, Gagny (May 16, 1979); worker-priest letter to Feltin (Nov. 21, 1953), p.1 in MDP (1953).

33. Tiberghien, Pacalet interviews; Henri Perrin, *Itinéraire de Henri Perrin* (Paris: Seuil, 1958), pp.365–366; "La Déclaration du cardinal Liénart," *Semaine Religieuse de Lille* (Jan. 10, 1954) in *Documentation Catholique* (Feb. 7, 1954), p.137; Maurice Combe, interview, Lyon (June 14, 1979).

34. Jacques Hollande, letter to Marzio (Dec. 1, 1953), p.1 in MDP (1953); Georges Suffert, "La Victoire des prêtres-ouvriers," *L'Express* (Nov., 1963?),

pp.1–3 in Henri Barreau, private papers; André Depierre, interview, Montreuil (June 20, 1979).

35. "The Bishops' Letter to the Worker-Priests" (Jan. 19, 1954) in Petrie, *The Worker-Priests*, pp.172–175. For copies of the original French text, see "La Lettre des évêques aux prêtres-ouvriers," in *Documentation Catholique* (Mar. 7, 1954), pp.291–294 and pp.1–2 in Albert Bouche, private papers.

36. Petrie, *The Worker-Priests*, p.176. See also "Un 'communiqué' de 73 prêtres-ouvriers," *Documentation Catholique* (Feb. 7, 1954), p.150.

37. Petrie, *The Worker-Priests*, p.177.

38. Ibid., p.42; Siefer, *The Church*, p.325; Deliat, *Vingt ans*, pp.135–136; Loew, *Journal*, pp.349–353; Dillaye interview; Maurice Montuclard, interview, Lyon (June 14, 1983); "Communiqué des prêtres-ouvriers du Nord," 1p. in Jacques Screppel, private papers.

39. "Circular Letter from His Excellency Monseigneur de Provenchères to His Clergy" (Feb. 11, 1954) in Petrie, *The Worker-Priests*, pp.148–150.

40. Ibid., p.151.

41. Ibid., pp.151–152.

42. *Témoignage Chrétien*, Feb. 12, 1954 in *Documentation Catholique* (Mar. 21, 1954), pp.364–365; "Letter from the worker-priests of Toulouse to Cardinal Saliège" (Feb. 13, 1954) in Petrie, *The Worker-Priests*, pp.179–187; "Letter from the Worker-Priests of Limoges to Monseigneur Rastouil" (Feb. 14, 1954) in Petrie, *The Worker-Priests*, pp.187–195.

43. Mgr. Richaud, Lenten pastoral, *L'Acquitaine* (Feb. 19, 1954) in *Documentation Catholique* (Mar. 7, 1954), p.287; Mgr. Lallier, communiqué, *Semaine Religieuse de Nancy et de Toul* (Feb. 28, 1954) in *Documentation Catholique* (Mar. 7, 1954), p.290.

44. "Letter from the Worker-Priests of Paris to Cardinal Feltin" (Feb. 15, 1954) in Petrie, *The Worker-Priests*, p.200. For the original French, see "Une lettre de 31 prêtres-ouvriers à S.Em. le cardinal Feltin," in *Documentation Catholique* (Mar. 21, 1954), pp.359–364. Emile Poulat, letter, Jan. 11, 1986, p.5.

45. Ibid., p.201.

46. "Partie Officielle," Feb. 24, 1954 in *Documentation Catholique* (Mar. 7, 1954), pp.263–269.

47. Siefer, *The Church*, p.326; Perrin, *Itinéraire*, p.368; Deliat, *Vingt ans*, p.139. In the interviews granted to me by former worker-priests, I was impressed uniformly by the affection they retained for their colleagues who had chosen differently and by their refusal to bring any judgment against them.

48. Deliat, *Vingt ans*, pp.139–140; Perrin, *Itinéraire*, pp.370–373; Siefer, *The Church*, p.327; Petrie, *The Worker-Priests*, pp.48, 203–204.

49. "Letter from the Worker-Priests of Limoges" in Petrie, *The Worker-Priests*, p.187; Yves Congar, interview, Paris (May 15, 1979).

IX. THE IMPACT OF THE WORKER-PRIESTS

1. "Soutien de prêtre aux foyers chrétiens," *Masses Ouvrières* (Aug.–Sept., 1947), pp.69–70; Joseph Cardijn, "Les Responsabilités des prêtres devant les problèmes actuels de la jeunesse ouvrière," *Masses Ouvrières* (Mar.–Apr., 1948), pp.178–181; "Mission et Action Catholique," *Masses Ouvrières* (July, 1948), pp.1–5.

2. "Une église, un monde ouvrier, un témoignage," *Masses Ouvrières* (Nov., 1953), p.5; R. Salanne, "Réflexions sur les décisions concernant les prêtres-ouvriers," *Lettre aux Fédéraux* (Mar., 1954), pp.1, 3, 10; Secrétariat Général J.O.C., "Circulaire aux Fédérations" (Feb. 9, 1954), 1p in Dossier on worker-priests (J.O.C.).

3. Letter, St.-Brieuc, Mar. 4, 1954, pp.1, 15, 17, 19 in Dossier on worker-priests (J.O.C.); Joseph Jacquet, interview, Lyon (June 14, 1979); Louisette Blanquart, interview, Paris (June 22, 1979); René Boudot, interview, Cons-la-Grandville (June 4, 1980).

4. "Lettre aux membres de l'A.C.O.," *Témoignage* (Mar., 1954), pp.2–3, 6–7; Maxime Hua, interview, Paris (May 9, 1979); Maxime Hua, note, Jan. 23, 1954, 1p in Mission de Paris papers (hereafter referred to as MDP) (1954); "Quatriéme Partie-les témoignages sacerdotaux," pp.21–22, 25–25 in *Cahiers MDP* (1955).

5. "Quatrième Partie," p.30.

6. Ibid., pp.23–31; "Les Témoignages des laïcs," pp.34–36 in *Cahiers MDP* (1955).

7. "Les Témoignages des laïcs," p.73.

8. Montarello, statement, 1954, p.1 in MDP (1954); "Une réunion de chrétiens militants ouvriers" (Feb. 19, 1954) in *Documentation Catholique* (Mar. 21, 1954), pp.366–367; "Un communiqué de 200 ouvriers chrétiens" in *Documentation Catholique* (Mar. 21, 1954), pp.365–366. Even as early as the Marseille controversy" of mid-1953, some A.C.O. groups rose to defend the worker-priests (see Groupe d'A.C.O. des Crottes, letter to Mgr. Delay, June 6, 1953, 1p. in François Vidal, private papers).

9. "Témoignages des prêtres de paroisse," p.18 in *Cahiers MDP* (1955); Père Retif, letter to Georges Mollard (Feb. 10, 1954), 1p. in Vidal papers.

10. "Lettre de M. le curé de la paroisse St. Michel de Marseille à Mgr. Delay, Archevêque" (May 8, 1953), p.1 in Vidal papers; "Lettre des prêtres de St. Louis à Mgr. l'évêque de Marseille" (May 19, 1953), p.1 in MDP (1953); Abbé Jean Clairefond, curé de N.-D. de Jerusalem, letter, Marseille (May 11, 1953), 1p in Vidal papers.

11. "Quatrième Partie," pp.3, 5–6, 27–28, 35, 46.

12. Gregor Siefer, *The Church and Industrial Society* (London: Darton, Longman and Todd, 1964), pp.321–323, 327; Jean Vinatier, *Le Cardinal Liénart et la Mission de France* (Paris: Centurion, 1978), pp.141–158; Louis Augros, interview, St. Symphorien-de-Laye (July 4, 1979); Jean Vinatier, interview, Fontenay-sous-Bois (June 7, 1980); Daniel Perrot, interview, Paris (May 10,

1979); Jean Villain, interview, Paris (June 6, 1979); Jean Villain, "L'Heure des prêtres-ouvriers," *Etudes* (Dec., 1953), pp.290–292; P. Maraîcher, "A propos des prêtres-ouvriers," *Jeunes Forces Rurales* (Oct. 16, 1953), p.10; "Et pourtant elle tourne," *Action Catholique Etudiante* (Feb., 1954), p.13; "Et pourtant elle tourne," *Action Catholique Etudiante* (Oct., 1953), p.9.

13. Yves Congar, interview, Paris (May 15, 1979); Maurice Montuclard, interview, Lyon (June 14, 1983); Maurice Combe, interview, Lyon (June 14, 1979); M.-D. Chenu, interview, Paris (May 15, 1979); Yves Congar, "L'Avenir des prêtres-ouvriers," *Témoignage Chrétien*, Sept. 25, 1953, p.1; François Le Guay, "Tels qu'ils sont," *Jeunesse de l'Eglise*, Oct., 1953, p.1.; M.-D. Chenu, "Le Sacerdoce des prêtres-ouvriers," *Vie Intellectuelle* (Feb., 1954), pp.175–176, 181; "L'Affaire des Dominicans," *La Quinzaine*, May 15, 1954, p.3; "Journal à plusieurs voix," *Esprit* (Mar., 1954), pp.407–409. Not all the Dominican theologians were as openly supportive; some tried to emphasize the truth found on both sides of the controversy. For one such example, see A.M. Carre, "Pourquoi des prêtres-ouvriers?" *Vie Intellectuelle* (Nov., 1953), pp.16–20, 22, 27–36.

14. J.-M. Domenach, interview, Paris (May 17, 1979); J.-M. Domenach, "Journal à plusieurs voix," *Esprit* (Oct.–Nov., 1953), pp.636, 639; Jean Lacroix, "L'Eglise et la mission," *Esprit* (Dec., 1953), pp.711–714, 716; Albert Beguin, "Les Prêtres-Ouvriers et l'espérance des pauvres," *Esprit* (Mar., 1954), pp.325, 336–337, 341.

15. Josse Alzin, *Jésus Incognito* (Paris: Téqui, 1953), p.1; Daniel-Rops, *Carrefour*, Sept. 24, 1953 in *Documentation Catholique* (Oct. 18, 1953), p.1298; Jean-Robert Hennion in *Problèmes du catholicisme français* (Paris: Julliard, 1954), pp.171–184; Pierre Andreu, *Grandeurs et erreurs des prêtres-ouvriers* (Paris: Amiot-Dumont, 1955), p.242. Andreu published a second work on the subject *Histoire des prêtres-ouvriers*, (Paris: Nouvelles Editions, Latines, 1960) which he dedicated to Jacques Loew.

16. Domenach interview; "Appeal Signed by 600 Christians . . . ," in John Petrie, *The Worker-Priests* (London: Routledge and Kegan Paul, 1956), pp.177–179; "Un manifeste d'un groupe d'intellectuels catholiques," *Le Monde* (Feb. 25, 1954), in *Documentation Catholique* (Mar. 21, 1954), pp.367–368.

17. Georges Hourdin, interview, Paris (June 21, 1979); Aline Coutrot and François Dreyfus, *Les Forces religieuses dans la société française* (Paris: Colin, 1965), pp.135, 142; Hourdin, *Problèmes du catholicisme* p.26. Hourdin's weekly *Vie Catholique* and his other periodicals had a circulation in excess of 500,000.

18. "La Rencontre nationale de 'Quinzaine,' . . ." *La Quinzaine*, July 15–Aug. 1, 1953, pp.4–6; "Un Communiqué . . . ," *La Quinzaine*, Dec. 1, 1952, p.3; "L'Emotion des chrétiens témoigne de leur fidelité," *La Quinzaine* Mar. 15, 1954, pp.1–3; M.C., "Le Prêtre-Ouvrier," *La Quinzaine*, Jan. 15 1952, pp.8–9; "Les Prêtres-Ouvriers et la classe ouvrière," *La Quinzaine*, Jan. 15, 1954, pp.1–2.

19. "La Déclaration officielle," *Témoignage Chrétien*, Nov. 20, 1953, p.6; "Au suject des 'prêtres de la mission ouvrière'," *Témoignage Chrétien*, Feb. 12, 1954, pp.1, 3.

20. Joseph Folliet, "Carnet d'un sociologue," *La Croix*, Oct. 13, 1953, p.7; Émile Gabel, "Evangéliser avec l'église," *La Croix*, Feb. 23, 1954, p.6.

21. Coutrot and Dreyfus, *Forces*, p.143; William Bosworth, *Catholicism and Crisis in Modern France* (Princeton, N.J.: University Press, 1962), p.235; Jean Le Cour Grandmaison, "Un communiqué et une lettre," *France Catholique*, June 20, 1952, p.1; Jean de Fabregues, "La Place des prêtres-ouvriers dans l'église," *France Catholique*, Feb. 5, 1954, p.1. For examples of these other press organs, see *Documentation Catholique's* press excerpts for the first three months of 1954.

22. Jeannette Vermeersch, "Notre lutte pour un gouvernement de paix," *France Nouvelle*, May 31, 1952, p.7; "La Réduction du nombre des prêtres-ouvriers," *L'Humanité*, Sept. 17, 1953, p.5; Jean Cazalbou, "Le Vatican au service de la Maison-Blanche," *France Nouvelle*, Oct. 17, 1953, p.9. This book is not the place to debate whether the Communist Party was the workers' preferred party or not. The author is convinced that it was. For arguments in support of that opinion, see Richard F. Hamilton, *Affluence and the French Worker in the Fourth Republic* (Princeton, N.J.: University Press, 1967).

23. "Unité! Unité!" *L'Humanité*, Apr. 3, 1953, p.5; Henri Barreau, interview, Gagny (May 16, 1979); Lucien Trilles, interview, Avignon (May 26, 1980); Jean Bratteau, interview, Paris (June 19, 1980); R. Launet, letter to "Comrade Depierre André", Paris (Apr. 2, 1954), p.1 in MDP (1954).

24. "Plus de 400 chrétiens ont signé ce texte," *La Quinzaine*, Feb. 15, 1954, p.10; "Le Prêtre dans le monde ouvrier," p.61 in MDP (1954); "Que les prêtres-ouvriers restent parmi nous, tels qu'ils sont," *La Quinzaine*, Oct. 1, 1953, pp.11–12.

25. François Mauriac, "Pour un nouveau concordat," *Le Figaro*, Feb. 16, 1954 in *Documentation Catholique* (Mar. 21, 1954), pp.370–371; "Interventions politiques" in *Documentation Catholique* (Mar. 21, 1954), p.372; Georges Bidault, interview, Paris (May 18, 1979); Bernard Chauveau, interview, Boulogne-Billancourt (May 11, 1979); Robert Pacalet, interview, Lyon (July 5, 1979); Joseph Robert, interview, Hellemes (July 12, 1979); François Vidal, interview, Marseille (June 2, 1983); Albert Guichard, interview, Paris (June 21, 1983); Jean Legendre, interview, Plateau d'Assy (June 6, 1983); Emile Poulat, interview, Paris (May 20, 1983).

26. Howard Schomer, "The Worker-Priests—One Year Later," *The Christian Century* 72 (March 16, 1955), pp.329–331. For a quick overview of this newspaper coverage, see *Documentation Catholique* (Oct. 18, 1953), pp.1297–1299 (Feb. 7, 1954), pp.133–139; (Mar. 21, 1954), pp.369–377; John Petrie, *The Worker-Priests*, pp.54–94.

27. *Le Monde*, Jan. 10–11, 1954 in *Documentation Catholique* (Feb. 7, 1954), pp.137–138; Henri Bénazet, *L'Aurore*, Feb. 11, 1954 and André Frossard, *L'Aurore*, (Feb. 24, 1954) both in Petrie, *The Worker-Priests*, pp.80–93; François Mauriac, *Le Figaro*, (Jan. 12, 1954) in *Documentation Catholique*, (Feb. 7, 1954), p.139 and (Oct. 6, 1953) in *Documentation Catholique* (Oct. 18, 1953), p.1299.

28. Emile Poulat, *Naissance des prêtres-ouvriers* (Paris: Centurion, 1965), pp.20, 30; Daniel Pézeril, *Rue Notre Dame* (London: Burns Oats, 1953); Daniel

Pézeril, interview, Paris (June 12, 1979); Gilbert Cesbron, *Les Saints vont en enfer* (Paris: R. Laffont, 1952).

29. Poulat, *Naissance,* pp.15–16, 23, 26, 30.

30. "Priest-Workmen: Their Present Position in France," *Blackfriars* XXXIII, 392 (Nov., 1952), p.467; John Fitzsimons, "Second Thoughts on the Priest-Workers," *Blackfriars* XXXV, 407 (Feb., 1954), pp.60–61; Canon Roger Lloyd, "Pays de Mission?," *The Spectator,* May 30, 1947, pp.618–619; *Church Times,* Dec. 19, 1952 in *Documentation Catholique* (Nov. 29, 1953), p.1484; Michael Gedge, "Priests, Politics and the Pope," *The Spectator,* Nov. 13, 1953, p.533; David L. Edwards, ed., *Priests and Workers* (London: SCM Press, 1961), pp.5, 131.

31. "Les Jésuites et les 'Prêtres-Ouvriers'," *Relations* (Feb., 1954), p.45; Jules Brosseau, "René Giroux, prêtre-ouvrier," *Relations* (Nov., 1970), p.305; Louis Rougier, "French Worker-Priest Idea Backfires," *Saturday Night,* Mar. 27, 1954, pp.7–8.

32. Friedrich Heer, "The Priest-Workers in France," *Cross Currents,* IV, 3 (Spr.–Sum., 1954), pp.262–274; Jacques Leclerq, "Holiness and the Temporal," *Cross Currents* 4 (Win., 1954), pp.92–108; Bertha Mugraver, "Variations in Pastoral Role in France," *American Catholic Sociological Review* 11 (Mar., 1950), pp.15–24; "Abolishes Term 'Worker-Priest'," *The Tablet,* Jan. 30, 1954, p.2; Monsignor Jean Calvet, "Worker-Priests of France," *Commonweal,* July 29, 1949, pp.385–386; Robert Barrat, "Heroes of the French Church," *Commonweal,* Jan. 8, 1954, pp.346–347; Sally Whelan Cassidy, "The Catholic Revival," *Catholic World* (Nov., 1953), pp.131–133; Michael de la Bedoyere, "From My Window in Fleet Street," *Catholic World* (Dec., 1954), pp.215–219; "Priest-Worker Crisis in France," *America,* Oct. 17, 1953, p.58.

33. Dorothy Day, "French Worker Priests and the Little Brothers of de Foucauld," *Catholic Worker,* Mar., 1954, pp.2, 4.

34. "Editorial-French Hierarchy Ends the Worker-Priests," *Christian Century,* Feb. 10, 1954, p.163; Howard Schomer, "The Worker-Priests-One Year Later," *Christian Century,* Mar. 16, 1955, pp.329–331; "No More Prêtres-Ouvriers?" *Time,* Sept. 28, 1953, p.48; "Letter from Paris," *New Yorker,* Oct. 24, 1953, pp.78–79; Egon Pohoryles, "Vatican Boomerang," *The Nation,* Oct. 24, 1953, p.332; Frank Gorrell, "Paris Dispatch," *New Republic,* Apr. 5, 1954, p.6; John Cogley, "They Are Priests and Workers Both," *New York Times Magazine,* Dec. 26, 1965, pp.6–7, 33–36.

35. "Rencontre entre les prêtres-ouvriers ayant quitté le travail et NN. SS. le Cardinal Feltin, de Bazelaire, Lallier" (July 16, 1954), pp.2–7 in MDP (1954); "Entretien avec les évêques," July 18, 1954, pp.1–12 in René Boudot, private papers.

36. Msgr. Robert Frossard, interview, Paris (July 2, 1979); Feltin letter, July 7, 1954, 1p in MDP (1954); Bernard Tiberghien, interview, Dunkerque (June 12, 1980); Jean Volot, interview, Paris (May 19, 1980); Alfred Ancel, interview, Lyon (June 14, 1979); Alfred Ancel, *Cinq ans avec les ouvriers* (Paris: Centurion, 1963).

37. "Lettre de S. Em. le cardinal Pizzardo," *Le Monde,* Sept. 15, 1959 in

Documentation Catholique (Oct. 4, 1959), p.1224; J.-M. Domenach, "Les Prêtres au travail et l'incroyance contemporaine," *Esprit* (Dec., 1959), pp.711–721.

38. Jean Vinatier, *Le Cardinal Liénart,* pp.173–184; Cogley, "They Are Priests," p.33.

39. "Un communiqué de S. Em. le cardinal Gerlier" (Mar., 1954) in Joseph Sanguedolce, *Joseph Gouttebarge,* pp.57–64 in Robert Pacalet, private papers; Henri Barreau, letter to Cardinal Feltin (c. Sept., 1955), pp.1–2 in Henri Barreau, private papers; Aldo Bardini, interview, Bagnolet (May 10, 1980); letter to Feltin (Jan. 14, 1961), pp.1–3 in Aldo Bardini, private papers; Pierre Veuillot (Aug. 23, 1964), in Jean Olhagaray, private papers; J.-M. Marzio, p.1 in MDP (1954); Roger Deliat, *Vingt ans chez Renault* (Paris: Editions Ouvrières, 1973), pp.51–96; "Pentecôte 66" (May 28–30, 1966) in Robert Pacalet, private papers; Maurice Combe, letters to his bishop (Aug. 27, 1982), (Nov. 5, 1982) and (Nov. 14, 1982) in Maurice Combe, private papers; Jacques Jaudon, interview, Grenoble (June 15, 1983); Bernard Cagne, interview, Paris (June 21, 1979); André Piet, *A travers le reél* (Paris: Pensée universelle, 1978).

40. Tiberghien, Domenach, Cagne, Augros, Legendre, Perrot, Montuclard, interviews; Albert Courtoy, interview, Liège, Belgium (June 8, 1983); Philbert Talé, interview, Antony (June 1, 1983); Francis Laval, interview, St. Etienne (May 19, 1983); Louis Augros, *De l'église d'hier à l'église de demain* (Paris: Cerf, 1980); Jacques Loew, interview, Fribourg, Swit. (May 14, 1980).

41. Volot interview; Edwards, *Priests and Workers; Le Groupe PRROQ, le monde ouvrier et l'église,* brochure printed by the PRROQ (Montreal: 2402 est rue Ste.-Catherine, 1982).

42. H. Karl Reko, "Determinative Factors in the Ability of Christ Seminary-Seminex Graduates to Conduct Worker-Priest Ministries in the United States," unpublished study (c. 1980), pp.15, 76–77; *The Worker Pastor,* brochure published by the Planning and Specialized Ministry Group, Personnel Commission of the Metropolitan New York Synod, LCA (c. 1980); Robert Pfaff, interview, Paris (June 10, 1983).

43. Reko, "Determinative Factors," pp.64, 149–157; Fred Ludolph, conversation, Waterloo, Ontario (Oct., 1983); Vinatier, *Cardinal Liénart,* p.183.

44. Cogley, "They Are Priests," p.36; *Courrier p.o.* (May, 1980), pp.4, 9–16, 23–24; Christel Peyrefitte, "Le Clergé français est-il en crise?" *Commentaire* 1, 2 (Summer, 1978), p.168; Congar interview; Francis Dumortier and Roger Biteau, "Depuis 1944, les prêtres-ouvriers," *Masses Ouvrières* (June, 1979), pp.29–41; "Prêtres-ouvriers en 1979," *Lettre—Temps Présent* (Apr., 1979), pp.10–13; Antoine Jourjon, Jean Burellier, Michel Lafond, interviews, Lyon (June 14, 1979).

45. Day, "French Worker Priests," p.4.

INDEX